THE
WORLD'S GREATEST
DOG STORIES

By the same author

Captain-General and Rebel Chief, The Life of James, Duke of Monmouth

Lionel Edwards: His Life and Work

The World's Greatest Horse Stories

The Book of Foxhunting
Victorian and Edwardian Field Sports from Old Photographs
British and Irish Hunts and Huntsmen, 3 vols.

The World of Polo

Sefton: The Story of a Cavalry Horse

A Dog called Sannet

THE WORLD'S GREATEST DOG STORIES

Selected and introduced by

J. N. P. Watson

Foreword by Her Grace Lavinia,
Duchess of Norfolk, CBE, President
of the National Canine Defence League

CENTURY PUBLISHING

LONDON

This selection first published in Great Britain by
Century Publishing Co. Ltd,
Portland House, 12–13 Greek Street,
London W1V 5LE

British Library Cataloguing in Publication Data
The World's greatest dog stories.
  1. Dogs—Literary collections
  I. Watson, J.N.P.
  808.8'036   PN6071.D6

ISBN 0 7126 1077 4

Phototypeset by Wyvern Typesetting Limited, Bristol
Printed and bound in Great Britain by Anchor Brendon Ltd,
Tiptree, Essex

CONTENTS

Contents

ADVERSITY

COMEDY

OBITUARY

ACKNOWLEDGEMENTS

I am extremely grateful for the generous cooperation of many writers and artists and to their publishers and representatives for allowing me to quote from their books and reproduce their drawings.

In particular I should like to thank Cassell Ltd and Curtis Brown Ltd for the passage from Eric Knight's *Lassie Come Home*; Messrs Chatto and Windus Ltd and the executors of the late Virginia Woolf for the quotation from her biographical *Flush*; to Rex Bellamy and the Editor of *Country Life* for his true story, *Mystery in the Peaks*; Messrs Eyre and Spottiswoode Ltd for allowing me to use the description of the alsatian's ejection into the sea from Svend Fleuron's *Flax, A Police Dog*; to Gollancz Ltd for the passage from the biography of the Northern Ireland Army hero, *Rats*, by Max Halstock; to Prentice Hall Ltd and the author for their permission to quote from *Dog Kill*, by Al Dempsey; and to Hamlyn Ltd for the piece from K. F. Barker's *Me and My Dog* and its accompanying illustrations.

To David Higham Ltd and the authors for the extracts from *The Plague Dogs* by Richard Adams and *The Lord God Made Them All* by James Herriot; to Hodder and Stoughton Ltd and the author for the episode from *The Incredible Journey*, by Sheila Burnford; to Methuen Ltd for the extract from Konrad Lorenz's *Man Meets Dog*; to Martin Secker and Warburg Ltd for permitting the description of the birth of alsatian puppies, from J. R. Ackerley's *My Dog Tulip*, to be used, and also for the quotation from Edward Hyams's translation of *Niki: The Story of a Dog* by the Hungarian author, Tibor Dery; to A. P. Watt Ltd for the excerpts from Rudyard Kipling's short story *Garm – A Hostage* and his comic poem *Thy Servant*; and to Anthony C. Mason for permission to quote from his grandfather Cecil Aldin's, *Time I Was Dead* and to reproduce a selection of his drawings.

My thanks are also especially due to Joy Hawken for her cooperation in completing her apt and masterly drawings to accompany so many of the quotations; to Audrey Guy who typed all the passages from the books; and, finally (but most warmly of all), to my wife, Lavinia, who typed all the introductions and correspondence connected with this anthology.

JNPW

The author is donating his proceeds to the National Canine Defence League and the Universities Federation for Animal Welfare.

FOREWORD

BY HER GRACE LAVINIA, DUCHESS OF NORFOLK, C.B.E.
President of the National Canine Defence League

Those of us who identify with, or feel an affinity with, dogs of one breed or another are likely to have read the most famous stories about them – tales such as Jack London's *Call of the Wild* and *White Fang*, Rudyard Kipling's *Garm – A Hostage*, Sir Percy Fitzpatrick's *Jock of the Bushveldt*, Virginia Woolf's *Flush* and Richard Adams's *The Plague Dogs*. But we need to be reminded of them, to dip into them, if only briefly, again. In this anthology the editor has included a great many more than the 'Greatest' of his title.

Presenting us with eighty and more authors, he follows the concise biographies of the more celebrated of them with summaries of their stories and one or more of his selected quotations from them. As the reader will see, the whole collection has been most skilfully edited and grouped.

Anyone who has read certain of those familiar articles of John Watson's in *Country Life* or his other anthology, *The World's Greatest Horse Stories* or more particularly his equine biography, *Sefton: The Story of a Cavalry Horse*, will recognize in the undercurrent theme of this collection the same strong feeling for animals which he displayed in those books.

These pages are, in my opinion, also greatly enhanced by the illustrations. The jacket painting and more than half the drawings are by Joy Hawken, one of the best animal artists now at work in Britain. Most of the remainder, all thoughtfully chosen, are from original editions. I would like to congratulate the publishers on the excellent presentation of the book, which I recommend as being of great entertainment value to all who, like me, love dogs.

Lavinia Norfolk.

Wild Dog crawled into the cave and laid his head on the Woman's lap, and said: 'O, my Friend and Wife of my Friend, I will help your Man to hunt through the day, and at night I will guard the Cave. . .'

When the Man waked up he said: 'What is Wild Dog doing here?' And the Woman said: 'His name is not Wild Dog any more, but the First Friend, because he will be our friend for always and always and always.'

Rudyard Kipling, *Just So Stories*

THE DOG IN LITERATURE

Man's first meaningful encounter with a dog on the literary stage was in the eighth century BC. It occurs in that sad juncture in the *Odyssey* when Homer shows the disguised Ulysses returning home after the Trojan War and the subsequent adventures, having been away for a total of twenty years. The hero's aged hound, Argus, with whom he had enjoyed many happy days of sport and companionship when they were young together, is the only being who recognizes his master. Ulysses approaches his palace, accompanied by Emmaeus the swineherd; this – according to Pope's translation (*c.* 1720) – is the unhappy sequel:

> Thus, near the gates conferring as they drew,
> Argus, the dog, his ancient master knew;
> He, not unconscious of the voice and tread,
> Lifts to the sound his ear, and rears his head;
> Bred by Ulysses, nourished at his board,
> But ah! not fated long to please his lord,
> To him, his swiftness and his strength were vain;
> The voice of glory called him o'er the main.
> Till then in every sylvan chase renown'd,
> With *Argus! Argus!* rang the woods around;
> With him pursued the youth the goat or fawn,
> Or traced the mazy leveret o'er the lawn;
> Now left to man's ingratitude he lay,
> Unhoused, neglected in the public way.
> He knew his lord – he knew, and strove to meet,
> In vain he strove to crawl, to kiss his feet;
> Yet (all he could) his tail, his ears, his eyes,
> Salute his master and confess his joys.
> Soft pity touch'd the mighty master's soul,
> Adown his cheek a tear unbidden stole. . . .
> The dog whom Fate had granted to behold
> His lord, when twenty tedious years had roll'd,
> Takes a last look, and, having seen him, dies;
> So closed forever faithful Argus' eyes.

We know from archaeologists that the process of training and

domesticating dogs began at least 9000 years before Homer's time. The wolf, the jackal and the wild dog scavenged on bones and offal left behind by early man, the hunter, who in his turn needed dogs to guard his home, scent and bring down his game, tend his flocks, and, in the last resort, give his own body for food. It was a general practice among the ancient races to issue instructions that, when they died, their dogs should be killed and buried with them. Rudyard Kipling's little fable quoted on page 10 suggests how it all started.

Georges Buffon (1707–88), the French naturalist and zoologist, thought that without dogs man could never have dominated the world:

> We may see of what importance this species is in the order of nature. By supposing for a moment that they had never existed; without the assistance of the dog, how could man have been able to tame, and reduce into slavery, other animals? How could he have hunted, discovered, and destroyed wild and obnoxious animals? To keep himself in safety and to render himself master of the living universe, it was necessary to begin by making himself friends among animals, in order to oppose them to others. The first art, then, of mankind, was the education of dogs, and the fruit of this art was the conquest and peaceable possession of the earth.

Seven centuries or so after poor Argus died, Roman writers were eulogizing dogs as well as any Greek. 'Dogs watch for us faithfully,' said Cicero; 'they love and worship their masters; they hate strangers; their power of tracking by scent is extraordinary; great is their keenness in the chase. What can all this mean but that they were made for man's advantage?' 'And do not leave to the last the care of dogs,' urges Virgil, 'but rear together on fattening whey the swift whelps of Sparta and the keen Molossian hound. Never with such guardians shall you fear the thief in the stables by night, or the onslaught of wolves. . . .' While in this verse, dedicated to the little bitch Issa, Martial echoes the Roman affection wonderfully:

Issa is naughtier than Catallus's sparrow,
Issa is purer than the kiss of a dove,
Issa is more winsome than all girls,
Issa is dearer than jewels of India,
Issa is the pet bitch of Publius.
You think she is speaking if she whines;
She feels both sadness and joy.
She lies resting on his neck, and sleeps
So that no breathing is heard.
And when compelled by the requirements of her inside
She proves traitor to the coverlet by not one drop.
But with coaxing paw she rouses and warns
To be put down from the bed; and asks to be taken up.
Such is the modesty of the chaste little dog
That she is ignorant of Venus; nor can we find
A husband worthy of so tender a girl.
Lest death take her completely off,
Publius has expressed her in a painting,
In which you will see Issa so like
That not even she herself is so like herself.
Accordingly, compare Issa with the picture:
See which you will think is the real dog,
And which the painted one.

In medieval, as in ancient, times – when hunting was not only necessary for food, but was the main diversion of princes and nobles – praise was mostly reserved for the venatic breeds. Hence the most effusive recognition of dog merit comes in such works as Gaston de Foix's *La Chasse*, William Twici's *The Craft of Hunting*, Edward, Duke of York's *Master of Game* and George Tuberville's *Book of Hunting*. Moving on to the sixteenth century, a more gentle reference is found in Thomas Stapleton's contemporary *Life of More*, Sir Thomas More's celebrated compassion for animals being portrayed in this poignant anecdote:

Sir Thomas his last wife loved little doggs to play withall. It happened that she was presented with one which had been stolen from a poor beggar woman. The poor beggar challenged her dogg, having spied it in the arms of one of the serving men that gave attendance upon my ladie. The dogg was denied her, so there was great hold and keep about it.

At length Sir Thomas had notice of it, so caused both his wife and the beggar to come before him in his hall, and said, 'Wife, stand you at the upper end of the hall, because you are a gentlewoman, and goodwife, stand there beneath, for you shall have no wrong'.

He placed himself in the middest, and held the dogg in his hands, saying to them, 'Are you content that I shall decide this controversie that is between you concerning this dogg?' 'Yea,' [quoth they]. 'Then,' said he, 'each of you call the dogg by his name, and to whom the dogg cometh she shall have it.'

The dogg came to the poor woman, so he caused the dogg to be given her, and gave her besides a French crown, and desired her that she would bestowe the dogg upon his ladie. The poor woman was well apaide with his fair speeches and his almes, and so delivered the dogg to my ladie.

Writing at about the same time, Francis Bacon exhorted his readers to: 'Mark what Generosity and Courage he [a dog] will put on, when he finds himself maintained by a Man; who to him is instead of a *God* or *Melior Natura*; which Courage is manifestly such as that Creature, without that confidence of a better nature than his owne, could never attaine.' Significantly, two centuries later, Robert Burns finds dogs to have 'better natures' than Men: 'Man is the God of the dog, whose . . . whole soul is wrapt up in his God! all the powers and facilities of his nature are devoted to his service! and these powers and facilities are ennobled by the intercourse. Divines tell us that it just ought to be so with the Christian, but the dog puts the Christian to shame.'

Another contemporary scholar, Montaigne, gives us an evocative glimpse of a sixteenth-century guide dog:

Animals are not incapable . . . of being instructed after our method. . . . But I observe this effect with the greatest admiration, which nevertheless is very common, in the dogs that lead the blind, both in the country and in cities; I have taken notice how they stop at certain doors, where they are wont to receive alms; how they avoid the encounter of coaches and carts, even there where they have sufficient room to pass; I have seen them, by the trench of a town, forsake a plain and even path and take a worse, only to keep their masters further from the ditch; – how could a man have made this dog understand that it was his office to look to his master's safety, and to despise his own conveniency to serve him? And how had he the knowledge that a way was wide enough for him that was not so for a blind man? Can all this be apprehended without ratiocination?

Here is Shakespeare, in *A Midsummer Night's Dream*, evoking human delight in the chase and in hound music, in a dialogue between Theseus, King of Athens, and Hippolyta, Queen of the Amazons, to whom he is betrothed:

THESEUS. We will, fair Queen, up to the mountain's top
And mark the musical confusion
Of hounds and echo in conjunction.
HIPPOLYTA. I was with Hercules and Cadmus once
When in a wood of Crete they bay'd the bear
With hounds of Sparta; never did I hear
Such gallant chiding, for, besides the groves,
The skies, the mountains, every region near,
Seem'd all one mutual cry. I never heard
So musical a discord, such sweet thunder.
THESEUS. My hounds are bred out of the spartan kind,
So flew'd, so sanded; and their heads are hung
With ears that sweep away the morning dew;
Crook-knee'd and dew-lapp'd like Thessalian bulls;
Slow in pursuit, but match'd in mouth like bells,
Each under each. A cry more tuneable
Was never holla'd to, nor cheer'd with horn,
In Crete, in Sparta, nor in Thessaly.
Judge when you hear.

In *Two Gentlemen of Verona* enter Launce, clownish servant to Proteus, with Crab, the cur for whom he professes to be scapegoat:

LAUNCE. When a man's servant shall play the cur with him, look you, it goes hard; one that I brought up of a puppy, one that I saved from drowning, when three or four of his blind brothers and sisters went to it. I have taught him, even as one would say precisely, 'Thus I would teach a dog.' I was sent to deliver him as a present to Mistress Silvia from my master, and I came no sooner into the dining-chamber but he steps me to her trencher and steals her capon's leg. O! 'tis a foul thing when a cur cannot keep himself in all companies. I would have, as one should say, one that takes upon him to be a dog indeed, to be, as it were, a dog at all things. If I had not more wit than he, to take a fault upon me that he did, I think verily he had been hanged for't; sure as I live, he had suffered for't: you shall judge. He thrusts himself into the company of three or four gentleman-like dogs under the duke's table: he had not been there – bless the mark! – a pissing-while, but all the chamber smelt him. 'Out with the dog!' says one; 'What cur is that?' says another; 'Whip him out,' says the third; 'Hang him up,' says the Duke. I, having been acquainted with the smell before, knew it was Crab, and goes me to the fellow that whips the dogs. 'Friend,' quoth I, 'you mean to whip the dog?' 'Ay, marry, do I,' quoth he. 'You do him more wrong,' quoth I, ''twas I did the thing you wot of.' He makes no more ado, but whips me out of the chamber. How many masters would do this for his servant? Nay, I'll be sworn, I have sat in the stocks for puddings he had stolen, otherwise he had been executed; I have stood on the pillory for geese he hath killed, otherwise he had suffered for't; thou thinkest not of this now. Nay, I remember the trick you served me when I took leave of Madam Silvia: did I not bid thee still mark me and do as I do? When didst thou see me heave up my leg and make water against a gentlewoman's farthingale? Didst thou ever see me do such a trick?

Three or four hundred years ago, people showed their affection for dogs, made fools of themselves over them, just as readily as they do today. Here is an Oxford scribe's mockery, during the Civil War, at the relationship between Prince Rupert and his beloved Boy:

First in respect to Civill (or rather uncivill) affaires, I find it very Loose and Strumpet-like. For he salutes and kisseth the Prince, as close as any Christian woman would; and the Prince salutes and kisseth him back again as favorily, as he would (I will not say any Alderman's wife, but) any Court-Lady, and is as little offended with his Breathing. Then they lye perpetually in one bed, sometimes the Prince upon the Dog, and sometimes the Dog upon the Prince; and what this may in time produce, none but the close Committee can tell. Next to his Master, he loves the King, and the King's Children, and cares very little for any other. . . .

Boy's death at the Battle of Marston Moor was greeted with exultation by the Roundheads. One of the 'King's Children' who would have known that dog was the future Charles II. Apart from the fact that the King Charles spaniel was named after him, his affection for dogs was widely acknowledged. Here is the wording of a notice posted in Whitehall in the year of his coronation:

We must call upon you again for a Black Dog, between a Greyhound and a Spaniel, no white about him, only a streak on his Breast, and his Tayl a little bobbed. It is His Majesty's own Dog, and doubtless was stoln, for the Dog was not born nor bred in England, and would never forsake His master. Whoever finds him may acquaint any at Whitehall, for the Dog was better known at Court than those who stole him. Will they never leave robbing his Majesty? Must he not keep a Dog? This Dog's place at Court (though better than some imagine) is the only place which nobody offers to beg.

After the Restoration, Pepys left some nice vignettes. Following a visit to the Council Chamber, his diary tells us that 'All I observed was the silliness of the King, playing with his dog all the while and not minding the business.' In September 1661, Pepys wrote this memoir:

To Dr Williams who did carry me into his garden, where he hath abundance of grapes: and he did show me how a dog that he hath do kill all the cats that come thither to kill his pigeons; and do afterwards bury them; and do it with so much care that they shall be quite covered; that if the tip of the tail hangs out, he will take up the cat again and dig the hole deeper; which is strange. And he tells me he do believe he hath killed above an hundred cats.

Another seventeenth-century classic is Isaak Walton's *The Compleat Angler*, which contains a eulogy on the wiles and voices of hounds at least as enthusiastic as Shakespeare's in *A Midsummer Night's Dream*:

I am a lover of Hounds; I have followed many a pack of dogs many a mile, and heard many merry Huntsmen make sport and scoff at Anglers. . . . And for the dogs that we use, who can commend their excellency to that height which they deserve? How perfect is the hound at smelling, who never leaves or forsakes his first scent, but follows it through so many changes and varieties of other scents, even over, and in, the water, and into the earth! What music doth a pack of dogs then make to any man, whose heart and ears are so happy as to be set to the tune of such instruments! How will a right Greyhound fix his eye on the best Buck in a herd, single him out, and follow him, and him only, through a whole herd of rascal game, and still know and then kill him! For my hounds, I know the language of them, and they know the language and meaning of one another, as perfectly as we know the voices of those with whom we converse daily.

Who, from their childhood reading, does not remember Robinson Crusoe's dog? Daniel Defoe, writing during the reign of George I, sets the scene at just about the time Charles II ascended the throne. Jotting his memoirs in the little hut he has built on his desert island, Crusoe insists that 'I must not forget that we had in the ship a Dog and two Catts. . . . As for the Dog he jump'd out of the Ship of himself, and swam on shore . . . and was a trusty servant to me many Years. I wanted nothing that he could fetch me, nor any Company that he could make up to me. I only wanted to have him talk to me, but that he would not do.'

How many lonely men and women, before and since, have longed for their dogs to speak to them? How many more have been content with the speech that comes through the eyes? Like Washington Irving's engaging, daydreaming, henpecked Rip Van Winkle, for example:

Rip's sole domestic adherent was his dog Wolf, who was as much henpecked as his master; for Dame Van Winkle regarded them as companions in idleness, and even looked upon Wolf with an evil eye, as the cause of his master's going so often astray. True it is, in all points of spirit befitting an honourable dog, he was as courageous an animal as ever scoured the woods – but what courage can withstand the ever-during and all-besetting terrors of a woman's tongue? The moment Wolf entered the house his crest fell, his tail drooped to the ground or curled between his legs, he sneaked about with a gallows air, casting many a sidelong glance at Dame Van Winkle, and at the least flourish of a broomstick or ladle, he would fly to the door with yelping precipitation. . . . Poor Rip was at last reduced almost to despair; and his only alternative to escape from the labour of the farm and the clamour of his wife was to take gun in hand, and stroll away into the woods. Here he would sometimes seat himself at the foot of a tree, and share the contents of his wallet with Wolf, with whom he sympathised

as a fellow-sufferer in persecution. 'Poor Wolf,' he would say, 'thy mistress leads thee a dog's life of it; but never mind, my lad, whilst I live thou shalt never want a friend to stand by thee!' Wolf would wag his tail, look wistfully in his master's face, and if dogs can feel pity, I verily believe he reciprocated the sentiment with all his heart.

That feeling of a dog's rapport shining through his whole body, particularly the eyes, is well expressed in a verse from 'Jocelyn' by Alphonse de Lamartine (1790–1869):

Faithful Spaniel.
No! when thy love by death shall be o'erthrown
It will revive and in some heaven unknown . . .
We shall love on as we were wont to love
Instinct and soul is one to him above!
Where friendship sheds o'er love its honoured name
Where nature lights a pure and hallowed flame
God will no more extinguish his soft light
That shines not brighter in the stars of night
Than in the faithful spaniel's anxious eye.

George Eliot (1819–80) shows, in this passage from *Adam Bede*, that she does not know whether to envy or pity their dumbness:

Poor dogs! I've a strange feeling about the dumb things, as if they wanted to speak, and it was a trouble to 'em because they couldn't. I can't help being sorry for the dogs a lump, though perhaps there's no need. But they may well have more in them than they know how to make us understand, for we can't say half what we feel with all our words.

That satirical novelist and playwright, Jerome K. Jerome (1859–1927), while appreciating the selflessness of the genus, attributes the quality, ultimately, to the dog's lack of reason. This is what he has to say in *Idle Thoughts of an Idle Fellow*:

He is very imprudent, a dog is, he never makes it his business to inquire whether you are in the right or in the wrong, never bothers as to whether you are going up or down on life's ladder, never asks whether you are rich or poor, silly or wise, sinner or saint. You are his pal. That is enough for him, and come luck or misfortune, good repute or bad, honour or shame, he is going to stick to you, to comfort you, guard you, give his life for you if need be – foolish, brainless, soulless dog.

Dickens, Flaubert, Surtees, Walpole, Trollope, Barrie and Galsworthy all introduced dogs into their novels, either as vehicles and mediums to elicit traits in their human characters, or as characters in their own right. One of the most famous titles in English detective fiction is *The Hound of the Baskervilles* by Sir Arthur Conan Doyle. But as that is not, in essence, a dog story, I have omitted it from this collection. Perhaps before the twentieth century, no great writer either loved his own dogs so much, or showed greater insight into a dog's virtues, than Sir Walter Scott (1771–1832). 'The misery of keeping a dog,' he opined, 'is his dying so soon; but, to be sure, if he lived for fifty years and then died, what would become of me?' The Waverley novels abound in dogs. The Dandie Dinmont was named after a character in *Guy Mannering*.

Roswal, in *The Talisman*, propounds Scott's opinion that 'the Almighty, who gave the dog to be companion of our pleasures and our toils, hath invested him with a nature noble and incapable of deceit. He forgets neither friend nor foe, remembers, and with what accuracy, both benefit and injury. He hath a share of man's intelligence, but no share of man's falsehood.' John Gibson Lockhart (1794–1854), who married Scott's elder daughter Sophia and wrote the classic *Life of Scott*, records his father-in-law's reaction following the death of a favourite:

> He was buried on a fine moonlight night, in the little garden behind the house in Castle Street, immediately opposite to the window at which Scott usually sat writing. My wife told me that she remembered the whole family standing in tears about the grave as her father himself smoothed down the turf above Camp, with the saddest expression of face she had ever seen in him. He had been engaged to dine abroad that day, but apologised on account of the death of a dear old friend; and Mr MacDonald Buchanan was not at all surprised that he should have done so, when it came out next morning that Camp was no more.

The modern compassion for animals, such as it is, dawned in Britain in Scott's day. Following the dedicated work in Parliament of men like Richard Martin and William Wilberforce during the first three decades of the nineteenth century, the first meaningful law for the protection of animals was passed in 1822. The RSPCA was founded, to Scott's great satisfaction, in 1824, when he was fifty-three. There was very little popular writing concerning dogs, unless about those useful to man – harriers, foxhounds and gundogs, for instance – until the middle of the nineteenth-century. Most of the stories in this anthology were published after that time.

I have divided my choice into five sections, under the headings 'Affection', 'Triumph', 'Adversity', 'Comedy' and 'Obituary'. Some of the extracts are pure fiction, others largely based upon experience. Some of the passages are not from stories at all, but are simply philosophical comments about dogs. In the first four sections many of the stories comprise a fluctuation, a seesaw, of triumph, tragedy and comedy, of love and rejection, of gaiety and misery, for the dogs concerned. The passages I have quoted are appropriate to their category.

Man's love of dogs down the ages is reflected and epitomized in the gravestones he has erected and the epitaphs he has written for them. Reading some of them, it is not difficult to envisage the joy those bodies lying in the cold earth gave their owners in the days of their love and vitality. The best of the epitaphs are contained in the fifth section. And, since some of the most vivid and endearing writings come from poets' pens, I have interspersed the book with verses.

The reader, questioning whether this is a truly comprehensive collection, may object that such a high proportion of the stories originate from the English-speaking world. If so, that may be fair comment, although there must be countless stories about dogs in other languages which, although quite good, failed to merit translation. Nevertheless, Austria, Belgium, Denmark, France, Germany, Hungary and Sweden are all represented. Whether the reader agrees with my choices or concurs with my comments or not, I hope he or she enjoys reading these abridgements and extracts as much as I have enjoyed compiling them.

AFFECTION

Greyfriars Bobby ──────────────────

John Brown

This story comes from the pen of Dr John Brown (1810–82) whose *Horae Subsecivae* (Odd Hours) includes several authentic accounts of dog behaviour. 'The True Story of Greyfriars Bobby', which is perhaps the most moving of them, concerns a shaggy little terrier, beloved of a Midlothian farmer called Gray. Brown tells how Bobby accompanied Gray to the market in Edinburgh every Wednesday:

It was Gray's custom, as the time-gun announced the hour of one from the Castle heights, to repair to a small restaurant in the neighbourhood of Greyfriars' dining rooms. Here Bobby and his master had their midday meal, which in the case of the doggie consisted regularly of a bun, probably followed by a canine bonne bouche in the way of a bone.

In 1858 Gray died, and was laid to rest in the historic churchyard of Greyfriars, aptly named by Sir Walter Scott 'The Westminster of Scotland'. On the third day following the funeral, and just as the echoes of the time-gun were dying away, the occupants of Traill's rooms were surprised to see a dog, the picture of woe and hunger, enter the doorway and approach the proprietor, upon whom he gazed with a most beseeching expression.

Traill immediately recognized in this visitor the once happy and well-cared-for Bobby. Stirred with compassion, he gave a bun to the silent pleader, who then, without waiting to eat it, ran out of the shop, carrying his newly found meal in his mouth. Next day, at the same hour, Bobby again appeared, and a repetition of events followed; but on the third day, Traill, whose curiosity and interest were now thoroughly aroused, determined to follow the dog, and thus discover his destination. This was soon reached, for Bobby, bun in mouth, made straight for Greyfriars' Churchyard, where, approaching the grave of his master, he lay down and began to eat his scanty meal. It was now evident that a chief, if not the only mourner of the kind-hearted farmer, had been his four-footed friend, Bobby, who, after following his late master's funeral, had then refused to leave the newly formed mound which marked his grave, until forced to do so by the pangs of hunger. Bobby's plight, and the locality of his new domicile, having come to the knowledge of the occupants of his former home, he was brought back, it is said, three times. However,

all efforts to make him relinquish his chosen post proved unavailing, and each attempt was followed by a speedy return to the same spot in Greyfriars.

The Greyfriars superintendent who, hitherto, had done his best to enforce the 'Dogs not Admitted' notice, made Bobby an exception, and '. . . here, at or near his master's grave, Bobby continued to spend both days and nights, taking refuge only in rough weather under a tombstone hard by, and stoutly resisting all friendly advances made by compassionate strangers. . . . In course of time a shelter was erected for Bobby's protection.' The little terrier, who never failed to report to the kind-hearted proprietor of the Greyfriars' dining rooms for his bun on the boom of the one o'clock gun each day, lived until 1872, being buried, like his master in Greyfriars churchyard, 'where his not far distant grave, in a flower-bed near the main entrance, is often pointed out to visitors.'

Wylie

John Brown

Horae Subsecivae also includes John Brown's touching memoir on the collie bitch, Wylie, who remained so devoted to her former work, that when she was sold into a life of mere domestic companionship, could not forbear to return to round up sheep at the weekly cattle market:

Our next friend was an exquisite shepherd's dog; fleet, thin-flanked, dainty, and handsome as a small greyhound, with all the grace of silky waving black and tan hair. . . .

We had been admiring the beauty and gentleness and perfect shape of Wylie, the finest collie I ever saw, and said, 'What are you going to do with Wylie?' [Old Adam, the shepherd, was going to live with his son in Glasgow.] ''Deed,' says he, 'I hardly ken. I canna think o' sellin' her, though she's worth four pound and she'll no like the toun.' I said, 'Would you let me have her?' and Adam, looking at her fondly – she came up instantly to him and made much of him – said, 'Ay, I wull, if ye'll be gude to her'; and it was settled that when Adam left for Glasgow she should be sent into Albany Street by the carrier.

She came, and was at once taken to all our hearts, even grandmother liked her; and though she was often pensive, as if thinking of her master and her work on the hills, she made herself at home, and behaved in all respects like a lady. When out with me, if she saw sheep in the streets or road, she got quite excited, and helped the work, and was curiously useful, the being so making her wonderfully happy. And so her life went on, never doing wrong, always blithe and kind and beautiful. But some months after she came there was a mystery about her; every Tuesday evening she disappeared; we tried to watch her, but in vain, she was always off by nine p.m. and was away all night, coming back next day, wearied and all over mud, as if she had travelled far. She slept all next day. This went on for some months and we could make nothing of it. Poor dear creature, she looked at us wistfully when she came in, as if she would have told us if she could, and was especially fond, though tired.

Well, one day I was walking through the Grass-market, with Wylie at my heels, when two shepherds started, and looking at her, one said, 'That's her; that's the wonderful wee bitch that naebody kens.' I asked him what he meant, and he told me that for months past she had made her appearance by the first daylight at the 'Buchts' or sheep pens in the cattle market, and worked incessantly, and to excellent purpose, in helping the shepherds to get their sheep and lambs in. 'She's a perfect meeracle; flees aboot like a speerit, and never gangs wrang; wears but never grups, and beats a' oor dowgs. A meeracle, and as soople as a maukin.' Then he related how they all knew her, and said, 'There's that wee fell yin; we'll get them in noo.' They tried to coax her to stop and be caught, but no, she was gentle, but off; and for many a day that 'wee fell yin' was spoken of by these rough fellows. She continued this amateur work until she died, which she did in peace.

Riquet ———————————————

Anatole France

The following story, which comes from *The Amethyst Ring*, by Anatole France (1844–1924), demonstrates wonderfully how, step by step, a dog is gifted to insinuate itself into a man's heart:

Seated at his table one morning in front of the window, against which the leaves of the plane-tree quivered, M. Bergeret, who was trying to discover how the ships of Aeneas had been changed into nymphs, heard a tap at the door, and forthwith his servant entered, carrying in front of her, opossum-like, a tiny creature whose black head peeped out from the folds of her apron, which she had turned up to form a pocket. With a look of anxiety and hope upon her face, she remained motionless for a moment; then she placed the little thing upon the carpet at her master's feet.

'What's that?' asked M. Bergeret. It was a little dog of doubtful breed, having something of the terrier in him, and a well-set head, a short, smooth coat of a dark tan colour, and a tiny little stump of a tail. His body retained its puppylike softness, and he went sniffing at the carpet.

'Angélique,' said M. Bergeret, 'take this animal back to its owners.'

'It has no owner, Monsieur.'

M. Bergeret looked silently at the little creature who had come to examine his slippers, and was giving little sniffs of approval. M. Bergeret was a philologist, which perhaps explains why at this juncture he asked a vain question.

'What is he called?'

'Monsieur,' replied Angélique, 'he has no name.'

M. Bergeret seemed put out at this answer: he looked at the dog sadly, with a disheartened air.

Then the little animal placed its two front paws on M. Bergeret's slipper, and holding it thus, began innocently to nibble it. With a sudden access of compassion M. Bergeret took the tiny nameless creature upon his knees. The dog looked at him intently, and M. Bergeret was pleased at his confiding expression.

'What beautiful eyes!' he cried.

The dog's eyes were indeed beautiful, the pupils of a golden-flecked chestnut set in warm white. And his gaze spoke of simple, mysterious thoughts, common alike to the thoughtful beasts and simple men of the earth.

Tired, perhaps, with the intellectual effort he had made for the purpose of entering into communication with a human being, he closed his beautiful eyes, and yawning widely, revealed his pink mouth, his curled-up tongue, and his array of dazzling teeth.

M. Bergeret put his hand into the dog's mouth, and allowed him to lick it, at which old Angélique gave a smile of relief.

'A more affectionate little creature doesn't breathe,' she said.

'Where did you find him?' asked M. Bergeret.

'Well, Monsieur, it was M. Dellion's chef gave him to me.'

'With the result,' continued M. Bergeret, 'that we now have this soul to care for.'

'What soul?' asked Angélique.

'This canine soul. An animal is, properly speaking, a soul; I do not say an immortal soul. And yet, when I came to consider the positions this poor little beast and myself occupy in the scheme of things, I recognize in both exactly the same right to immortality.'

After considerable hesitation old Angélique, with a painful effort which made her upper lip curl up and reveal her two remaining teeth, said:

'If Monsieur does not want a dog, I shall return him to M. Dellion's chef; but you may safely keep him, I assure you. You won't see or hear him.'

She had hardly finished her sentence when the puppy, hearing a heavy van rolling down the street, sat bolt upright on M. Bergeret's knees, and began to bark both loud and long, so that the window-panes resounded with the noise.

M. Bergeret smiled.

'He is a watch dog,' said Angélique, by way of excuse. 'They are by far the most faithful.'

'Have you given him anything to eat?' asked M. Bergeret.

'Of course,' returned Angélique.

'What does he eat?'

'Monsieur must be aware that dogs eat bread and meat.'

Somewhat piqued, M. Bergeret retorted that in her eagerness she might very likely have taken him away from his mother before he was old enough to leave her; upon which he was lifted up again and re-examined, only to make sure of the fact that he was at least six months old.

M. Bergeret put him down on the carpet, and regarded him with interest. . . .

'We must give him a name. . . .'

And he cudgelled his brains, trying to hit upon a name for the little living thing who was busily engaged in nibbling the fringe of the carpet. . . . 'What day is it?' he asked at last.

'The ninth,' replied Angélique. 'Thursday, the ninth.'

'Well, then!' said M. Bergeret, 'can't we call the dog Thursday, like Robinson Crusoe, who called his man Friday for the same reason?'

'As Monsieur wishes,' said Angélique, 'but it isn't very pretty.'

'Very well,' said M. Bergeret, 'find a name for the creature yourself, for after all, you brought him here.'

'Oh, no,' said the servant. 'I couldn't find a name for him; I'm not clever enough. When I saw him lying on the straw in the kitchen, I called him Riquet, and he came up and played about under my skirts.'

'You called him Riquet, did you?' cried M. Bergeret. 'Why didn't you say so before? Riquet he is and Riquet he shall remain; that's settled. Now be off with you, and take Riquet with you. I want to work.'

'Monsieur,' returned Angélique, 'I am going to leave the puppy with you. I will come for him when I get back from market.'

'You could quite well take him to market with you,' retorted M. Bergeret.

'Monsieur, I am going to church as well. . . .'

'Eh!' ejaculated M. Bergeret. 'Shut him up in the kitchen or some other convenient place, and do not wor—'

He did not finish his sentence, for Angélique had vanished, purposely pretending not to hear, that she might leave Riquet with his master. She wanted them to grow used to one another, and also wanted to give poor, friendless M. Bergeret a companion. Having closed the door behind her, she went along the corridor and down the steps.

M. Bergeret set to work again and plunged head foremost into his *Virgilius nauticus*. He loved the work; it rested his thoughts, and became a kind of game that suited him, for he played it all by himself. On the table beside him were several boxes filled with pegs, which he fixed into little squares of cardboard to represent the fleet of Aeneas. Now while he was thus occupied he felt something like tiny fists tapping at his legs. Riquet, whom he had quite forgotten, was standing on his hind legs patting his master's knees, and wagging his little stump of a tail. When he tired of this, he let his paws slide down the trouser leg, then got up and began his coaxing once again. And M. Bergeret, turning away from the printed lore before him, saw two brown eyes gazing up at him lovingly.

'What gives a human beauty to the gaze of this dog,' he thought, 'is probably that it varies unceasingly, being by turns bright and vivacious or serious and sorrowful, because through these eyes his little dumb soul finds expression for thought that lacks nothing in depth or sequence. . . .'

Riquet was agitating his paws in frantic fashion, and M. Bergeret, who was anxious to return to his philological amusements, said kindly, but shortly:

'Lie down, Riquet!'

Upon which Riquet went and thrust his nose against the door through which Angélique had passed out. And there he remained, uttering from time to time plaintive, meek little cries. After a while he began to scratch, making a gentle rasping noise on the polished floor with his nails. Then the whining began again, followed by more scratching. Disturbed by these sounds, M. Bergeret sternly bade him keep still.

Riquet peered at him sorrowfully with his brown eyes, then, sitting down, he looked at M. Bergeret again, rose, returned to the door, sniffed underneath it, and waited afresh.

'Do you want to go out?' asked M. Bergeret.

Putting down his pen, he went to the door, which he held a few inches open. After making sure that he was running no risk of hurting himself on the way out, Riquet slipped through the doorway and marched off with a composure that was scarcely polite. On returning to his table, M. Bergeret, sensitive man that he was, pondered over the dog's action. He said to himself:

'I was on the point of reproaching the animal for going without saying either goodbye or thank you, and expecting him to apologize for leaving me. It was the beautiful human expression of his eyes that made me so foolish. I was beginning to look upon him as one of my own kind.'

After making this reflection, M. Bergeret applied himself anew to the metamorphosis of the ships of Aeneas, a legend both pretty and popular, but perhaps a trifle too simple in itself for expression in such noble language . . . He was almost on the point of grasping the solution . . . when he heard a noise like the rattling of chains at his door, a noise which, although not alarming, struck him as curious. The disturbance was presently accompanied by a shrill whining, and M. Bergeret . . . immediately concluded that these importunate wails must emanate from Riquet.

As a matter of fact, after having looked vainly all over the house for Angélique, Riquet had been seized with a desire to see M. Bergeret again. Solitude was as painful to him as human society was dear. In order to put an end to the noise, and also because he had a secret desire to see Riquet again, M. Bergeret got up from his armchair and opened the door, and Riquet entered the study with the same coolness with which he had quitted it; but as soon as he saw the door close behind him he assumed a melancholy expression, and began to wander up and down the room like a soul in torment.

He had a sudden way of appearing to find something of interest beneath the chairs and tables, and would sniff long and noisily; then he would walk aimlessly about, or sit down in a corner with an air of great humility, like the beggars who are to be seen in church porches. Finally he began to bark at a cast of Hermes which stood upon the mantelshelf, whereupon M. Bergeret addressed him in words full of just reproach.

'Riquet! such vain agitation, such sniffing and barking, were better suited to a stable than the study of a professor. . . . Since you came into this chamber of study your hoarse voice, your unseemly snufflings and your whines, that sound like steam-whistles, have constantly confused my thoughts and interrupted my reflections. And now you have made me lose the drift of an important passage in Servius, referring to the construction of one of the ships of Aeneas. Know thee, Riquet, my friend, that this is the house of silence and the abode of meditation, and that if you are anxious to stay here you must become literary. Be quiet!'

Thus spake M. Bergeret. Riquet, who had listened to him with mute astonishment, approached his master, and with suppliant gesture placed a timid paw upon the knee, which he seemed to revere in a fashion that savoured of long ago. Then a kind thought struck M. Bergeret. He picked him up by the scruff of his neck, and put him upon the cushions of the ample easy chair in which he was sitting. Turning himself round three times, Riquet lay down, and then remained perfectly still and silent. He was quite happy. M. Bergeret was grateful to him, and as he ran through Servius, he occasionally stroked the close-cropped coat, which, without being soft, was smooth and very pleasant to the touch. Riquet fell into a gentle doze, and communicated to his master the generous warmth of his body, the subtle, gentle heat of a living, breathing thing. And from that moment M. Bergeret found more pleasure in his *Virgilius nauticus. . . .*

His reflections were running thus when old Angélique, breathless and perspiring, entered the study. She first opened the door, and then she knocked, for she never permitted herself to enter without knocking. If she had not done so before she opened the door, she did it after, for she had good manners, and knew what was expected of her. She went in, therefore, knocked, and said:

'Monsieur, I have come to relieve you of the dog.'

M. Bergeret heard these words with decided annoyance. He had not as yet inquired into his claims to Riquet, and now realized that he had none. The thought that Madame Borniche might take the animal away from him filled him with sadness; yet, after all, Riquet did belong to her. Affecting indifference, he replied:

'He's asleep; let him sleep!'

'Where is he? I don't see him,' remarked old Angélique.

'Here he is,' answered M. Bergeret, 'in my chair.'

With her two hands clasped over her portly figure, old Angélique smiled, and in a tone of gentle mockery ventured:

'I wonder what pleasure the creature can find in sleeping there behind Monsieur!'

'That,' retorted M. Bergeret, 'is his business.'

Then, as he was of an inquiring mind, he immediately sought of Riquet his reasons for the selection of his resting-place, and lighting on them, replied with his accustomed candour:

'I keep him warm, and my presence affords a sense of security; my comrade is a chilly and homely little animal.' Then he added: 'Do you know, Angélique, I shall go out presently and buy him a collar.'

Half Wild – Half Tame _____

James Oliver Curwood, who was born in Owosso, Michigan, in 1878, enjoyed a wide reputation as a writer of stories dealing with animal life coupled with human adventure. His stories, like those of Jack London, were set in the wild northland of America. *Kazan* is one of the most poignant sagas in dog literature. Kazan, the hero, who has found his soulmate in the she-wolf Grey Wolf, is a sledgedog attached to a caring family of wood folk. This excerpt makes one of the strongest comments in fiction on the link between – and, at the same time, the chasm dividing – humans and animals:

Half a mile away, at the summit of a huge mass of rock which the Indians called the Sun Rock, Kazan and Grey Wolf had found a home; and from here they went down to their hunts on the plain, and often the girl's voice reached up to them, calling 'Kazan! Kazan! Kazan!'

Through all the long winter, Kazan hovered thus between the lure of Joan and the cabin – and Grey Wolf.

Then came Spring – and the Great Change.

The rocks, the ridges and the valleys were taking on a warmer glow. The poplar buds were ready to burst. The scent of balsam and of spruce grew heavier in the air each day, and all through the wilderness, in plain and forest, there was the rippling murmur of the spring floods finding their way to Hudson's Bay. In that great bay, there was the rumble and crash of the ice fields thundering down in the early break-up through the Roes Welcome – the doorway to the Arctic, and for that reason there still came with the April wind an occasional sharp breath of winter.

Kazan had sheltered himself against that wind. Not a breath of air stirred in the sunny spot the Wolf-dog had chosen for himself. He was more comfortable than he had been at any time during the six months of terrible winter – and as he slept, he dreamed.

Grey Wolf, his wild mate, lay near him, flat on her belly, her forepaws reaching out, her eyes and nostrils as keen and alert as the smell of man could make them. For there was that smell of man, as well as of balsam and spruce, in the warm spring air. She gazed anxiously and sometimes steadily at Kazan as he slept. Her own grey spine stiffened when she saw the tawny hair along Kazan's back bristle at some dream vision. She whined softly as his upper lip snarled back, showing his long white fangs. But for the most part Kazan lay quiet, save for the muscular twitchings of legs, shoulders and muzzle, which always tell when a Dog is dreaming; and as he dreamed there came to the door of the cabin out on the plain a blue-eyed girl-woman, with a big brown braid over her shoulder, who called through the cup of her hands, 'Kazan, Kazan, Kazan!'

The voice reached faintly to the top of the Sun Rock, and Grey Wolf flattened her ears. Kazan stirred, and in another instant he was awake and on his feet. He leaped to an outcropping ledge, sniffing the air and looking far out over the plain that lay below them.

Over the plain, the woman's voice came to them again, and Kazan ran to the ridge of the rock and whined. Grey Wolf stepped softly to his side and laid her muzzle on his shoulder. She had grown to know what the Voice meant. Day and night she feared it, more than she feared the scent or sound of man.

Since she had given up the pack and her old life for Kazan, the Voice had become Grey Wolf's greatest enemy, and she hated it. It took Kazan from her. And wherever it went, Kazan followed.

Night after night it robbed her of her mate, and left her to wander alone under the stars and the moon, keeping faithfully to her loneliness, and never once responding with her own tongue to the hunt-calls of her wild brothers and sisters in the forests and out on the plains. Usually she would snarl at the Voice, and sometimes nip Kazan lightly to show her displeasure. But today, as the Voice came a third time, she slunk back into the darkness of a fissure between two rocks, and Kazan saw only the fiery glow of her eyes.

Kazan ran nervously to the trail their feet had worn up to the top of the Sun Rock, and stood undecided. All day, and yesterday, he had been uneasy and disturbed. Whatever it was that stirred him seemed to be in the air, for he could not see it or scent it. But he could *feel* it. He went to the fissure and sniffed at Grey Wolf; usually she whined coaxingly. But her response today was to draw back her lips until he could see her white fangs.

A fourth time the Voice came to them faintly, and she snapped fiercely at some unseen thing in the darkness between the two rocks. Kazan went again to the trail, still hesitating. Then he began to go down. It was a narrow winding trail, worn only by the pads and claws of animals; for the Sun Rock was a huge crag that rose almost sheer up for a hundred feet above the tops of the spruce and balsam, its bald crest catching the first gleams of the sun in the morning and the last glow of it in the evening. Grey Wolf had first led Kazan to the security of the retreat at the top of the rock.

When he reached the bottom he no longer hesitated, but darted swiftly in the direction of the cabin. Because of that instinct of the wild that was still in him, he always approached the cabin with caution. He never gave warning, and for a moment Joan was startled when she looked up from her baby and saw Kazan's shaggy head and shoulders in the open door. The baby struggled and kicked in her delight, and held out her two hands with cooing cries to Kazan. Joan, too, held out a hand.

'Kazan!' she cried softly. 'Come in, Kazan!'

Slowly the wild red light in Kazan's eyes softened. He put a forefoot on the sill, and stood there, while the girl urged him again. Suddenly his legs seemed to shrink a little under him, his tail drooped and he slunk in with that doggish air of having committed a crime. The creatures he loved were in the cabin, but the cabin itself he hated. He hated all cabins, for they all breathed of the club and the whip and bondage. Like all Sledge-dogs, he preferred the open snow for a bed, and the spruce-tops for shelter.

Joan dropped her hand to his head, and at its touch there thrilled through him that strange joy that was his reward for leaving Grey Wolf and the wild. Slowly he raised his head until his black muzzle rested on her lap, and he closed his eyes while that wonderful little creature that mystified him so – the baby – prodded him with her tiny feet, and pulled his tawny hair. He loved these baby-maulings even more than the touch of Joan's hand.

Motionless, sphinx-like, undemonstrative in every muscle of his body, Kazan stood, scarcely breathing. More than once this lack of demonstration had urged Joan's husband to warn her. But the Wolf that was in Kazan, his wild aloofness, even his mating with Grey Wolf, had made her love him more. She understood, and had faith in him.

In the days of the last snow, Kazan had proved himself. A neighbouring trapper had run over with his team, and the baby Joan had toddled up to one of the big huskies. There was a fierce snap of jaws, a scream of horror from Joan, a shout from the men as they leaped towards the pack. But Kazan was ahead of them all. In a grey streak that travelled with the speed of a bullet, he was at the big husky's throat. When they pulled him off, the husky was dead. Joan thought of that now, as the baby kicked and tousled Kazan's head.

'Good old Kazan,' she cried softly, putting her face down close to him. 'We're glad you came, Kazan, for we're going to be alone tonight – baby and I. Daddy's gone to the post, and you must care for us while he's away.'

She tickled his nose with the end of her long shining braid. This always delighted the baby, for in spite of his stoicism Kazan had to sniff and sometimes to sneeze, and twig his ears. And it pleased him, too. He loved the sweet scent of Joan's hair.

'And you'd fight for us, if you had to, wouldn't you?' she went on. Then she rose quietly. 'I must close the door,' she said. 'I don't want you to go away again today, Kazan. You must stay with us.'

Kazan went off to his corner, and lay down. Just as there had been some strange thing at the top of the Sun Rock to disturb him that day, so now there was a mystery that disturbed him in the cabin. He sniffed the air, trying to fathom its secret. Whatever it was, it seemed to make his mistress different too. And she was digging out all sorts of odds and ends of things about the cabin, and doing them up in packages. Late that night, before she went to bed, Joan came and snuggled her hand close down beside him for a few moments.

'We're going away,' she whispered, and there was a curious tremble that was almost a sob in her voice. 'We're going home, Kazan. We're going away down where his people live – where they have churches, and cities, and music, and all the beautiful things in the world. And we're going to take *you*, Kazan!'

Kazan didn't understand. But he was happy at having the woman so near to him, and talking to him. At these times, he forgot Grey Wolf. The Dog that was in him surged over his quarter-stream of wildness, and the woman and the baby alone filled his world. But after Joan had gone to her bed, and all was quiet in the cabin, his old uneasiness returned. He rose to his feet and moved stealthily about the cabin, sniffing at the walls, the doors and the things his mistress had done into packages. A low whine rose in his throat. Joan, half-asleep, heard it, and muttered:

'Be quiet, Kazan. Go to sleep – go to sleep.'

Long after that, Kazan stood rigid in the centre of the room, listening, trembling. And faintly he heard, far away, the wailing cry of Grey Wolf. But tonight it was not the cry of loneliness. It sent a thrill through him. He ran to the door, and whined, but Joan was deep in slumber and did not hear him. Once more he heard the cry, and only once. Then the night grew still. He crouched down near the door.

Joan found him there, still watchful, still listening, when she awoke in the early morning. She came to open the door for him, and in a moment he was gone. His feet seemed scarcely to touch the earth as he sped in the direction of the Sun Rock. Across the plain he could see the cap of it already painted with a golden glow.

He came to the narrow winding trail, and wormed his way up it swiftly.

Grey Wolf was not at the top to greet him. But he could smell her, and the scent of that other thing was strong in the air. His muscles tightened; his legs grew tense. Deep down in his chest there began the low rumble of a growl. He knew now what that strange thing was that had haunted him, and made him uneasy. It was *life*. Something that lived and breathed had invaded the home which he and Grey Wolf had chosen. He bared his long fangs, and a snarl of defiance drew back his lips. Stiff-legged, prepared to spring, his neck and head reaching out, he approached the two rocks between which Grey Wolf had crept the night before. She was still there. And with her was *something else*. After a moment the tenseness left Kazan's body. His bristling crest drooped until it lay flat. His ears shot forward, and he put his head and shoulders between the two rocks, and whined softly. And Grey Wolf whined. Slowly Kazan backed out, and faced the rising sun. Then he lay down, so that his body shielded the entrance to the chamber between the rocks.

Grey Wolf was a mother.

The Tragedy on Sun Rock

All that day Kazan guarded the top of the Sun Rock. Fate, and the fear and brutality of masters, had heretofore kept him from fatherhood, and he was puzzled. Something told him now that he belonged to the Sun Rock, and not to the cabin. The call that came to him from over the plain was not so strong. At dusk Grey Wolf came out from her retreat, and slunk to his side, whimpering, and nipped gently at his shaggy neck. It was the old instinct of his father's that made him respond by caressing Grey Wolf's face with his tongue. Then Grey Wolf's jaws opened, and she laughed in short panting breaths, as if she had been hard run. She was happy, and as they heard a little snuffling sound from between the rocks, Kazan wagged his tail, and Grey Wolf darted back to her young.

The babyish cry and its effect upon Grey Wolf taught Kazan his first lesson in fatherhood. Instinct again told him that Grey Wolf could not go down to the hunt with him now – that she must stay at the top of the Sun Rock. So when the moon rose, he went down alone, and towards dawn returned with a big white Rabbit between his jaws. It was the wild in him that had made him do this, and Grey Wolf ate ravenously. Then he knew that each night hereafter he must hunt for Grey Wolf – and the little whimpering creatures hidden between the two rocks.

The next day, and still the next, he did not go to the cabin, though he heard the voices of both the man and the woman calling him. On the fifth he went down, and Joan and the baby were so glad that the woman hugged him, and the baby kicked and laughed and screamed at him, while the man stood by cautiously, watching their demonstrations with a gleam of disapprobation in his eyes.

'I'm afraid of him,' he told Joan for the hundredth time. 'That's the Wolf-gleam in his eyes. He's of a treacherous breed. Sometimes I wish we'd never brought him home.'

'If we hadn't – where would the baby – have gone!' Joan reminded him, a little catch in her voice.

'I had almost forgotten that,' said her husband. 'Kazan, you old devil, I guess I love you, too.' He laid his hand caressingly on Kazan's head. 'Wonder how he'll take to life down there?' he asked. 'He has always been used to the forests. It'll seem mighty strange.'

'And so – have I – always been used to the forests,' whispered Joan. 'I guess that's why I love Kazan – next to you and the baby. Kazan – dear old Kazan!'

This time Kazan felt and scented more of the mysterious thing in the cabin. Joan and her husband talked incessantly of their plans when they were together; and when the man was away, Joan talked to the baby, and to him. And each time he came down to the cabin during the week that followed, he grew more and more restless, until at last the man noticed the change in him.

'I believe he knows,' he said to Joan one evening. 'I believe he knows we're preparing to leave.' Then he added: 'The river was rising again today. It will be another week before we can start, perhaps longer.'

That same night the moon flooded the top of the Sun Rock, with a golden light, and out into the glow of it came Grey Wolf, with her three little whelps toddling behind her. There was much about these soft little balls that tumbled about him and snuggled in his tawny coat that reminded Kazan of the baby. At times they made the same queer, soft little sounds, and they staggered about on their four little legs just as helplessly as baby Joan made her way about on two. He did not fondle them, as Grey Wolf did, but the touch of them, and their babyish whimperings, filled him with a kind of pleasure that he had never experienced before.

The moon was straight above them, and the night was almost as bright as day, when he went down again to hunt for Grey Wolf. At the foot of the rock, a big white Rabbit popped up ahead of him, and he gave chase. For half a mile he pursued, until the Wolf instinct in him rose over the Dog, and he gave up the futile race. A Deer he might have overtaken, but small game the Wolf must hunt as the Fox hunts it; and he began to slip through the thickets slowly and as quietly as a shadow. He was a mile from the Sun Rock when two quick leaps put Grey Wolf's supper between his jaws. He trotted back slowly, dropping the big seven-pound Snow-shoe Hare now and then to rest.

When he came to the narrow trail that led to the top of the Sun Rock, he stopped. In that trail was the warm scent of strange feet. The Rabbit fell from his jaws. Every hair in his body was suddenly electrified into life. What he scented was not the scent of a Rabbit, a Marten or a Porcupine. Fang and claw had climbed the path ahead of him. And then, coming faintly to him from the top of the rock, he heard sounds which sent him up with a terrible whining cry. When he reached the summit he saw in the white moonlight a scene that stopped him for a single moment. Close to the edge of the sheer fall to the rocks, fifty feet below, Grey Wolf was engaged in a death-struggle with a huge grey Lynx. She was down – and under, and from her there came a sudden sharp terrible cry of pain.

Kazan flew across the rock. His attack was the swift assault of the Wolf, combined with the greater courage, the fury and the strategy of the husky. Another husky would have died in that first attack. But the Lynx was not a Dog or a Wolf. It was 'Mow-lee, the Swift', as the Sarcees had named it – the quickest creature in the wilderness. Kazan's inch-long fangs should have sunk deep in its jugular. But in a fractional part of a second, the Lynx had thrown itself back like a huge soft ball, and Kazan's teeth buried themselves in the flesh of its neck instead of the jugular. And Kazan was not now fighting the fangs of a Wolf in the pack, or of another husky. He was fighting claws – claws that ripped like twenty razor-edged knives, and which even a jugular hold could not stop.

Once he had fought a Lynx in a trap, and he had not forgotten the lesson the battle had taught him. He fought to pull the Lynx *down*, instead of forcing it on its back, as he would have done with another Dog or a Wolf. He knew that when on its back, the fierce Cat was

most dangerous. One rip of its powerful hind-feet could disembowel him. Behind him he heard Grey Wolf sobbing and crying, and he knew she was terribly hurt. He was filled with the rage and strength of two Dogs, and his teeth met through the flesh and hide of the Cat's throat. But the big Lynx escaped death by half an inch. It would take a fresh grip to reach the jugular, and suddenly Kazan made the deadly lunge. There was an instant's freedom for the Lynx, and in that moment it flung itself back, and Kazan gripped at its throat – *on top.*

The Cat's claws ripped through his flesh, cutting open his side – a little too high to kill. Another stroke and they would have cut to his vitals. But they had struggled close to the edge of the rock wall; and suddenly, without a snarl or a cry, they rolled over. It was fifty or sixty feet to the rocks of the ledge below, and even as they pitched over and over in the fall, Kazan's teeth sank deeper. They struck with terrific force, Kazan uppermost. The shock sent him half a dozen feet from his enemy. He was up like a flash, dizzy, snarling, on the defensive. The Lynx lay limp and motionless where it had fallen. Kazan came nearer, still prepared, and sniffed cautiously. Something told him that the fight was over. He turned and dragged himself slowly along the edge to the trail, and returned to Grey Wolf.

Grey Wolf was no longer in the moonlight. Close to the two rocks lay the limp and lifeless bodies of the three pups. The Lynx had torn them to pieces. With a whine of grief, Kazan approached the two boulders and thrust his head between them. Grey Wolf was there, crying to herself in that terrible sobbing way. He went in, and began to lick her bleeding shoulders and head. All the rest of that night she whimpered with pain.

With dawn she dragged herself out to the lifeless little bodies on the rock.

And then Kazan saw the terrible work of the Lynx. For Grey Wolf was blind – not for a day or a night, but blind for all time. A gloom that no sun could break had become her shroud. And perhaps again it was that instinct of animal creation, which often is more wonderful than man's reason, that told Kazan what had happened. For he knew now that she was helpless – more helpless than the little creatures that had gambolled in the moonlight a few hours before. He remained close beside her all that day.

Vainly that day did Joan call for Kazan. Her voice rose to the Sun Rock, and Grey Wolf's head snuggled closer to Kazan, and Kazan's ears dropped back, and he licked her wounds. Late in the afternoon Kazan left Grey Wolf long enough to run to the bottom of the trail and bring up the Snow-shoe Rabbit. Grey Wolf nuzzled the fur and flesh, but would not eat. Still a little later Kazan urged her to follow him to the trail. He no longer wanted to stay at the top of the Sun Rock, and he no longer wanted Grey Wolf to stay there. Step by step he drew her down the winding patch away from her dead puppies. She would move only when he was very near her – so near that she could touch his scarred flank with her nose.

They came at last to the point in the trail where they had to leap down a distance of three or four feet from the edge of a rock, and here Kazan saw how utterly helpless Grey Wolf had become. She whined, and crouched twenty times before she dared make the spring, and then she jumped stiff-legged, and fell in a heap at Kazan's feet. After this Kazan did not have to urge her so hard, for the fall impinged on her the fact that she was safe only when her muzzle touched her mate's flank. She followed him obediently when they reached the plain, trotting with her foreshoulder to his hip.

Kazan was heading for a thicket in the creek bottom half a mile away, and a dozen times in that short distance Grey Wolf stumbled and fell. And each time she fell Kazan learned a little more of the limitations of blindness. Once he sprang off in pursuit of a Rabbit, but he had not taken twenty leaps when he stopped and looked back. Grey Wolf had not moved an inch. She stood motionless, sniffing the air – waiting for him! For a full minute Kazan stood, also waiting. Then he returned to her. Ever after this he returned to the point where he had left Grey Wolf, knowing that he would find her there.

All that day they remained in the thicket. In the afternoon, he visited the cabin. Joan and her husband were there, and both saw at once Kazan's torn side and his lacerated head and shoulders.

'Pretty near a finish fight for him,' said the man, after he had examined him. 'It was either a Lynx or a Bear. Another Wolf could not do that.'

For half an hour, Joan worked over him, talking to him all the time, and fondling him with her soft hands. She bathed his wounds in warm water, and then covered them with a healing salve, and Kazan was filled again with that old restful desire to remain with her always, and never to go back into the forests. For an hour she let him lie on the edge of her dress, with his nose touching her foot, while she worked on baby things. Then she rose to prepare supper, and Kazan got up – a little wearily – and went to the door. Grey Wolf and the gloom of the night were calling him, and he answered that call with a slouch of his shoulders and a drooping head. Its old thrill was gone. He watched his chance, and went out through the door. The moon had risen when he rejoined Grey Wolf. She greeted his return with a low whine of joy, and nuzzled him with her blind face. In her helplessness she looked happier than Kazan in all his strength.

From now on, during the days that followed, it was a last great fight between blind and faithful Grey Wolf and the woman. If Joan had known of what lay in the thicket, if she could once have seen the poor creature to whom Kazan was now all life – the sun, the stars, the moon, and food – she would have helped Grey Wolf. But as it was, she tried to lure Kazan more and more to the cabin, and slowly she won.

At last the great day came, eight days after the fight on the Sun Rock. Kazan had taken Grey Wolf to a wooded point in the river two days before, and there he had left her the preceding night when he went to the cabin. This time a stout babiche thong was tied to the collar round his neck, and he was fastened to a staple in the log wall. Joan and her husband were up before it was light next day. The sun was just rising when they all went out, the man carrying the baby, and Joan leading him. Joan turned and locked the cabin door, and Kazan heard a sob in her throat as they followed the man down to the river. The big canoe was packed and waiting. Joan got in first, with the baby. Then, still holding the babiche thong, she drew Kazan up close to her, so that he lay with his weight against her.

The sun fell warmly on Kazan's back as they shoved off, and he closed his eyes, and rested his head on Joan's lap. Her hand fell softly on his shoulder. He heard again that sound which the man could not hear, the broken sob in her throat, as the canoe moved slowly down to the wooded point.

Joan waved her hand back at the cabin, just disappearing behind the trees.

'Good-bye!' she cried sadly. 'Good-bye –' And then she buried her face close down to Kazan and the baby, and sobbed.

The man stopped paddling.

'You're not sorry – Joan?' he asked.

They were drifting past the point now, and the scent of Grey Wolf came to Kazan's nostrils, rousing him, and bringing a low whine from his throat.

'You're not sorry – we're going?' Joan shook her head.

'No,' she replied. 'Only I've – always lived here – in the forests – and they're home.'

The point with its white finger of sand, was behind them now. And Kazan was standing rigid, facing it. The man called to him and Joan lifted her head. She, too, saw the point, and suddenly the babiche leash slipped from her fingers, and a strange light leaped in her blue eyes as she saw what stood at the end of that white tip of sand. It was Grey Wolf. Her blind eyes were turned towards Kazan. At last Grey Wolf, the faithful, understood. Scent told her what her eyes could not see. Kazan and the man-smell were together. And they were going – going – going –

'Look!' whispered Joan.

The man turned. Grey Wolf's feet were in the water. And now, as the canoe drifted farther and farther away, she settled back on her haunches, raised her head to the sun which she could not see, and gave her last long wailing cry for Kazan.

The canoe lurched. A tawny body shot through the air – and Kazan was gone.

The man reached forward for his rifle. Joan's hand stopped him. Her face was white.

'Let him go back to her! Let him go – let him go!' she cried. 'It is his place – with her.'

And Kazan, reaching the shore, shook the water from his shaggy hair, and looked for the last time towards the woman. The canoe was drifting slowly around the first bend. A moment more and it disappeared.

Grey Wolf had won.

Garm – A Hostage _____

Rudyard Kipling

Few writers have possessed such strong feelings for animals as Rudyard Kipling (1865–1936), as his *Jungle Book* tales well show. I was engrossed with his stories from the time I could first read. When I lay in bed in a London hospital as a small boy, in 1936 – recovering from a tonsils and adenoids operation – I was visited by a literary friend of my parents, who spotted the Kipling books on my bedside table. 'Oh, I know him well! Would you like me to ask him to autograph them for you?' she offered. But, alas, she returned the following week with the books, a headshake and a regretful smile. Kipling had just died.

Born in India and working as a journalist there during the 1880s, he was intimately familiar with the society of the British Raj. So his backgrounds always provide a rich and accurate comment on the place and period, as they do in 'Garm – A Hostage', one of my early favourites and surely one of the best half-dozen dog stories ever told.

The narrator opens by describing a visit to the local regimental barracks one evening to watch their amateur theatricals, when a drunk soldier staggers in front of his carriage and is knocked down. The narrator takes him home, bandages him, gives him a bed for the night and drives him back in the morning. The soldier, who is called Stanley, returns to the narrator's house three days later with his white bull-terrier, saying 'E's for you.' He puts the dog through a number of tricks, makes him lie down as though he were dead, then runs back to barracks.

The narrator describes the dog as 'one of the finest – of old-fashioned breed, two parts bull and one terrier – that I have ever set eyes on'. After the bull terrier saves his little bitch Vixen from attack by a ferocious pack of pariahs, the narrator calls him Garm of the Bloody Breast ('who was a great person in his time'). But Garm soon proves miserable at being parted from Stanley, who, just as miserable at being parted from Garm, comes every day to visit him secretly in the narrator's garden. The narrator explains the situation to an Irishman, Private Ortheris, a great friend of Stanley's:

'. . . And now Stanley's in my garden crying over his dog. Why doesn't he take him back? They're both unhappy.'

'Unhappy! There's no sense in the little man any more. But 'tis his fit.'

'What *is* his fit? He travels fifty miles a week to see the brute, and he pretends not to notice me. . . . I'm as unhappy as he is. Make him take the dog back.'

'It's his penance he's set himself. I told him by way of a joke, after you'd run him over so convenient that night, whin he was drunk – I said if he was a Catholic he'd do penance. Off he went wid that fit in his little head *an'* a dose of fever, and nothin' would suit but given' you the dog as a hostage.'

'Hostage for what? I don't want hostages from Stanley.'

'For his good behaviour. He's keepin' straight now, the way it's no pleasure to associate wid him.'

Stanley, sick and fevered with sorrow, is sent to the hills with the

other regimental invalids, but, to the narrator's great consternation, he even walks the fourteen miles from there to visit Garm. Kipling continues:

Next evening who should turn up but Stanley. The officer had sent him back fourteen miles by rail with a note begging me to return the [officer's] retriever if I had found him, and, if I had not, to offer huge rewards. The last train to camp left at half-past ten, and Stanley stayed till ten talking to Garm. I argued and entreated, and even threatened to shoot the bull-terrier, but the little man was as firm as a rock, though I gave him a good dinner and talked to him most severely. Garm knew as well as I that this was the last time he could hope to see his man, and followed Stanley like a shadow. The retriever said nothing, but licked his lips after his meal and waddled off without so much as saying 'Thank you' to the disgusted dog-boy.

So that last meeting was over, and I felt as wretched as Garm, who moaned in his sleep all night. When we went to the office he found a place under the table close to Vixen, and dropped flat till it was time to go home. There was no more running out into the verandahs, no slinking away for stolen talks with Stanley. As the weather grew warmer the dogs were forbidden to run beside the cart, but sat at my side on the seat, Vixen with her head under the crook of my left elbow, and Garm hugging the left handrail. . . .

Living with the dog as I did, I never noticed that he was more than ordinarily upset by the hot weather, till one day at the Club a man said: 'That dog of yours will die in a week or two. He's a shadow.' Then I dosed Garm with iron and quinine, which he hated; and I felt very anxious. He lost his appetite, and Vixen was allowed to eat his dinner under his eyes. Even that did not make him swallow, and we held a consultation on him, of the best man-doctor in the place; a lady-doctor, who cured the sick wives of kings; and the Deputy Inspector-General of the veterinary service of all India. They pronounced upon his symptoms, and I told them his story, and Garm lay on a sofa licking my hand.

'He's dying of a broken heart,' said the lady-doctor suddenly.

''Pon my word,' said the Deputy Inspector-General, 'I believe Mrs Macrae is perfectly right – as usual.'

The best man-doctor in the place wrote a prescription, and the veterinary Deputy Inspector-General went over it afterwards to be sure that the drugs were in the proper dog-proportions; and that was the first time in his life that our doctor ever allowed his prescriptions to be edited. It was a strong tonic, and it put the dear boy on his feet for a week or two; then he lost flesh again. I asked a man I knew to take him up to the Hills with him when he went, and the man came to the door with his kit packed on the top of the carriage. Garm took in the situation at one red glance. The hair rose along his back; he sat down in front of me and delivered the most awful growl I have ever heard in the jaws of a dog. I shouted to my friend to get away at once, and as soon as the carriage was out of the garden Garm laid his head on my knee and whined. So I knew his answer, and devoted myself to getting Stanley's address in the Hills.

My turn to go to the cool came in late August. We were allowed thirty days' holiday in a year, if no one fell sick, and we took it as we could be spared. My chief and Bob the Librarian had their holiday first, and when they were gone I made a calendar, as I always did, and hung it up at the end of my cot, tearing off one day at a time till they returned. Vixen had gone up to the Hills with me five times before; and she appreciated the cold and the damp and the beautiful wood fires as much as I did.

'Garm,' I said, 'we are going back to Stanley at Kasauli. Kasauli – Stanley; Stanley – Kasauli.' And I repeated it twenty times. It was not Kasauli really, but another place. Still I remembered what Stanley had said in my garden on the last night, and I dared not change the name. Then Garm began to tremble; then he barked; and then he leaped up at me, frisking and wagging his tail.

'Not now,' I said, holding up my hand. 'When I say "Go", we'll go, Garm.' I pulled out the little blanket coat and spiked collar that Vixen always wore up in the Hills to protect her against sudden chills and thieving leopards, and I let the two smell them and talk it over. What they said of course I did not know, but it made a new dog of Garm. His eyes were bright; and he barked joyfully when I spoke to him. He ate his food, and he killed his rats for the next three weeks, and when he began to whine I had only to say 'Stanley – Kasauli; Kasauli – Stanley' to wake him up. I wish I had thought of it before.

We came to Umballa in the hot misty dawn, four or five men, who had been working hard for eleven months, shouting for our dâks – the two-horse travelling carriages that were to take us up to the Kalka at the foot of the Hills. It was all new to Garm. He did not understand carriages where you lay at full length on your bedding, but Vixen knew and hopped into her place at once, Garm following. . . .

There was a river to be forded, and four bullocks pulled the carriage, and Vixen stuck her head out of the sliding-door and nearly fell into the water while she gave directions. Garm was silent and curious, and rather needed reassuring about Stanley and Kasauli. So we rolled, barking and yelping, into Kalka for lunch, and Garm ate enough for two. . . .

Suddenly Kadir Buksh said, over his shoulder: 'Here is Solon'; and Garm snored where he lay with his head on my knee. Solon is an unpleasant little cantonment, but it has the advantage of being cool and healthy. It is all bare and windy, and one generally stops at a rest-house nearby for something to eat. I got out and took both dogs with me, while Kadir Buksh made tea. A soldier told us we should find Stanley 'out there', nodding his head towards a bare, bleak hill.

When we climbed to the top we spied that very Stanley, who had given me all this trouble, sitting on a rock with his face in his hands, and his overcoat hanging loose about him. I never saw anything so lonely and dejected in my life as this one little man, crumpled up and thinking, on the great grey hillside.

Here Garm left me.

He departed without a word, and, so far as I could see, without moving his legs. He flew through the air bodily, and I heard the whack of him as he flung himself at Stanley, knocking the little man clean over. They rolled on the ground together, shouting and yelping, and hugging. I could not see which was dog and which was man, till Stanley got up and whimpered.

He told me that he had been suffering from fever at intervals, and was very weak. He looked all he said, but even while I watched, both man and dog plumped out to their natural sizes, precisely as dried apples swell in water. Garm was on his shoulder, and his breast and feet all at the same time, so that Stanley spoke all through a cloud of Garm – gulping, sobbing, slavering Garm. He did not say anything that I could understand, except that he had fancied he was going to die, but that now he was quite well, and that he was not going to give up Garm any more to anybody under the rank of Beelzebub.

Then he said he felt hungry, and thirsty, and happy.

We went down to tea at the rest-house, where Stanley stuffed himself with sardines and raspberry jam, and beer, and cold mutton and pickles, when Garm wasn't climbing over him; and then Vixen and I went on.

Garm saw how it was all at once. He said goodbye to me three times, giving me both paws one after another, and leaping on my shoulder. He further escorted us, singing Hosannas at the top of his voice, a mile down the road. Then he raced back to his own master.

Vixen never opened her mouth, but when the cold twilight came, and we could see the lights of Simla across the hills, she snuffled with her nose at the breast of my ulster. I unbuttoned it, and tucked her inside. Then she gave a contented little sniff, and fell fast asleep, her head on my breast, till we bundled out at Simla, two of the four happiest people in all the world that night.

The Power of the Dog

Rudyard Kipling

There is sorrow enough in the natural way
From men and women to fill our day;
But when we are certain of sorrow in store,
Why do we always arrange for more?
Brothers and sisters, I bid you beware
Of giving your heart to a dog to tear.

Buy a pup and your money will buy
Love unflinching that cannot lie –
Perfect passion and worship fed
By a kick in the ribs or a pat on the head.
Nevertheless it is hardly fair
To risk your heart for a dog to tear.

When the fourteen years which Nature permits
Are closing in asthma, or tumour, or fits,
And the vet's unspoken prescription runs
To lethal chambers or loaded guns,
Then you will find – it's your own affair
But . . . you've given your heart to a dog to tear.

When the body that lived at your single will
When the whimper of welcome is stilled (how
   still!)
When the spirit that answered your every mood
Is gone – wherever it goes – for good,
You will discover how much you care
And will give your heart to a dog to tear!

We've sorrow enough in the natural way,
When it comes to burying Christian clay.
Our loves are not given, but only lent,
At compound interest of cent per cent.
Though it is not always the case, I believe,
That the longer we've kept 'em, the more do we
    grieve:
For, when debts are payable, right or wrong,
A short-time loan is as bad as a long –
So why in Heaven (before we are there!)
Should we give our hearts to a dog to tear?

The Galsworthys' Dogs

John and Ada Galsworthy

If a man does not soon pass beyond the thought 'By what shall this dog profit me?' into the large state of simple gladness to be with dog, he shall never know the very essence of that companionship which depends not on the points of dog, but on some strange and subtle mingling of mute spirits. For it is by muteness that a dog becomes for one so utterly beyond value, with him one is at peace where words play no torturing tricks. When he just sits loving and knows that he is being loved, those are the moments that I think are precious to a dog: when, with his adoring soul coming through his eyes, he feels that you are really thinking of him.

That extract was written by the dramatist and novelist John Galsworthy (1867–1933), who brought dog characters into *The Forsyte Saga*, *The Patrician*, *The Stoic* and other books. Aunt Juley in *On Forsyte Change*, in defiance of her relations, eventually keeps the Pomeranian who 'adopts' her in the park. This passage shows Aunt Juley's dilemma:

Dear, dear! That little white dog was running about a great deal. Was it lost? Backwards and forwards, round and round! What they called – she believed – a Pomeranian, quite a new kind of dog. And, seeing a bench, Mrs Septimus Small bent, with a little backward heave to save

her 'bustle', and sat down to watch what was the matter with the
white dog. The sun, glaring out between two Spring clouds, fell on
her face, transfiguring the pouting puffs of flesh, which seemed trying
to burst their way through the network of her veil. Her eyes, of a
Forsyte grey, lingered on the dog with the greater pertinacity in that of
late – owing to poor Tommy's [their cat's] disappearance, very
mysterious – she suspected the sweep – there had been nothing but
'Polly' at Timothy's to lavish her affection on. This dog was draggled
and dirty, as if it had been out all night, but it had a dear little pointed
nose. She thought, too, that it seemed to be noticing her, and at once
had a swelling-up sensation beneath her corsets. Almost as if aware of
this, the dog came sidling, and sat down on its haunches in the grass, as
though trying to make up its mind about her. Aunt Juley pursed her
lips in the endeavour to emit a whistle. The veil prevented this, but she
held out her gloved hand. 'Come, little dog – nice little dog!' It seemed
to her dear heart that the little dog sighed as it sat there, as if relieved
that at long last someone had taken notice of it. But it did not
approach. The tip of its bushy tail quivered, however, and Aunt Juley
redoubled the suavity of her voice: 'Nice little fellow – come then!'

The little dog slithered forward, humbly wagging its entire body,
just out of reach. Aunt Juley saw that it had no collar. Really, its nose
and eyes were sweet!

'Pom!,' she said. 'Dear little Pom!'

The dog looked as if it would let her love it, and sensation increased
beneath her corsets.

'Come, pretty!'

Not, of course, that he was pretty, all dirty like that; but his ears
were pricked, and his eyes looked at her, bright, and rather round their
corners – most intelligent! Lost – and in London! It was like that sad
little book of Mrs – What *was* her name – not the authoress of *Jessica's
First Prayer*? – dear, dear! Now, fancy forgetting that! The dog made a
sudden advance, and curved like a C, all fluttering, was now almost
within reach of her gloved fingers, at which it sniffed. Aunt Juley
uttered a purring noise. Pride was filling her heart that out of all the
people it *might* have taken notice of, she should be the only one. It had
put out its tongue now, and was panting in the agony of indecision.
Poor little thing! It clearly didn't know whether it dared try another
master – not, of course, that she could possibly take it home, with all
the carpets, and dear Ann so particular about everything being nice,
and – Timothy! Timothy would be horrified! And yet – ! Well, they
couldn't prevent her stroking its little nose. And she too panted

slightly behind her veil. It *was* agitating! And then, without either of them knowing how, her fingers and the nose were in contact. The dog's tail was now perfectly still; its body trembled. Aunt Juley had a sudden feeling of shame at being so formidable; and with instinct inherited rather than acquired, for she had no knowledge of dogs, she slid one finger round an ear and scratched. It *was* to be hoped he hadn't fleas! And then! The little dog leaped on her lap. It crouched there just as it had sprung, with its bright eyes upturned to her face. A strange dog – her dress – her Sunday best! It *was* an event! The little dog stretched up, and licked her chin. Almost mechanically Aunt Juley rose. And the little dog slipped off. Really she didn't know – it took such liberties! Oh! dear – it *was* thin, fluttering round her feet! What would Mr Scoles say? Perhaps if she walked on! She turned towards home, and the dog followed her skirt at a distance of six inches. The thought that she was going to eat roast beef, Yorkshire pudding, and mincepies, was almost unbearable to Aunt Juley, seeing it gaze up as if saying: 'Some for me! Some for me!' Thoughts warred within her: must she 'shoo' and threaten it with her parasol? Or should she – ? Oh! This would never do! Dogs could be *so* – she had heard? And then – the responsibility! And fleas! Timothy couldn't endure fleas! And it might not know how to behave in a house! Oh, no! She really couldn't! The little dog suddenly raised one paw. Tt, tt! Look at its little face! And a fearful boldness attacked Aunt Juley. Turning resolutely towards the gate of the Gardens, she said in a weak voice: 'Come along, then!' And the little dog came. It was dreadful!

While she was trying to cross the Bayswater Road, two or three of those dangerous hansom cabs came dashing past – so reckless! – and in the very middle of the street a 'growler' turned round, so that she had to stand quite still, and, of course, there was no policeman. The traffic was really getting beyond bounds. If only she didn't meet Timothy coming in from his constitutional, and could get a word with Smither – a capable girl – and have the little dog fed and washed before anybody saw it. And then? Perhaps it could be kept in the basement till somebody came to claim it. But how could people come to claim it if they didn't know it was there? If only there were someone to consult! Perhaps Smither would know a policeman – only she hoped not – policemen were rather dangerous for a nice-looking girl like Smither, with her colour, and such a figure, for her age. Then, suddenly, realising that she had reached home, she was seized by panic from head to heel. There was the bell – it was not the epoch of latchkeys; and there the smell of dinner – yes, and the little dog had

smelt it! It was now or never. Aunt Juley pointed her parasol at the dog
and said very feebly: 'Shoo!' But it only crouched. She couldn't drive
it away! And with an immense daring she rang the bell. While she
stood waiting for the door to be opened, she almost enjoyed a
sensation of defiance. She was doing a dreadful thing, but she didn't
care! Then, the doorway yawned, and her heart sank slowly towards
her high and buttoned boots.

'Oh, Smither! This poor little dog has followed me. Nothing has
ever followed me before. It must be lost. And it looks so thin and
dirty. What *shall* we do?'

The tail of the dog, edging into the home of that rich smell,
fluttered.

'Aoh!' said Smither – she was young! 'Paw little thing! Shall I get
Cook to give it some scraps, Ma'am?' At the word 'scraps' the dog's
eyes seemed to glow.

'Well,' said Aunt Juley, 'you do it on your own responsibility,
Smither. Take it downstairs quickly.'

She stood breathless while the dog, following Smither and its nose,
glided through the little hall and down the kitchen stairs. The pit–pat
of its feet roused in Aunt Juley the most mingled sensations she had
experienced since the death of Septimus Small.

She went up to her room, and took off her veil and bonnet. What
was she going to say? She went downstairs without knowing. . . .

Galsworthy's wife, Ada, was at least as great a dog-lover as her
husband. In 1935 Heinemann published her little tribute *The Dear
Dogs*, in which she describes, with great affection, all her favourites,
including this Dalmatian:

Dalmatian Dick was my special property and delight. He did his best
to assume drawing-room manners, but the chief manifestation of
them was, unfortunately, a gradual annexation of the softest place on
the softest of the Chesterfields; and this he would dispute with
anyone. Being a large dog, with an easy growl and none too good a
temper, this was very awkward. I always felt that, owing to some
kink in body or mind, there was an insuperable barrier to knowing all
about Dickie; I longed so to fathom what lay behind his lovely,
mournful moss-agate eyes. A strange dog, so irritable, yet so
affectionate! He was not strong, physically, and gave terrifying
exhibitions of hysteria from time to time. Quite obviously, he would
see a phantom, and with head up would pursue it with howls and

screams through the long corridor running from end to end of the house; and behind him ran his distracted, sympathising owners, of whom he was for the moment quite oblivious. His vet told us that Dalmatians were, as a breed, peculiarly subject to hysteria. The vet himself had a thrilling experience with our Dickie. For some small ailment it was judged best to transport Dickie to the vet's establishment some five miles away; being about to return home after his visit to us, the kindly man offered to take the dog in his open car, which he was driving. Dickie started willingly enough, for the two were very good friends. However, halfway up Bury Hill, noted for length, steepness, twistiness, and the cheerful amount of traffic coming round its corners at most times, Dickie was overcome by hysteria. It must have been something of a feat, driving up that steep hill with one hand, and holding a temporarily demented dog, large and very wilful, with the other.

In those days it was a spectacular cortège that left our house for the early-morning ride on the Downs: a dark iron-grey mare; a red setter; a Dalmatian dog, a black spaniel, all streaming up Bury Hill at 7.45 a.m. Dickie, as was to be expected of a Dalmatian [or carriage dog], followed the horse's heels perfectly, the others, not so well; Rex was wild, as I have said, and Jon remarkably impudent in traffic. I am credibly informed that he was once seen being very, very gently pushed down Bury Hill by an indulgent car. When the daily ride was topped up with half a dozen jumps over hurdles, Jon apparently laid careful plans for being trodden on by the horses as they came over. He was nearly always discovered wallowing just under their alighting feet. Luckily the horses knew his ways. Dickie, on the other hand, was a lovely sight, placing his straight, clean forelegs neatly together and pouring himself over the jumps in perfect style and rhythm with his horses. Rex was usually some distance away, leading his own life, at a canter, nose down to some scent or other. . . .

Ada invited her husband to contribute a postscript to *The Dear Dogs* and this is what he wrote:

He is by far the nearest thing to man on the face of the earth; the one link that we have spiritually with the animal creation; the one dumb creature into whose eyes we can look and tell pretty well for certain what emotion, even what thought is at work; the one dumb creature which – not as a rare exception, but almost always – steadily feels the sentiment of love and trust.

I have observed that before men can be gentle and broad-minded with each other, they are always gentle and broad-minded about beasts. These dumb things, so beautiful – even the plain ones – in their different ways, and so touching in their dumbness, do draw us to magnanimity, and help the wings of our hearts to grow.

There is a great comfort in the companionship of a dog, with its ever-ready touching humility, which human companionship, save of the nearest, does not bring.

Little Lizzie

Somerville and Ross

Those vivid and amusing tales of Irish country life at the end of the Victorian era, headed by *Some Experiences of an Irish R.M.*, in which Edith Œnone Somerville (1858–1949) and her cousin Violet Martin ('Martin Ross') (1862–1915) collaborated, rarely progressed for long without horses, dogs and cats taking the stage. The following vignette of terrier affection, taken from *An Enthusiast*, is, I think, especially dog-sensitive:

Little Lizzie was sitting in the stable yard waiting for his return; she crept into the house after him, and followed him to the room known as his office. She watched him as he threw himself down in an arm-chair and began to try and read a book, and then betook herself to her own basket in a remote corner. She did not lie down, but sat with her head up, and her small eyes fixed on him as if he were a hole from which, at any moment, a rat's head might emerge. Lizzie never obtruded her affection on the god of her adoration; she disapproved of demonstrations as much, even, as Mrs Palliser, but she, unlike Mrs Palliser, had a soul as sensitive as an aneroid to variations of mood. When Dan dropped the book, and leaned back in his chair with a long sigh of nerve-tension she understood that he was troubled, and consequently in need of the prop of her presence. She noiselessly left her basket and stole across the room, and abruptly poked a nose as sharp and fine as a fox's into the big listless hand that hung near to the floor over the edge of the chair. The hand instinctively gathered the little head into it, fondlingly. She waited an instant, and then, with a hop sparingly adjusted to the effort of reaching Dan's knee, she landed herself in the haven where she would be, and having given the god's chin a lick so brief and stern and dry as to suggest the striking of a match, she settled down, with a slight groan, on his knees.

'Thank you, Lizzie,' said Dan, who was always polite to dogs, 'that's very kind of you. But I'm afraid you can't help me much.'

The Most Perfect Creation of God? _____

Axel Munthe

The Swedish author of that classic autobiography *The Story of San Michele*, Axel Munthe (1857–1949), who became a doctor in Paris at a precociously early age and was described by his publishers as 'the friend of European royalty and of most of the literary, social and historical personalities of the day', showed an extraordinary rapport with animals as well as humans. His compassion is mirrored in the heartfelt way in which he wrote of the sick beasts he attended in the Jardin des Plantes, and in which he condemned vivisection, the contemporary killing of songbirds for luxury food and man's inhumanity to the nonhuman species in general. No animal features more strongly in *The Story of San Michele* than the dog:

Never forget that the mentality of one dog is totally different from that of another. The sharp wit that sparkles in the quick eye of a fox-terrier, for instance, reflects a mental activity totally different from the serene wisdom which shines in the calm eye of a St Bernard or an old sheep-dog. The intelligence of dogs is proverbial, but there is a great difference of degree, already apparent in the puppies as soon as they open their eyes. There are even stupid dogs, though the percentage is much smaller than in man. On the whole it is easy to understand the dog and to learn to read his thoughts. The dog cannot dissimulate, cannot deceive, cannot lie because he cannot speak. The dog is a saint. He is straightforward and honest by nature.

If, in exceptional cases, there appear in a dog some stigmas of hereditary sin traceable to his wild ancestors, who had to rely on cunning in their fight for existence, these stigmas will disappear when his experience has taught him that he can rely upon straight and just dealings from us. If these stigmas should remain in a dog who is well treated, the dog is not normal; he is suffering from moral insanity, and should be given a painless death. These cases are extremely rare. A dog gladly admits the superiority of his master over himself, accepts his judgement as final, but, contrary to what many dog-lovers believe, he does not consider himself as a slave. His submission is voluntary and he expects his own small rights to be respected. He looks upon his master as his king, almost as his god; he expects his god to be severe if need be, but he expects him to be just. He knows that his god can read his thoughts, and he knows it is no good to try to conceal them. . . .

The dog can read his master's thoughts, can understand his varying moods, and foretell his decision. He knows by instinct when he is not wanted, lies quite still for hours when his king is hard at work as kings often are, or at least ought to be. But when his king is sad and worried he knows that his time has come, and he creeps up and lays his head on his lap. Don't worry! Never mind if they all abandon you, I am here to replace all your friends and to fight all your enemies! Come along and let us go for a walk and forget all about it! . . .

Alas! the life of a dog is so short, and there are few of us who have not been in mourning for a lost friend. Your first impulse, and your first words after you have laid him to rest under a tree in the park, are that you never wish to have another dog; no other dog could ever be to you what he has been. You are mistaken. It is not *a* dog we love; it is *the* dog. They are all more or less the same; they are all ready to love you and be loved by you. They are all representatives of the most lovable and, morally speaking, most perfect creation of God. If you loved your dead friend in the right way, you cannot do without another. Alas! he also will have to part from you, for those beloved by the gods die young.

To a Black Greyhound

Julian Grenfell

Shining black in the shining light
  Inky black in the golden sun,
Graceful as the swallow's flight,
  Light as swallow, winged one,
Swift as driven hurricane –
  Double-sinewed stretch and spring,
Muffled thud of flying feet,
  See the black dog galloping,
    Hear his wild foot-beat.

See him lie when the day is dead,
  Black curves curled on the boarded floor.
Sleepy eyes, my sleepy-head –
  Eyes that were aflame before.
Gentle now, they burn no more,
  Gentle now and softly warm,
With the fire that made them bright
  Hidden – as when after storm
    Softly falls the night.

God of speed, who makes the fire –
　　God of peace, who lulls the same –
God who gives the fierce desire,
　　Lust for blood as fierce as flame –
God who stands in Pity's name –
　　Many may ye be or less,
Ye who rule the earth and sun:
　　Gods of strength and gentleness,
　　　Ye are ever one.

To Fulfil Our Every Wish and Whim ____

Maurice Maeterlinck

The next excerpt comes from 'My Dog' by Maurice Maeterlinck (1862–1949), the Belgian dramatist and essayist who won the Nobel Prize for literature in 1911. This brief essay, which is in mourning for his Pelléas, opens with these words: 'I have lost, within these last few days, a little bull-dog. He had just completed the sixth month of his brief existence. He had no history. His intelligent eyes opened to look out upon the world, to love mankind, then closed again on the cruel secrets of death.' The essay includes a panegyric to dogdom:

We have not to gain his confidence or his friendship: he is born our friend; while his eyes are still closed, already he believes in us; even before his birth, he has given himself to man. But the word 'friend' does not exactly depict his affectionate worship. He loves us and reveres us as though we had drawn him out of nothing. He is, before all, our creature, full of gratitude and more devoted than the apple of our eye. He is our intimate and impassioned slave, whom nothing discourages, whom nothing repels, whose ardent trust and love nothing can impair. He has solved, in an admirable and touching manner, the terrifying problem which human wisdom would have to solve if a divine race came to occupy our globe. He has loyally, religiously, irrevocably recognized the superiority of man and has surrendered himself to him body and soul, with not an after-thought, with no idea of drawing back, reserving of his independence, his instinct and his character only the small part indispensable to the continuation of the life prescribed by nature to his species. With a certainty, an unconstraint and a simplicity that surprise us a little, deeming us better and more powerful than all that exists, he betrays, for our benefit, the whole of the animal kingdom to which he belongs and, without scruple, denies his race, his kin, his mother and even his young.

But he loves us not only in his consciousness and his intelligence: the very instinct of his race, the entire unconsciousness of his species, it appears, think only of us and dream only of being useful to us. To serve us better, to adapt himself better to our different needs, he has adopted every shape and been able infinitely to vary the faculties, the aptitudes which he places at our disposal. Is he to aid us in the pursuit of game in the plains? His legs lengthen inordinately, his muzzle tapers, his lungs widen, he becomes swifter than the deer. Does our prey hide under wood? The docile genius of the species, forestalling our desires, presents us with the basset, a sort of serpent, almost without feet, which steals into the closest thickets. Do we ask that he should drive our flocks? The same compliant genius grants him the requisite size, intelligence, energy and vigilance. Do we intend him to watch and defend our house? His head becomes round and monstrous, in order that his jaws may be more powerful, more formidable and more tenacious. Are we taking him to the South? His hair grows shorter and lighter, so that he may faithfully accompany us under the rays of a hotter sun. Are we going up to the North? His feet grow larger, the better to tread the snow; his fur thickens, in order that the cold may not compel him to abandon us. Is he intended only for us to play with, to amuse the leisure of our eyes, to adorn and liven the home? He clothes himself in a sovereign grace and elegance, he makes himself smaller than a doll to sleep on our knees by the fireside, or even consents, should our fancy demand it, to appear a little ridiculous to please us.

You shall not find, in nature's immense crucible, a single living being that has shown a like suppleness, a similar abundance of forms, the same prodigious faculty of accommodation to our wishes. This is because, in the world which we know, among the different and primitive geniuses of life that preside over the evolution of the several species, there exists not one, excepting that of the dog, that ever gave a thought to the presence of man.

It will, perhaps, be said that we have been able to transform almost as thoroughly certain of our domestic animals: our fowls, our pigeons, our ducks, our cats, our horses, our rabbits, for instance.

Yes, perhaps; although such transformations are not comparable with those undergone by the dog, and although the kind of service which these animals render us remains, so to speak, invariable. In any case, whether this impression be purely imaginary or correspond with a reality, it does not appear that we feel in these transformations the same inexhaustible and engaging good-will, the same sagacious and exclusive love. For the rest, it is quite possible that the dog, or rather the inaccessible genius of his race, troubles scarcely at all about us and that we have merely known how to make use of various aptitudes offered by the abundant chances of life. It matters not: as we know nothing of the substance of things, we must needs cling to appearances; and it is sweet to establish that, at least in appearance, there is, on the planet where, like disowned kings, we live in solitary state, a being that loves us.

A Child's Dream ————————————

Frances Cornford

I had a little dog, and my dog was very small;
He licked me in the face, and he answered to my call;
Of all the treasures that were mine, I loved him most of all.

His nose was fresh as morning dew and blacker than the night;
I thought that it could even snuff the shadows and the light;
And his tail he held bravely, like a banner in a fight.

His body covered thick with hair was very good to smell;
His little stomach underneath was pink as any shell;
And I loved him and honoured him, more than words can tell.

We ran out in the morning, both of us, to play,
Up and down across the fields for all the sunny day;
But he ran so swiftly – he ran right away.

I looked for him, I called for him, entreatingly. Alas,
The dandelions could not speak, though they had seen him pass.
And nowhere was his waving tail among the waving grass.

The sun sank low – I ran; I prayed: 'If God has not the power
To find him, let me die. I cannot bear another hour.'
When suddenly I came upon a great yellow flower.

And all among its petals, such was Heaven's grace,
In that golden hour, in that golden place,
All among its petals, was his hairy face.

Surely a Dog Has a Soul? ————

James Douglas

Among the lesser-known authors who attempted to fathom the motivations of dogs was James Douglas. In recounting his experiences during the 1920s with Bunch his Sealyham he presents, in *The Bunch Book*, his theory on the canine psyche:

Before we laugh at the love lavished on dogs by the nation of lonely women we should try to understand the hidden forces at work in each woman's heart. A fat old woman waddling behind a fat old dog is a figure of comedy, but she is also a figure of tragedy.

She looks ludicrous and her dog looks ludicrous, but the relation

between them is not ludicrous, for no kind of love is ludicrous when it is probed to its depths, although all love is ludicrous if it is seen only on the surface.

When a lonely woman loves a dog she is trying to keep her soul alive. Without some sort of love the soul is dead, for love is its way of breathing. We do not know why we need love in order to preserve the sense of being alive. But we need it as our blood needs the air supplied to it by our lungs.

If we are choking for lack of air in pneumonia we are re-enlivened by inhaling oxygen. The oxygen vitalises the blood and keeps the heart going. It may be that the love of a dog is like oxygen. It takes the place of human love. It keeps the heart going.

It is certain that many human beings fail to fulfil and realise and complete themselves by the mastery of human love. They have shut themselves out from it or they have been shut out. Whether their exile is voluntary or involuntary does not matter. This life is not integrated and unified. It has asked for unity and has not got it.

A human life without love is in a state of asphyxiation. It is gasping for breath. I suspect that the majority of human beings go through their existence in this condition. They suffer permanently from atrophy of the affections. They lack the power to love and to be loved. They do not know that they are dying till they are dead.

It is no exaggeration to say that when a woman has nobody to love her she goes to the dogs, and the sooner she goes to the dogs the better, for if she cannot find a human creature to love or to be loved by, a dog is the next best thing, because we have humanised dogs so successfully that we are accustomed to say a dog is 'almost human'.

When I say that man has humanised the dog I do not mean only that he has tamed him, domesticated him, and taught him to perform tricks. I mean that he has discovered the soul of the dog and mingled his own soul with it. The nature of the human soul is an unfathomable and indefinable mystery. There are some who deny its existence. They say that man is a machine.

But a machine is incapable of love. I hold that the will and the power to love are a proof of the existence of the soul. We do not love with the reason, with the mind, with the brain. We love with the immortal and indestructible essence of our being, with that part of us which is above our mechanism and outside it and separate from it.

Now a dog possesses this will and power to love as really as we possess it. As I watch Bunch dogging the footsteps of Eva Alexandra, following her wherever she goes, gazing at her in dumb adoration while she is reading or sewing, I recognize the pure quality of love.

I see the soul of Bunch looking out through his eyes, and I cannot draw any distinction between his soul and the human soul. I see no reason why my soul should be more immortal than his soul. Probably there are beings who are as much higher in the scale of life as I am higher than Bunch. They might possibly deny my right to a soul because I am in a lower order of life which they cannot comprehend. But beings higher than they might also deny their right to a soul.

It may be that a man is only a little lower than the angels and that a dog is only a little lower than a man. I am constantly surprised by what I may call the personality of Bunch, his quiddity, his difference from other dogs. This is his spiritual quality, the shape and texture and colour of his soul.

Here may be found the origin of that curious doctrine of Pythagoras, the transmigration of souls. In a shadowy fashion I have detected in the soul of Bunch a strange resemblance to a human being who was once very dear to me. This resemblance and verisimilitude I cannot explain. It is a haunting presence which I did not invent or imagine. In some way the soul of Bunch reminds me of the soul of the dead man.

When I try to analyse it I know that it is conveyed by the expression

of the eyes and by no other vehicle. Now it is the soul that is perceived in the eyes. It is the soul that looks out through them. I cannot explain this miracle, but it is plain if you compare a blind man's face with the face of a seeing man. The blind man's soul is shuttered. It presses against his features, but the pressure is dim and blurred.

Death looks like sleep if the eyes are closed, but if they are open they are not awake. The soul has vanished from them. It is not only that they do not see, but that we do not see the soul looking through them. The brain is still there, but the owner of the brain is not there. He is elsewhere.

It is said that a dog can see a ghost. There is strong evidence to prove that he has a sense of the supernatural and supernormal. If this be so, it goes far to prove that he has a soul. I know that Bunch seems to be aware of forces which elude my perception. He communicates to me his disquiet and discomfort.

His dreams puzzle me. We take too lightly the fact that a dog dreams like a human being.

Alsatian Birth _____

J. R. Ackerley

My Dog Tulip, one of the most charming dog biographies ever written, was the inspiration of another Englishman, J. R. Ackerley. It was published in 1956. Ackerley watched over his Alsatian like a devoted father trying to interpret every plea and satisfy every need of a dumb daughter. Although he lived in a London flat he took immense trouble to give her all the exercise she needed. His devotion is well expressed in this account of her giving birth:

Tulip was in her box. She had understood its purpose after all. She was lying there in the shadows facing me, the front of her body upright, the rest inclined upon its side. Her ears crumpled back with pleasure at the sight of me; her amber eyes glowed with a gentle, loving look. She was panting. A tiny sound, like the distant mewing of gulls, came from the box; I could just discern, lying against her stomach, three small rat-like shapes. I think it is Major Hancock who says that a bitch is liable to hold up her labour if she is distracted or watched, and may

even devour her children to protect them. I accepted this in a general way; I knew, at the same time, that Tulip was glad that I was there. Nevertheless, I did not approach her box. Moving to a chair at some distance from her, I hid my face in my hands and observed her without seeming to do so. Suddenly she stopped panting, her face took on a look of strain, she uttered a muted, shuddering sound like a sigh, a movement passed over her recumbent body, and she raised her great tail so that it stood out straight and rigid from her rump. Immediately a dark package was extruded beneath it, and to this with a minimum of general effort, she brought her long nose round. Now I could not clearly see what she was doing, for her head interposed and obscured the operation; but I knew what was happening and I heard her tongue and teeth at work with liquid, guzzling noises. She was licking and nosing this package out of herself, severing the umbilical cord, releasing the tiny creature from its tissues and eating up the after-birth. In a few seconds she had accomplished all these tasks and was guiding her fourth child to her teats, cleansing it on the way.

It was a marvellous sight, to me very affecting; but I think that to anyone who did not know her and love her as I did, it must have been a solemn and moving thing to see this beautiful animal, in the midst of the first labour of her life, performing upon herself, with no help but unerringly, as though directed by some divine wisdom, the delicate and complicated business of creation. I guessed now that she was thirsty. Quietly leaving the room I warmed some milk for her. When I returned with a bowl she stretched her head eagerly forward. Kneeling in front of her I held it to her while she lapped. She licked my hand and laid her head heavily back on the blanket.

Half an hour elapsed before her next delivery; then another sigh, another spasm, and her tail lifted to eject the fifth. She produced eight puppies at half-hourly intervals and was not done until evening fell. I sat with her in the darkened room throughout. It was a beautiful thing to have seen. When it was plain that she had finished I went and kissed her. She was quite wet. She allowed me to touch her babies. They were still blind. I took one up; she was frightened and gently nuzzled my hand as though to say 'Take care!' But she had too much confidence in me to suppose that I would hurt them.

Appreciation of Man Friday and Joe _____

Sir Alfred Munnings

Sir Alfred Munnings (1878–1959), sometime President of the Royal Academy, renowned for his equestrian paintings, like nearly all horse-lovers was a lover of dogs too. In his autobiographical *An Artist's Life* he remarks that there was always a dog at his side as he painted. 'My dog Friday,' he said, remembering a friend of his youth:

only used me for his own amusement, and lay in the studio by the fire because it was warm – dreaming of rats which he drove out of their holes into the water, leaving naught but a chain of bubbles behind. His dreams would take him through these scenes again. He tried to bark, his feet quivering as he ran in his sleep. His master all the while losing time on something that would not come right – foolish fellow! Ah, why didn't I leave it? Why go on? Best to put it away if you can. Friday's dog-dreams would vanish, and he would awake, get up, stretch, shake himself and stand looking at me until I looked at him; then he wagged that tail of his and twisted his hind part round and went to the door, telling me it was time to stop.

I wasn't always wise enough, and much too obstinate to stop; and what I was painting would be scrapped the next morning. I should have listened to Friday. Poor Friday! I believe the watercolour which my mother had of him in her Norwich home is far better than I could do today. Something has left me since we two kept company in that carpenter's-shop studio long ago. . . .

And then there was Joe:

My dog, Joe, never left me, unless it was to go out with Friday, following my mother in her pony carriage at the rate of two and a half to four miles an hour. As I worked on *The Ford* he always expected me to throw something in the river for him to retrieve, or he would lie on a sack inside the engine-room door. His life suddenly came to an untimely end, and I was left utterly broken-hearted. We all were. He had gone out, as usual, with my mother on a journey to Harleston, and, joining in a fight with other curs in the High Street, was run over and killed by a butcher's cart. Butcher-carts were always driven at what we then thought a terribly reckless speed; and thus ended poor Joe's life. My mother, in tears, brought him home, stiff and stark. Fred Gray, who long ago, when I lived in Shearing's Farm, Mendham, had gone to fetch him for me after having bought him from a man near Bungay, dug his grave in tears, and old Gray and I were the mourners. The misery we suffered – that I suffered – on that afternoon was deep enough, and the memory of that scene at the end of the lawn by the old boathouse brings tears again. How often had Joe and I stepped into the boat in that old boathouse, either to go off sailing or painting! How he loved a boat and the river! He was the most faithful, queer little companion in the world, and he was gone! Another Welsh terrier, from Wales, called Taffy, took his place; but he was not the same, alas!

I would not call this an obituary notice, but rather an appreciation. I have told of those autumn and winter afternoon rides, when Joe accompanied me. During the day he was about the stables after rats, or around the hedges hoping to catch a rabbit, and if the weather was inclement, he lay on a rug near the stove in my studio. As the afternoon drew on to half past three, or as late as four o'clock, Joe would show signs of bottled-up impatience. He sometimes gave that little whine, such as terriers make, and shaking all over, he suddenly came to life as he saw his master lay down palette and brushes, take off the old painting-coat, and put on his hat. Soon he was dashing round to the stables, and immediately I was mounted he began his usual foolish trick of jumping up and trying to bite the mare's nose as she trotted out of the yard. This happened once too often, for as we were going into the road there was a frightful yelp; the mare had trodden on Joe's forefoot. This was a finisher for Joe. He was unable to accompany me for days. The vet was sent for to dress his foot, but next day Joe pulled off the bandage and was licking his crushed paw. Limping on three legs, he would go to the stables and see me off. Hour after hour he used to lie in his chair, patiently licking the wounded paw until it healed.

On these rides Joe always ran at least twenty yards ahead. One late winter afternoon we met the staghounds returning from hunting. There stood Joe, like a diminutive statue on three legs, in the middle of the road, his short tail erect, quivering, while the whole pack, with bristles raised, gathered round him. Their deep rumbling growls may have disconcerted this small hero, but he did not show the least sign of fear. At a word and the crack of whips from the hunt servants, the hounds passed on, my friend, Jack Cooke, the Master, saying, 'Turn your horse round and ride with us' – which I did. After we had ridden a mile or two, Cooke relating the doings of the day, he looked forward and said, 'What do you think of our leading hound?' and there at the head of the pack was my small dog, trotting along in the middle of the road with the hounds in his wake, as though he had done this sort of thing all his life!

While he was with me at Shearing's Farm I did not like sleeping in the room at the end of that ancient farmhouse without Joe, because I was sure it was haunted.

I forget how long I had this dog, but through many and many a long winter evening he was my sole companion, each of us occupying an armchair on either side of the hearth.

An Artist's Models _____

Cecil Aldin

Cecil Aldin, arguably the best dog artist who ever lived, swore that the eye was a dog's most important feature, whence the whole personality showed. His sketchbooks are full of drawings of dogs' eyes. Born in 1870, he was hard at work on dog models by the age of twelve. In his autobiography, *Time I Was Dead*, he recalls, with some nostalgia, the characters of two of his earliest sitters:

About 1886 I became the owner of my first dog model. How she came to me or where from I cannot remember, but Gyp, this little smooth-haired fox-terrier, was my first dog destined to earn her living as a model. Since that time I have had many for that purpose, but I think that Gyp, my first, was the best sitter and the most perfectly trained of them all. To her it was not only the necessary part of her day's work – it was a pleasurable game eagerly taken part in; and when I placed her on the 'throne' or chair upon which I wanted her to pose, I could always arrange a leg or her body propped up on books or cushions in any position. This pose she would hold like a professional human model for a quarter of an hour at a time. Another thing she learnt through constantly sitting for me was that whenever I picked up a sketch-book and pencil and looked at her she was expected to 'sit'. Any ordinary dog, if his master looks at him, will generally come towards him – this was not the case with Gyp. Instead of coming nearer to me when I took up pencil and sketch-book, or following after me, if I wanted to get a little farther away she would only follow my movements with her eyes as much as to say 'I am ready when you are'. Through constantly sitting she knew as well as I did that no sketch could be made if I was too close to her; at any rate, she understood that she was never to move or come nearer to me when she went through her daily food-earning performances. I trained her in the beginning by tying her up to the throne then walking away to make my drawing, always rewarding her after sitting with some little titbit she loved. In time she began to know that directly she saw me produce this tasty morsel that it was necessary for her, in order to enjoy it, to climb up on the throne and wait there until I brought it to

her. It became only a matter of showing it to her in the studio, and instead of coming towards me for it she straightaway took up a position on her raised platform. After I had had her for some years she was so expert that she would invariably take up a pose on this if I had another dog chained there sitting for me. This she would do entirely on her own initiative, although naturally I always gave her the usual reward. The whole time any other dog was sitting she would remain stationary on the throne. Like my mother's Scotch terrier, Gyp was my shadow, and always with me day and night. A dog you have with you as your constant companion is so much more amenable to teaching than one that is only with his master occasionally during the day. Gyp once had even to 'sit' literally standing on her head, her hind legs being propped high up against the back of an armchair and her head tucked down between her forelegs on the seat. This pose she held for five minutes at a time and funnily enough seemed quite happy about it, although I was rather pessimistic at first and was frightened the blood would all collect in her head and cause a fit or something of the sort.

Another terrier I had at that time went by the unromantic name of 'Spot'. He was rather a handsome dog – one that would have been described in *The Exchange and Mart* sales columns of that day as having an 'even marked black and tan head', but much broader in the face than the fox-terrier of today. His failing was that he loved journeying in railway carriages – it was well before the days of cars, or no doubt that mode of travelling would have been his pet fancy. From the day I first had him until his final disappearance Spot was always an anxiety. He was one of that very independent type of the dog world who can quite well go for long walks alone without failing to find their way home. Although I don't like to smirch his escutcheon I think he must have had a bar sinister somewhere in his pedigree. Mongrels will always do this – no mongrel ever dies or is stolen, they want no careful rearing; it is only the well-bred dog who is lost, stolen or strayed. Often Spot would be returned from the station near my suburban home by a friendly porter who would say that he had tried to get into every train to London all the morning, and the station-master had sent him back to me. Spot became almost as well known at my station as the terminus dogs at Paddington and Euston. If ever I took him by train his delight was unbounded, and he would always be the first to enter the carriage and immediately dive under the seat and remain there. I watched and followed him on one occasion when he tried to take his favourite mode of travel alone. For some time he prowled

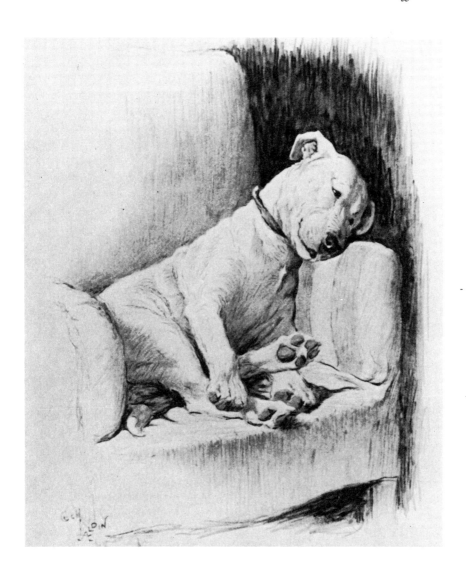

inquisitively round the platform smelling the interesting dog smells that cloakrooms and parcels-offices always contain, and when a train came in, followed a passenger into the carriage, all the time vigorously wagging his tail until he was pulled out from under the seat by a porter and once more safely placed on the platform. Time after time he would appear as each train came in, no matter how many times the station staff had pulled him out and hustled him off. I am sure he must often have had free journeys alone and evaded the eye of the officials.

73

Many times he was away for a day or more, having been noticed previously on the platforms; he probably boarded a train, got out at the next stop and made his way home the best he could. In the end I had to keep him chained up when I was away from my studio and could not have my dogs with me. He eventually disappeared completely, for, infatuated by this hobby of railway travelling, he was last seen as a fast train to the coast stopped to set down or pick up passengers. It was almost certain that Spot must have slipped into a carriage when the door was opened and been carried direct to the

seaport town. The station-master, everyone, made the most exhaustive enquiries, but Spot was never seen again by me. He had taken his last train journey from our station. As he was a very friendly dog, he may have 'palled' up with some passenger who, thinking he was lost, had kept him out of compassion. I had no anxiety about him as Spot was a dog who would never remain in a bad home and was a natural wanderer. A few dog natures are like that; they are very independent, easily make new friends and forget old ones. *All* 'doggy' humans are their masters, and if they find a master whom they think does not provide quite so good a home as another they have no scruples in 'walking out'. Someone will always feed a dog if he is not shy and is very friendly. It is the shy, nervous and half-starved stray who has the worst time. Spot was never that type; he made friends with anyone, but was very independent and self-possessed himself, much more like a chow than a fox-terrier in character.

A Foxhound's Love

Daphne Moore

Many stories have been recounted of the homing instinct of dogs, and of their magnetic will, when separated from their masters and mistresses, to be reunited with them. Daphne Moore, the leading writer on everything concerning hounds, included one such reminiscence in her book *Foxhounds*:

A true story of the love of a foxhound for her Master is perhaps one of the most extraordinary ever related. In the season of 1928–9, when he had the Tedworth Hounds, Sir Peter Farquhar acquired a bitch from the Bicester, Ramble (1925). She became very attached to him, so much so indeed, that although, in his own words, she 'hunted like the devil', she was constantly looking back to reassure herself that he was not far away, and she also refused to leave the kennels if, because of his military duties or for any other reason, he was unable to hack on to the meet with hounds. She was therefore given by Sir Peter to a friend of his who was Master of the Oxford Drag, for she had the makings of a very fast hound. This was early in the season, about November. Her new Master did his best to win her affection, but to no avail. She had already given her heart to Sir Peter and no substitute would satisfy her. The homing instinct prevailed.

Miraculously, she found her way back to the Tedworth kennels (from which she had been sent by rail, which makes her achievement even more amazing), a distance of about 120 miles. How long it took her I do not know; however, she arrived safe and sound, and it was with reluctance that Sir Peter dispatched her to Oxford for a second time. The Master of the Drag had implored him to return her, since she had proved herself brilliant on a drag. He promised to take good care of her, and this time she appeared to settle down well. She gradually accepted her new Master, and proved to be one of the best hounds in the pack.

May came, and hunting was now at an end. Sir Peter had moved to a new house some eight miles from the kennels, and the kennel staff had changed, old Fred Funnell being replaced by Jack Scarratt, whilst there was also a new kennelman. The Oxford Drag had also undergone a change, and there was a New Master of the draghounds.

Jack Scarratt reported seeing a strange bitch on several occasions near the kennels, but this was thought to be one of the Bulford Harriers which were kennelled a short distance away. One day, however, as Sir Peter drove up to his new house he saw a foxhound lying curled up in the porch – none other than Ramble! How she could ever have discovered the house (whose existence was not even known to Sir Peter in the days when Ramble was with him), having for the second time within a year accomplished that fantastic 120-mile journey, passes comprehension. The fact that, on both occasions, she travelled to Oxford by train serves to increase the inexplicability of the story. For a while she was kept as a pet, but a pet foxhound is really a contradiction in terms and very seldom proves to be a success. It is sad to relate that poor Ramble eventually met her death when she was knocked down by a passing car. At least she had the satisfaction of spending her latter days with the human of her choice, for whom she had travelled no less than 240 miles, and experienced untold dangers and privations.

Fantail

J. Orr-Ewing

Hound puppies are normally sent away from the hunt kennels to individual farmers and other hunt supporters when they are eight to ten weeks old, and are returned a year or so later to be 'entered'. Naturally most puppy-walkers become very attached to their charges. This narrative verse aptly describes the wrench felt by a puppy-walker when her charge is taken away:

> One day, the summer of '46,
> Two men drove up in a Morris van
> To Kissthornes Farm of the rose-red bricks;
> They left a bundle of black-and-tan,
> A small round bundle of tender age,
> To be faring forth on a pilgrimage.
>
> They called her Fantail, and, Birdsall bred,
> She could be setting the Thames on fire;
> From Middleton Timely her lovely head.
> Her nose from Farndale, her Derwent sire;
> And Fantail, born on a Sabbath day,
> Was 'blithe and bonny, and good and gay'.

And fair her lot by the fates decreed,
For Mrs Pearson of Kissthornes Farm
Possessed a heart that was warm indeed,
And promptly lost it to Fantail's charm:
As months sped by that were lightning-shod
She worshipped the ground on which Fantail trod.

So Fantail flourished and throve, and grew
A lovely creature of lissom grace,
Of eyes that shone with a love as true
As that she read in a woman's face:
Ah me! The pity that, soon or late,
Most puppies come to a hound's estate.

Few words were writ on the dreaded card:
'Will call for Fantail on Friday, Jim';
Few words – yet suddenly life was hard,
And love was cruel, and parting grim
For Mrs Pearson; and Fantail knew
A strange unhappiness reach her, too.

Black Friday dawned, and its noon crept by;
Her chores completed, her heart like lead,
With untouched dinner, and tear-dimmed eye,
Poor Mrs Pearson retired to bed,
Where all her being repeated, 'No!
I cannot bear to see Fantail go.'

Then mercy granted an aching heart
The boon of sleep – until six o'clock,
When sounds that came from a world apart
Awakened her with the land-girl's knock
And words, 'I'm ever so sorry, Mum.
They can't catch Fantail. Will you please come?'

When fate insists on her pound of flesh,
No 'dodge the column', no 'swing the lead',
Her gears slip in with a synchro-mesh;
Poor Mrs Pearson arose from bed,
And down and out to the yard she ran –
So Fantail left in the Kennel's van.

Three years went by . . . When the wind blew chill
By Kissthornes Covert one winter's day,
A crash of music, a holloa shrill,
A doubled horn said, 'A fox away!'
And Mrs Pearson ran out to see
The Chase flash by in its finery.

As she knelt to re-tie her shoe,
A bolt descended from out of space,
With joyous whimpers, the next she knew
A cold, wet muzzle that sought her face;
And swift the message in Fantail's eye,
'I love you still; but I have to fly!'

Away she sped; but she left behind
A woman happy in heart and mind;
For this world's woes there is but one balm,
And Fantail brought it to Kissthornes Farm.

Epilogue

The sequel: Still does the truth hold true:
In that same winter was Fantail wed
To Ringwood: came, on a Sunday, too,
Her puppies, thoroughly Birdsall bred.

A wave of wand, and a whispered charm
Brought Fantail's daughter to Kissthornes Farm.

Ringrose they called her, and rings she made
Round all the rest at the Puppy Show:
Then, higher yet, 'twas the lead she played
With sister, Ringlet, at Peterb'ro:
They made the lot of them look like hacks.
Unentered bitches from fourteen packs.

And fancy carried me far away:
The wind blew chill on a winter's day
When Fantail proved 'There is but one balm'.
Long may it flourish at Kissthornes Farm.

Stasi _____

Konrad Lorenz

A co-founder of that branch of zoology called ethology, the science of animal behaviour, Konrad Lorenz was born in Austria, in 1903, the son of a famous surgeon. He won the Nobel Prize in 1973, while his classics *King Solomon's Ring* and *On Aggression* were reprinted, worldwide, in a great many editions. Here, in *Man Meets Dog*, he tells of the remarkable devotion of his bitch, Stasi:

Stasi was born in our house in early spring, 1940, and was seven months old when I adopted her as my own and began to train her. In her outward appearance, as in her temperament, the characters of the Alsatian and the Chow were mixed in a particularly favourable way. With her sharp, wolf-like muzzle, wide cheekbones, slanting eyes and short, hairy ears, with her short, bushy tail and, above all, her wonderfully elastic and elegant movements, she resembled more than anything else a little female wolf; only the flaming golden-red of her coat betrayed very literally her Aureus [a particular species of wolf] blood. But the true gold was in her character. She learned the rudiments of canine education, walking on the lead, walking to heel, and 'lying down', astonishingly quickly. She was more or less spontaneously house-clean and safe with poultry, so that there was no need to teach her those attributes.

After two short months, my bond with this dog was broken by the force of destiny: I was called to the University of Königsberg as professor of psychology and I left my family, home and dogs on September 2nd, 1940. When I returned at Christmas for a short holiday, Stasi greeted me in a frenzy of joy, demonstrating that her great love for me was unchanged. She could do everything I had taught her, just as well as before, and was indeed exactly the same dog as I had left behind me four months previously. But tragic scenes were enacted when I began to prepare for my departure. Many dog-lovers will know what I mean. Even before the suitcase packing – the visible sign of departure – had started, the dog became noticeably depressed and refused to leave my side for an instant. With nervous haste, she sprang up and followed every time I left the room, even accompanying me to the bathroom. When the trunks were packed and my departure became imminent, the misery of poor Stasi waxed to the point of desperation, almost to a neurosis. She would not eat and her breathing became abnormal, very shallow and punctuated now and then by great, deep sighs. Before I left, we decided to shut her up, to prevent her making a violent attempt to follow me. But now, strangely, the little bitch, who had not left my side for days, retired to the garden, and would not come when I called her. The most obedient of all dogs had become refractory, and all our efforts to catch her were in vain. When, finally, with the usual retinue of children, a handcart and luggage, I started out for the station, a strange looking dog, with lowered tail, ruffled mane and wild eyes followed us at a distance of twenty-five yards. At the station I made a last attempt to catch her, but it was hopeless. Even when I boarded the train, she still stood in the defiant attitude of a rebellious dog, with lowered ears and ruffled mane, watching me suspiciously from a safe distance. The train began to pull out of the station, and still the dog stood rooted to the spot. But as the engine increased its speed, she suddenly shot forward, rushing alongside the train, and leaping up into it, three carriages in front of the one on whose platform I was still standing in order to prevent her jumping onto it. [On the Austrian local trains, there is a fairly spacious platform at each end of and communicating with the carriages.] I ran forward, seized her by the skin of her neck and rump and thrust her from the train, which was already moving quite fast. She landed dexterously on her feet, without falling. No longer in defiant attitude, but with ears pricked and head on one side, she watched the train until it was out of sight.

In Königsberg, I soon received disturbing news of Stasi: she had killed a whole series of our neighbour's hens, had started roaming restlessly about the district, was no longer house-trained and refused to obey anybody. Her only use now was as a watchdog, for she was becoming increasingly ferocious. After she had committed a long list of crimes – several hen murders, the burglary of a rabbit hutch, with much ensuing bloodshed, and finally the tearing of the postman's trousers, she was degraded to the status of a yard dog and sat in sorrowful solitude on the terrace adjoining the west side of our house. In actual fact, she was only solitary in regard to human company, for she shared a large and elegant kennel with our handsome Dingo dog. From shortly after Christmas until July, she was caged like a wild animal in the company of a wild animal.

On my return to Altenberg at the end of June 1940, I went straight into the garden to see Stasi. As I climbed the steps to the terrace, both dogs rushed at me furiously, as furiously as only dogs deprived of their freedom can. I stood still on the top step and the dogs came nearer, barking and growling angrily, for the direction of the wind was such that they could not pick up my scent. I wondered when they would recognize me visually, but they did not do this at all. Quite suddenly, Stasi scented me and what now took place I shall never forget: in the midst of a heated onrush, she stopped abruptly and stiffened to a statue. Her mane was still ruffled, her tail down and her ears flat, but her nostrils were wide, wide open, inhaling greedily the message carried by the wind. Now the raised crest subsided, a shiver ran through her body and she pricked up her ears. I expected her to throw herself at me in a burst of joy, but she did not. The mental suffering which had been so severe as to alter the dog's whole personality, causing this most tractable of creatures to forget manners, law and order for months, could not fade into nothingness in a second. Her hind legs gave way, her nose was directed skywards, something happened in her throat, and then the mental torture of months found outlet in the hair-raising yet beautiful tones of a wolf's howl. For a long time, perhaps for half a minute, she howled, then, like a thunderbolt she was upon me. I was enveloped in a whirlwind of ecstatic canine joy, she leapt to my shoulders, nearly tearing the clothes from my back, she – the exclusive, undemonstrative, whose greeting normally consisted of a few restrained tail-wags, the highest sign of whose affection was a head laid upon my knee – she, the silent one, whistled in her excitement like a locomotive, and cried in piercing tones, even louder than her howls of a few seconds before. Then she suddenly desisted, ran past me towards the gate, where she stopped, looking round at me over her shoulder, and begging to be let out. It was self-evident to her that, with my return, her imprisonment was also at an end, and she returned quite simply to the order of the day. Lucky animal, enviable robustness of the nervous system! A mental trauma whose cause is removed leaves in animals no after-effects which cannot be healed by a howl of thirty seconds' duration and a dance for joy of a minute and a half, healed so completely that the animal can return at once to normal.

As I went back to the house with Stasi at my side, my wife who saw me coming, cried 'Good heavens, the hens!' Stasi did not so much as look at a single hen. In the evening, when I brought her into the house, my wife warned me that the dog was no longer 'clean'. Stasi was as perfectly house-trained as she had ever been. She could still do everything I had taught her and was still the same dog which my scarcely two months of training had made her. During nine months of the deepest sorrow which can ever befall a dog, she had faithfully conserved all that she owed to me. And now followed for Stasi weeks

of the purest delight. During that summer vacation, she was my inseparable companion, and nearly every day we took long walks beside the Danube, often swimming in the river.

Ignorance —————————————————

C. R. Acton

Many dog-owners fail to appreciate that 'affection' should imply deep practical care and a close knowledge of a dog's needs. Barbara Wodehouse is now the doyenne of dog care and discipline. C. R. Acton, an expert, in particular, on hounds and other working breeds, was writing regularly between the 1930s and 1950s. One of his essays was included in the *Dog Annual* of 1951:

I have always maintained that dog-owning is a great responsibility, and that one should not keep a dog unless one is prepared to make a good deal of sacrifice, if necessary, on its behalf.

And it is important to add that no one should keep a dog unless he or she knows something about dogs. The trouble, of course, is that everyone thinks they know all that is necessary to look after a dog. Every dog-owner will reply, 'Oh yes! Of course I know all about dogs!' And yet, if one were to take a census one would find that the amount of ignorance amongst dog-owners is absolutely appalling.

To drive a motorcar in the public streets one has to pass an examination and receive – and pay for – a licence, yet no examination or licence is necessary for the man or woman who wants to drive a horse, or horses in the public streets, and no examination, but merely an inexpensive licence, for him or her who wishes to take dogs into the public streets, where the said dogs may quite conceivably cause trouble, fight, get run over and become a public nuisance in many ways, owing to the fact that they are not under control.

And that is the first piece of ignorance that I regret to say is very widespread. How many dogs does one see that are really under control? Very, very few, and the reason is – ignorance on the part of their owner.

Dogs should be taught to be strictly obedient, which is merely a matter of patience, sympathy and encouragement. It takes time, of course, but the results more than justify the time and trouble. If one can rely upon implicit obedience in one's dog one can take it anywhere and teach it to do more or less anything, and the first and, I might almost say, most important thing to teach a dog is to come when it is called, and to come at once. The dog can then be described as being 'under control', and will not be a nuisance to other people, or to other people's dogs. And, of course, it will not be a nuisance to itself, as if it is strictly obedient and walks to heel when it is told, it is unlikely to get run over, or to chase valuable stock, or to get mixed up in a fight, or any of the other vicissitudes of a disobedient and uncontrolled dog. I think that there are few scenes more ridiculous than the sight of a man or woman yelling away at a recalcitrant dog that is showing a complete disregard of its purple-faced owner, and that there are few scenes more regrettable than the sight of the same dog, when at last captured, receiving a heavy – and probably spiteful – thrashing for disobedience. It is the owner who has failed in the duty of properly teaching the dog who needs the thrashing.

Every dog is born with the character for lavishing affection and devotion on a human being. This is an acquired character that has grown up during the years that dogs have exchanged their wild lives for lives of companionship. It is more developed in some breeds than in others. But that affection and devotion, if properly fostered by patient and sympathetic teaching, and judicious encouragement, will prove the groundwork for implicit and willing obedience. I repeat the words: Patience, Sympathy, and judicious Encouragement.

A practice that is tantamount to cruelty is the misuse of the chain, and this, in most cases, is also due to ignorance.

I cannot conceive of a more miserable existence than of a wretched dog, day in day out, kept perpetually on a chain. Nor can I conceive why anyone should wish to keep a dog under those circumstances. A good house-dog, guard-dog, or companion should be loose. A dog perpetually on a chain can fulfil none of these definitions. He is just a miserable captive, and surely, in these so-called enlightened days, no one but a subhuman would wish to keep a captive in misery.

No dog should be thought of or treated as a captive. A dog's intelligence should be developed, and he should be well disciplined, well fed, and well exercised. Then he is likely to prove fully capable of becoming a companion, a house-dog or a guard-dog, according to his training, and will evince no desire to run away, so the chain at once becomes unnecessary.

To the one who says, 'Oh, I haven't the time for all that!' the only

reply is, 'Then you haven't the time, or the right, to keep a dog!' and that reply is unanswerable.

Overfeeding is another form of ignorance, and overfeeding is as bad in its way as neglect of a dog's meals. No overfed dog can be really happy or healthy. Their bodies become gross, and their active minds become vacant. The ideal to aim at in a dog is a strong active body, and a sharp active mind.

Another form of ignorance, and one that, I regret to say, is common in country districts, is the allowing loose of bitches in season. This is an appalling thing to do, but it usually springs from ignorance.

Apart from the possible harm to the bitch concerned through her being warded by a dog too big for her, a bitch in this condition, running loose, is frequently the cause of really terrible fights amongst the dogs that are always attracted to her.

The proper care of bitches is quite a subject of its own, and no owner should keep a bitch unless fully capable of looking after her carefully and thoroughly.

Teasing sounds a very small matter, but it may assume quite vast proportions in the mind of a trusting dog. Dogs hate being made fools of, and they hate being lied to, or deceived, by the master or mistress whom they trust, and teasing, to a dog, is tantamount to deception.

Ignorance crops up often in the assessment of exercise. A dog does not want as much exercise on a boiling hot afternoon as he does on a nice cool morning, for instance. That sounds obvious, but it is astonishing to note the number of unwilling dogs one sees dragged out for a Sunday afternoon walk, irrespective of the weather.

Any dog-owner may be forgiven for not possessing veterinary skill, but no dog-owner may be forgiven for not calling in the vet when something seems wrong with the dog, and the owner does not know what is the matter. Yet one often hears an owner say, 'Oh, I'm not going to panic. He'll be all right.' The veterinary surgeon is the antidote to ignorance on the owner's part, and it is really wicked not to make full use of the services of the skilled man.

Very few dog-owners are intentionally neglectful, or intentionally cruel, but Ignorance breeds Neglect, and it is a very short step from Neglect to Cruelty.

Shep and the Spotted Stray ─────────

Fred Gipson

Fred Gipson's stories are set mainly in Texas. His *Old Yeller*, which was published in 1956, is the story of a half-starved stray, which enters the lives of a family living on the Texas frontier in the 1860s. It steals a chunk of meat, but is nevertheless adopted, and repays the family several times over for their generosity by fighting off a variety of fierce intruders on the farm. But on many occasions it was mauled and was still severely crippled at the time of its last fight in which it saved the mother of the family from a rabid wolf. The wolf bit it and it had to be shot.

Dogs feature, too, on the lighter side in Gipson's novel *The Home Place* (1951). This comprises the adventures of a widower, Sam Crockett, who – with his sons and 'Grandpa Firth' – retires from Kansas City to his old Texan homeland. Towards the end of the novel a potential 'coon hound enters the boys' lives:

Grandpa Firth had promised them apple pie for supper, so when Steve and Chuck got off the school bus at the lane end, they held a foot race from there to the house to see who was to get the first and biggest piece.

Steve burst through the door, shouting, 'I won! I won!' and Yo-Yo came running towards him from the kitchen, his eyes shining with welcome.

Just then Grandpa Firth called out, 'You boys hush that racket a minute and listen.'

Steve and Chuck stopped and tried to listen, but they were

breathing so fast and their hearts were pounding blood against their eardrums so hard that they couldn't hear a thing.

They crept quietly into the kitchen to find the old man bent over, peering through the back window. Without looking at them, Grandpa said, 'You boys run down there to the cowshed and see what all that god-awful racket's about.' So they hurried out the back door to see squawking chickens and turkeys taking to the tall weeds in fright, while the milk calf, nearly grown now, bawled in terror and made frantic attempts to leap the cowpen fence.

From inside the cowshed came a banging and clattering and a roaring, yelping sound like no sound they'd ever heard before.

Big-eyed with wonder, Steve and Chuck hurried around the garden towards the cowpen, with Yo-Yo chasing after them, yelling for them to wait.

Before they got there, Grandpa's sheep-dog came racing up from the creek, with his hackles raised and a rumbling growl in his throat.

Shep cleared the fence with a mighty leap and dived into the cowshed.

Instantly, there was a clatter and scramble inside the shed, punctuated by Shep's furious roar and the shrill, ringing yelps of some creature in pain.

A spotted, half-grown dog came racing out of the shed with the savage Shep hard after him. The smaller dog ran blindly because of the chili can that enveloped his head and, when he rammed headlong into the cowpen, the recoil of the springy wire threw him back with such a force that Shep barely wheeled in time to catch him.

Shep was shaking the interloper like a jack rabbit when Steve and Chuck flung open the cowpen gate. They fell upon the black dog with shouts of indignation, kicking and hammering his head with their fists to make him release his catch.

They had to carry the starved and whimpering pup to the house and call on Grandpa's assistance with the can-opener before they could get the can off the pup's head.

Steve set the pup on the floor then and Grandpa eyed him disapprovingly. 'Think you oughta left him in the can,' he said. 'I never in my life seen such a rack of dog bones, for 'em to be still alive.'

Steve looked at the starved spotted pup, at his long, black ears, his tragic eyes, at the thin bony tail which he held clamped in fear up under his belly.

'But he's a hound pup, Grandpa,' Steve defended. 'Like Mr Spiller's 'coon hounds.'

Yo-Yo went up to stroke the back of the starved and cowering pup.

'Well, that don't make him no prettier,' Grandpa said.

'But we've been needing us a hunting dog,' Steve argued. 'One with a pretty voice that can trail a 'coon.'

'Feed him up, and I bet he'd make a dandy,' Chuck put in.

'Haw! If his hide'll hold feed,' Grandpa said. 'Poor and thin as that thing is, it'd crowd him to throw a shadder in bright sunlight.'

Yo-Yo went up to stroke the back of the starved and cowering pup. 'Chili dog!' he said.

At first the pup sank fearfully to the floor, twisted his head and licked Yo-Yo's hand. Yo-Yo laughed and patted his head. An instant later, the pup was reared up, with a foot on each of Yo-Yo's shoulders, wringing his whip tail and licking a smear of jelly from Yo-Yo's face.

'We can keep him, can't we, Grandpa?' Chuck begged.

'We'll name him Chili,' Steve said.

Grandpa grunted. 'You'll have to see your daddy about that,' he said. 'Me, I don't have no say in nothing around here.'

They had the pup out in the yard, lapping milk from a stew pan, when Sam and Stud Spiller drove up from the field in the jeep, with Stud's mule and plough loaded in the trailer.

'Where'd you get your dog, boys?' Stud asked, climbing out of the jeep to come look over the yard fence.

'Out of a chili can,' Grandpa said from the doorway.

'He's a stray,' Chuck said. 'He come here to our place and we're gonna keep him. We'll feed him up and make a 'coon hound out of him.'

'And we're going to name him Chili,' Steve added.

'Well, by golly, he looks like he'd make a 'coon hound all right,' Stud said. He turned to Sam, who had come up to stand beside him. 'Look at the old pup, Sam. Look at them ears and feet. Look how wide he is between the eyes. Why, give that thing a little training with them old pot hounds of mine, and I'd bet there ain't an old boar 'coon in the country that could out-smart him.'

It warmed Steve to hear such praise for the hound pup. Stud kept 'coon hounds, he ought to know. Steve looked anxiously up at his father.

'We can keep him, can't we, Daddy?'

Sam said to Stud, 'Don't you guess he belongs to somebody around here?'

'Doubt it,' Stud said. 'Look how he puts them feet down. Like he was walking in hot ashes. He's bound to've travelled a good long piece from home to've wore them feet that tender.'

Sam saw how breathlessly Chuck and Steve were awaiting his verdict and grinned. 'All right,' he said. 'If nobody comes to claim him right away, I guess you boys have got yourselves a 'coon hound.'

Chuck let out a whoop.

Steve's eyes shone with excitement. 'Gee!' he said. 'Gee, we'll train him till he's real good, then sometime I'll write to Ted Meadows and get him to come out here and go 'coon hunting with us.'

Chuck said, 'How long will it take us to get him fattened up a little, Mr Spiller?'

Stud laughed. 'Boys, that's the slickest trick of all. You can take the poorest old hound alive and throw one big feed into him, and he's fat the next morning.'

Sam and Stud got into the jeep again and drove towards Stud's house.

'Told you all along them boys would take to the country,' Stud said. 'Give 'em another year and you couldn't run 'em off to town with a stick!'

Mystery in the Peaks ————————————

Rex Bellamy

Here is a true story. It is about an old Peak District shepherd and the devotion of his bitch Tip. Rex Bellamy wrote it for *Country Life* in June 1984:

Joseph Tagg was no ordinary shepherd. He spent his life in Derwent Dale amid the Peak District's wild gritstone moorland. But he inspired respect, even renown over a much wider area. For many years Tagg was shepherd to the Duke of Norfolk. He became a sheep-farmer, was among the founders of the Hope Valley sheepdog trials in 1905, and had a succession of prize-winning dogs at trials throughout the country. In the 1920s he sold a sheepdog to an American for £1000, probably the first time an English shepherd had realized a four-figure sum from an overseas sale.

At the age of eighty-five Tagg had more or less retired, though he still had some land and a few sheep near Pike Low, a hill east of Derwent Dam. By that time he was part of the landscape, and a legend in his own lifetime. But on Saturday, 12 December 1953, Tagg and his dog Tip, a border collie bitch, vanished from the face of Derwent Dale. The search was unusually intensive and prolonged, but abortive. What was left of Tagg was found by chance on Saturday, 27 March 1954. Tip was dozing about five yards away. Somehow she had survived fifteen wintry weeks of heavy snow and fierce, bitter winds high on the flank of Bleaklow, one of the most hostile stretches of moorland in England.

Tagg's remains were buried in the Roman Catholic churchyard at Bamford. In his retirement he had lived nearby, in the hamlet of Yorkshire Bridge, with his niece and his dog. The headstone bears no precise date of death: just 'Dec. 1953'. Of course, no one knew whether Tagg died on the day he was last seen alive. Tip was nursed back to health – and to a fame that was not merely national but international. The British and American publics subscribed to a memorial erected as a tribute to her astonishing enduring devotion.

It is now thirty years since Tagg and Tip were found: thirty years since one of the most tragic and touching of the Peak District's unsolved mysteries first excited speculation in the scattered farms and villages dotted among those empty brown moors. Anniversaries that end with a nought arouse a special effort to dispel the clouds of memory. I have known Derwent Dale for more than forty years and on the thirtieth anniversary of Tagg's disappearance I stood again by his grave. Then I retraced most of the route he supposedly followed on that last walk. To help catch the mood I took along an old friend borrowed from the Hathersage Inn – Shadow (like Tip a border collie bitch). Thirty years on, we dogged the footsteps of Tagg and Tip on a similar December day.

Predictably, there was still no solution to the mystery that surrounds the puzzling location and odd circumstances of Tagg's death, nor any answers to the questions that were first asked thirty years ago. Why did Tagg digress from his usual territory to perish on a moor with which he and Tip were unfamiliar and had no cause to visit? Why had his boots been unlaced and, it seems, boots, jacket and waistcoat taken off? How had Tip survived? True, Tagg's memory was failing and this may explain why he ended where he did. Perhaps he got lost and died of old age and exhaustion. But what about the boots and clothing and the endurance of a dog that, at the age of eleven, was probably too old to hunt for food on those bare, wintry moors? Perhaps Tip lived on the sheep, rabbits and birds killed by the harsh weather.

The facts must be separated from the deduction and speculation. First the facts. Though only six weeks away from his eighty-sixth birthday, Tagg was still healthy, still tended those sheep near Pike Low, and had known Derwent Dale all his life. There was no cause for apprehension when, at 9.30 on that Saturday morning, he packed some sandwiches and set off with Tip to visit his sheep. At about 1.20 p.m. (with less than three hours of daylight left) a forestry worker saw them walking along a bridle road by Abbey Cottage at the foot of Abbey Brook. The cottage, which stood on the site of a medieval monastic settlement, is there no more. But some of its tiled flooring remains, on a patch of level ground between the bridle road and a group of rhododendron bushes.

Tagg was never seen alive again. The official search went on for nine days and was conducted by farmers, shepherds, gamekeepers, relatives, friends, ramblers, police dog-handlers and RAF rescue services. The unofficial search continued sporadically throughout those fifteen weeks that man and dog were missing. It transpired that one search party had lunched within 150 yards of Tagg and Tip. Shepherd and collie were eventually discovered – at an altitude of 1500 feet in the remote valley of Grinah Grain by an employee of the Derwent Valley Water Board who was helping to round up sheep. He recognized Tip. She raised a feeble wag but was reluctant to leave what was left of her master. Wet, weak and thin, she had to be carried over some rough ground to the security of her rescuer's lorry and, later, to a warm, caring home and the status of a celebrity. She lived a year longer. The Tip memorial was erected at the western end of Derwent Dam in May 1955.

Tagg was identified by the contents of his jacket pockets and, of course, by the presence of Tip. At the inquest the coroner recommended an open verdict and the jury decided that death was due to 'natural causes', adding that there was not enough evidence to be more precise. Tagg's bones were buried and everyone made a fuss of Tip. The National Canine Defence League awarded her a medal.

The rest is deduction and speculation. The accepted theory is that, having seen to his sheep, Tagg indulged a known whim to revisit the site of his birthplace and childhood home, Ronksley Farm. The most northerly farm in Derwent Dale, it stood at the foot of Linch Clough just beyond the abrupt terminus of today's minor road up the western shores of the dale's three reservoirs. Ronksley was demolished in 1910 because the fields below it were being submerged by the new Howden Reservoir. But Tagg retained a great affection for the place and, perhaps suspecting that there would be no more birthdays to come, presumably decided to take a last look at Ronksley while he could. This means that instead of going straight home from the Abbey Cottage area (perhaps crossing the dale at Derwent Dam and catching a bus to Ladybower), he walked in the opposite direction to cross the Derwent at Slippery Stones before turning south to Ronksley.

The popular theory about what happened next – about Tagg's route from Ronksley to Grinah Grain – is that he and Tip walked on down the road to the foot of Westend Clough and then, for some reason, left the road and ascended Westend Clough to the bleak fastness of Grinah Grain. Another, personal, theory is based on the fact that Tagg had vivid memories of a boyhood in which he must often have clambered up from Ronksley to explore Linch Clough. He may have explored it again 12 December 1953 – and Linch Clough would have led him directly, though strenuously, across Ronksley Moor to Grinah Grain. Via Westend Clough Tagg and Tip would have walked about fourteen miles in the day. Via Linch Clough, about twelve. Either way, shepherd and dog would have been tired – and treading unfamiliar moors in the gathering gloom of a December day.

As a shepherd, Tagg had mostly worked the eastern side of

Derwent Dale. The western side represented boyhood rather than manhood. And the sharp memories of youth – which come down from the shelf for a dusting with the onset of senility – would in Tagg's case be clouded and confused by bewildering changes in the landscape. Tagg the old man saw a reservoir where Tagg the boy had seen fields and the river Derwent. We shall never know what went through Tagg's mind that day.

The beautiful grandeur of Derwent Dale keeps its secrets. So do the windswept flanks of Grinah Grain. But the story of Joseph Tagg lives on in the vague date on a gravestone and the memorial of a dog's devotion.

Brick and the Stray Collie

W. Harold Thomson

That Terrier Brick, W. Harold Thomson's biography of his cairn, was published in 1929. Here's how Brick does an old man a good turn:

With my gallant-hearted terrier as my companion, I had called at Ben Warren's cottage, meaning to pass the time of day with Ben and his retriever, Joe. But we found a sad and lonely old man, and learned that, overnight, there must have been a welcoming stir in those happy hunting grounds to which the souls of good dogs go.

'He just sighed once an' then his head fell down, an' I was alone,' Ben said, the while he fumbled with a tattered tobacco-pouch. 'Ten years he's been with me, day an' night, rain or shine. . . Best friend I ever had – an' yet some folks say as dogs don't know nothing! Well, he's the last I'll have; for me there'll never be another Joe, an' I don't want a second-best dog for company.'

The sympathy which I gave to him was sincere, and I have the odd fancy that Brick, young though he is, added his sympathy to mine. Certainly he had sensed that something was gravely wrong, and when he and I were taking our earned ease by the study fire he put a feathery-tufted forepaw on one of my feet and looked up at me through eyes which said, I swear:

'What was the matter with that old man? And where was Joe?'

'Ben has lost Joe,' I told him. 'It's one of the things that hurts most in this world, Brick – to lose an old friend, I mean.'

Brick said no more on the subject then, nor for that matter did I, but less than a fortnight later he did something for which, surely, he will be rewarded.

Where he found the down-and-out, middle-aged collie I do not know, nor shall I ever know, but with jaunty confidence he brought the stray into the house.

'What's the idea, Brick?' I asked. 'We can't keep this poor chap. He looks as though he's been on the road for weeks. He's got no collar, and –'

Brick began that old trick of scratching at my leg, and as he did so, and as I looked at the thin vagrant he had introduced to me, I thought about Ben Warren. Why, I argued, should not Ben try second-best?

In the beginning the old man would not listen to me, and it was only when I pointed out that he was lonely, and that the collie was lonely, and that the alliance of two lonely people put an end to loneliness that he said:

'All right then. I'll take the poor chap – but it's for Joe's sake. See what I mean?'

'I see,' I said.

When Brick and I, pausing in the lane, looked back, we saw Ben leaning forward and gazing towards the little patch of garden.

We saw too how the collie lifted his head and licked at one of the old man's frail hands – and how that hand was laid on the head of the stray who was to be second-best.

TRIUMPH

The Dog of Montargis ───────────

Andrew Lang

The next dramatic account is from French history. I can find no record either of the period to which it belongs or who first related it. It came into English literature through the pen of the poet, anthropologist, historian and French scholar, Andrew Lang (1844–1912) and is included in his *Animal Story Book*:

For three days, Aubrey de Montdidier had not been seen by his friends and comrades in arms. On Sunday morning, he had attended mass in the Church of Our Lady, but it was noticed that in the afternoon he was absent from the great tournament which was held at Saint Katherine's.

This astonished his friend the young Sieur de Narsac, who had appointed to meet him there, that they might watch the encounter between a Burgundian knight and a gentleman from Provence, both renowned in tilting, who were to meet together for the first time that day in Paris.

It was unlike Aubrey to fail to be present on such an occasion; and his friends grew anxious, and began to question among themselves whether some accident might not have befallen him.

Early on the morning of the fourth day, de Narsac was awakened by a continuous sound, as of something scratching against his door. Starting up to listen, he heard, in the intervals of the scratching, a low whine, as of a Dog in pain. Thoroughly aroused, he got up and opened the door. Stretched before it, apparently too weak to stand, was a great gaunt Greyhound, spent with exhaustion and hunger. His ribs stood out like the bars of a gridiron beneath his smooth coat; his tongue hung down between his jaws, parched and stiff; his eyes were bloodshot, and he trembled in every limb.

On seeing de Narsac, the poor creature struggled to his feet, feebly wagged his tail, and thrust his nose into the young man's hands. Then only did de Narsac recognize in the half-starved skeleton before him the favourite Dog and constant companion of his friend, Aubrey de Montdidier.

It was clear from the poor animal's emaciated appearance that it was in the last stage of exhaustion. Summoning his servant, de Narsac ordered food and water to be brought at once; and the Dog devoured the huge meal set before it.

From his starved appearance, and from the voracity with which he devoured the food set before him, it was evident that he had had nothing to eat for some days.

No sooner was his hunger appeased, than he began to move uneasily about the room. Uttering low howls of distress from time to time, he approached the door; then, returning to de Narsac's side, he looked up in his face and gently tugged at his mantle, as if to attract attention. There was something at once so appealing and peculiar in the Dog's behaviour that de Narsac's curiosity was aroused, and he became convinced that there was some connection between the Dog's starved appearance and strange manner and the unaccountable disappearance of his master. Perhaps the Dog might supply the clue to Aubrey's place of concealment.

Watching the Dog's behaviour closely, de Narsac became aware that the dumb beast was inviting him to accompany him. Accordingly, he yielded to the Dog's apparent wish, and, leaving the house, followed him out into the streets of Paris.

Looking round from time to time to see that de Narsac was coming after him, the Greyhound pursued his way through the narrow, tortuous streets of the ancient city, over the Bridge, and out by the Porte St-Martin, into the open country outside the gates of the town. Then, continuing on its track, the Dog headed for the Forest of Bondy, a place of evil fame in those far-off days, as its solitudes were known to be infested by bands of robbers.

Stopping suddenly in a deep and densely wooded glade of the woods, the Dog uttered a succession of low, angry growls; then, tugging at de Narsac's mantle, it led him to some freshly turned-up earth, beneath a wide-spreading oak tree. With a piteous whine, the Dog stretched himself on the spot, and could not be induced by de Narsac to follow him back to Paris, where he straightaway betook himself, as he at once suspected foul play.

A few hours later, a party of men, guided to the spot by the young Sieur de Narsac, removed the earth and dead leaves and ferns from the hole into which they had been hastily flung, and discovered the murdered body of Aubrey de Montdidier. Hurriedly a litter was constructed of boughs of trees and, followed by the Dog, the body was borne into Paris, where it was soon afterwards buried.

From that hour, the Greyhound attached himself to the Sieur de Narsac. It slept in his room, ate from his table, and followed close at his heels when he went out of doors.

One morning, as the two were threading their way through the crowded Rue St-Martin, de Narsac was startled by hearing a low, fierce growl from the Greyhound. Looking down, he saw that the creature was shaking in every limb; his smooth coat was bristling, his tail was straight and stiff, and he was showing his teeth. In another moment, he had made a dart from de Narsac's side, and had sprung on a young gentleman named Macaire, in the uniform of the king's bodyguard who, with several comrades in arms, was sauntering along on the opposite side of the street. There was something so sudden in the attack that the Chevalier Macaire was almost thrown to the ground. With their walking-canes, he and his friends beat off the Dog, and on de Narsac coming up, it was called away, and, still trembling and growling, followed its master down the street.

A few days later, the same thing occurred. De Narsac and the Chevalier Macaire chanced to encounter each other walking in the royal park. In a moment, the Dog had rushed at Macaire and, with a fierce spring at his throat, had tried to pull him to the ground. De Narsac and some officers of the king's bodyguard came to Macaire's assistance, and the Dog was called off.

The rumour of the attack reached the ears of the king, and mixed with the rumours were whisperings of a long-standing quarrel between Macaire and Aubrey de Montdidier. Might not the Dog's strange and unaccountable hatred for the young officer be a clue to the mysterious murder of his late master?

Determined to sift the matter to the bottom, the king summoned de Narsac and the Dog to his presence at the Hôtel St-Pol. Following close on his master's heels, the Greyhound entered the audience-room, where the king was seated, surrounded by his courtiers. As de Narsac bowed low before his sovereign, a short, fierce bark was heard from the Dog; and, before he could be held back, he had darted in among the startled courtiers, and had sprung at the throat of the Chevalier Macaire, who, with several other knights, formed a little group behind the king's chair.

It was impossible longer to doubt that there was some ground for the surmises that had rapidly grown to suspicion, and that had received sudden confirmation from the fresh evidence of the Dog's hatred.

The king decided that there should be a trial by the judgement of God, and that a combat should take place between man, the accused, and Dog, the accuser. The place chosen for the combat was a waste, uninhabited plot of ground, frequently selected as a duelling-ground by the young gallants of Paris.

In the presence of the king and his courtiers, the strange unnatural combat took place that afternoon. The knight was armed with a short thick stick; the Dog was provided with an empty barrel, as a retreating ground from the attacks of his adversary.

At a given signal, the combatants entered the lists. The Dog seemed quite to understand the strange duel on which it was engaged. Barking savagely, and darting round his opponent, he made attempts to leap at his throat; now on this side, now on that he sprang, jumping into the air, and then bounding back out of reach of the stick. There was such swiftness and determination about his movements, and something so unnatural in the combat, that Macaire's nerve failed him. His blows beat the air, without hitting the Dog; his breath came in quick short gasps; there was a look of terror on his face; and for a moment, overcome by the horror of the situation, his eye quailed and sought the ground.

At that instant, the Dog sprang at his throat, and pinned him to the

earth. In his terror, he called out, and acknowledged his crime, and implored the king's mercy. But the judgement of God had decided. The Dog was called off before it had strangled its victim, but the man was hurried away to the place of execution, and atoned that evening for the murder of the faithful Greyhound's master.

The Dog has been known to posterity as the Dog of Montargis, as in the Castle of Montargis there stood for many centuries a sculptured stone mantlepiece, on which the combat was carved.

Buck's Great Feat _____

Jack London

Who receives the accolade as the greatest writer of novels about dogs? If that question were put to a universal vote the answer would almost certainly be the American Jack London (1876–1916), whose career began as a sailor on the lower deck and who took part in the Klondike gold rush of 1897. His characterization of dogs, especially draught dogs, and his ability to portray their endearing and admirable qualities are second to none. Having shared the same rigours as a great variety of dog-owning frontiersmen, prospectors and Indians, London witnessed, often in the most stark circumstances, the triumphs and tragedies and the interrelations of their dogs.

Buck, the hero of *The Call of the Wild*, half St Bernard, half sheepdog and originally the property of an American judge, is stolen by a servant and sold to a fierce, unsympathetic gold prospector. After many adventures, in which he changes hands – some cruel, some kind – many times and fights his way into the place of top dog of a sledge team, he is eventually bought by John Thornton, through whom he learns the real love of a man for the first and last time. In the end Thornton and his companions are slaughtered by Indians. Having avenged the murder, Buck joins the she-wolf who has already become his mate: hence 'The Call of the Wild'. This extract tells how Thornton wins a thousand-dollar bet that Buck can drag a sledge weighing a thousand pounds over a distance of a hundred yards, which proves to be the greatest triumph in the dog's life:

That winter, at Dawson, Buck performed another exploit, not so heroic, perhaps, but one that put his name many notches higher on the totem-pole of Alaskan fame. This exploit was particularly gratifying to the three men; for they stood in need of the outfit which it furnished, and were enabled to make a long-desired trip into the virgin East, where miners had not yet appeared. It was brought about by a conversation in the Eldorado Saloon, in which men waxed boastful of their favourite dogs. Buck, because of his record, was the target for these men, and Thornton was driven stoutly to defend him. At the end of half an hour one man stated that his dog could start a sled with five hundred pounds and walk off with it; a second bragged six hundred for his dog; and a third, seven hundred.

'Pooh! pooh!' said John Thornton, 'Buck can start a thousand pounds.'

'And break it out? and walk off with it for a hundred yards?' demanded Matthewson, a Bonanza King, he of the seven hundred vaunt.

'And break it out, and walk off with it for a hundred yards,' John Thornton said coolly.

'Well,' Matthewson said, slowly and deliberately, so that all could hear, 'I've got a thousand dollars that says he can't. And there it is.' So saying, he slammed a sack of gold dust of the size of a bologna sausage down upon the bar.

Nobody spoke. Thornton's bluff, if bluff it was, had been called. He could feel a flush of warm blood creeping up his face. His tongue had tricked him. He did not know whether Buck could start a thousand pounds. Half a ton! The enormousness of it appalled him. He had great faith in Buck's strength and had often thought him capable of starting such a load; but never, as now, had he faced the possibility of it, the eyes of a dozen men fixed upon him, silent and waiting. Further, he had no thousand dollars; nor had Hans or Pete.

'I've got a sled standing outside now, with twenty fifty-pound sacks of flour on it,' Matthewson went on with brutal directness, 'so don't let that hinder you.'

Thornton did not reply. He did not know what to say. He glanced from face to face in the absent way of a man who has lost the power of thought and is seeking somewhere to find the thing that will start it going again. The face of Jim O'Brien, a Mastodon King and old-time comrade, caught his eyes. It was a cue to him, seeming to rouse him to do what he would never have dreamed of doing.

'Can you lend me a thousand?' he asked, almost in a whisper.

'Sure,' answered O'Brien, thumping down a plethoric sack by the side of Matthewson's. 'Though it's little faith I'm having, John, that the beast can do the trick.'

The Eldorado emptied its occupants into the street to see the test. The tables were deserted, and the dealers and gamekeepers came forth to see the outcome of the wager and to lay odds. Several hundred men, furred and mittened, banked around the sled within easy distance. Matthewson's sled, loaded with a thousand pounds of flour, had been standing for a couple of hours, and in the intense cold (it was sixty below zero) the runner had frozen fast to the hard-packed snow. Men offered odds of two to one that Buck would not budge the sled. A quibble arose concerning the phrase 'break out'. O'Brien contended that it was Thornton's privilege to knock the runners loose, leaving Buck to break it out from a dead standstill. Matthewson insisted that the phrase included breaking the runners from the frozen grip of the snow. A majority of the men who had witnessed the making of the bet decided in his favor, whereat the odds went up to three to one against Buck.

There were no takers. Not a man believed him capable of the feat. Thornton had been hurried into the wager, heavy with doubt; and now that he looked at the sled itself, the concrete fact, with the regular team of ten dogs curled up in the snow before it, the more impossible the task appeared. Matthewson waxed jubilant.

'Three to one!' he proclaimed. 'I'll lay you another thousand at that figure, Thornton. What d'ye say?'

Thornton's doubt was strong in his face, but his fighting spirit was aroused – the fighting spirit that soars above odds, fails to recognize the impossible, and is deaf to all save the clamor for battle. He called Hans and Pete to him. Their sacks were slim, and with his own the three partners could rake together only two hundred dollars. In the ebb of their fortunes, this sum was the total capital; yet they laid it unhesitatingly against Matthewson's six hundred.

The team of ten dogs was unhitched, and Buck, with his own harness, was put into the sled. He had caught the contagion of the excitement, and he felt that in some way he must do a great thing for John Thornton. Murmurs of admiration at his splendid appearance went up. He was in perfect condition, without an ounce of superfluous flesh, and the one hundred and fifty pounds that he weighed were so many pounds of grit and virility. His furry coat shone with the sheen of silk. Down the neck and across the shoulders, his mane, in repose as it was, half bristled and seemed to lift with every movement, as that excess of vigour made each particular hair alive and active. The great breast and heavy forelegs were no more than in proportion with the rest of the body, where the muscles showed in tight rolls underneath the skin. Men felt these muscles and proclaimed them as hard as iron, and the odds went down to two to one.

'Gad, sir! Gad, sir!' stuttered a member of the latest dynasty, a king of the Skookum Benches. 'I offer you eight hundred for him, sir, before the test; eight hundred just as he stands.'

Thornton shook his head and stepped to Buck's side.

'You must stand off from him,' Matthewson protested. 'Free play and plenty of room.'

The crowd fell silent; only could be heard the voices of the gamblers vainly offering two to one. Everybody acknowledged Buck a magnificent animal, but twenty fifty-pound sacks of flour bulked too large in their eyes for them to loosen their pouch-strings.

Thornton knelt down by Buck's side. He took his head in his two hands and rested cheek on cheek. He did not playfully shake him, as was his wont, or murmur soft love curses; but he whispered in his ear. 'As you love me, Buck. As you love me,' was what he whispered. Buck whined with suppressed eagerness.

The crowd was watching curiously. The affair was growing mysterious. It seemed like a conjuration. As Thornton got to his feet, Buck seized his mittened hand between his jaws, pressing in with his teeth and releasing slowly, half reluctantly. It was the answer, in terms, not of speech, but of love. Thornton stepped well back.

'Now, Buck,' he said.

Buck tightened the traces, then slacked them for a matter of several inches. It was the way he had learned.

'Gee!' Thornton's voice rang out, sharp in the tense silence.

Buck swung to the right, ending the movement in a plunge that took up the slack and with a sudden jerk arrested his one hundred and fifty pounds. The load quivered, and from under the runners arose a crisp crackling.

'Haw!' Thornton commanded.

Buck duplicated the manoeuvre, this time to the left. The crackling turned into a snapping, the sled pivoting and the runners slipping and grating several inches to the side. The sled was broken out. Men were holding their breaths, intensely unconscious of the fact.

'Now, MUSH!'

Thornton's command cracked out like a pistol-shot. Buck threw himself forward, tightening the traces with a jarring lunge. His whole

body was gathered compactly together in the tremendous effort, the muscles writhing and knotting like live things under the silky fur. His great chest was low to the ground, his head forward and down, while his feet were flying like mad, the claws scarring the hard-packed snow in parallel grooves. The sled swayed and trembled, half-started forward. One of his feet slipped, and one man groaned aloud. Then the sled lurched ahead in what appeared a rapid succession of jerks, though it never really came to a dead stop again . . . half an inch . . . an inch . . . two inches. . . . The jerks perceptibly diminished; as the sled gained momentum, he caught them up, till it was moving steadily along.

Men gasped and began to breathe again, unaware that for a moment they had ceased to breathe. Thornton was running behind, encouraging Buck with short, cheery words. The distance had been measured off, and as he neared the pile of firewood which marked the end of the hundred yards, a cheer began to grow and grow, which burst into a roar as he passed the firewood and halted at command. Every man was tearing himself loose, even Matthewson. Hats and mittens were flying in the air. Men were shaking hands, it did not matter with whom, and bubbling over in a general incoherent babel.

But Thornton fell on his knees beside Buck. Head was against head, and he was shaking him back and forth. Those who hurried up heard him cursing Buck, and he cursed him long and fervently, and softly and lovingly.

'Gad, sir! Gad, sir!' spluttered the Skookum Bench king. 'I'll give you a thousand for him, sir, a thousand, sir – twelve hundred, sir.'

Thornton rose to his feet. His eyes were wet. The tears were streaming frankly down his cheeks. 'Sir,' he said to the Skookum Bench king, 'no sir. You can go to hell, sir. It's the best I can do for you.'

Buck seized Thornton's hand in his teeth. Thornton shook him back and forth. As though animated by a common impulse, the onlookers drew back to a respectful distance; nor were they again indiscreet enough to interrupt.

White Fang Is Not Denied _____

Jack London

In the opening scene of *White Fang* two desperate men drive their sledge across the wastes of the Yukon territory of Canada towards their base fort. They are shadowed by a pack of famished wolves. First the wolves steal the men's rations, then their dogs, and, finally, they get the men themselves. One member of the pack is Kiche, formerly the property of the Indian chief Grey Beaver. Half dog, half wolf, she is the pack member who, with her coaxing whines, lures the sledge dogs, one by one, to their deaths at night. She is to be the dam, by another member of the pack, of White Fang who, by chance, in his turn becomes Grey Beaver's property.

After experiencing Grey Beaver's harsh discipline and many adventures, White Fang is bought by an odious man called Beauty Smith in exchange for a quantity of whisky. Smith keeps White Fang as a fighting dog and gives him the most unpleasant time of his life. The dog's saviour is a mining engineer, Weedon Scott, who shows him for the first time – as Buck is shown by Thornton in *The Call of the Wild* – how a human has the facility to love a dog. During Scott's first absence, White Fang is sick with sorrow and heartache. When Scott starts for California and leaves his wolf-dog with his partner, Matt, White Fang breaks out and joins the steamer just before it sets sail. Scott relents. In California White Fang is nearly killed himself when he fights and slays an escaped convict who breaks into the Scotts' house with the purpose of killing Weedon Scott's father, the judge who had convicted him. As in *The Call of the Wild*, the story ends happily with the mating and fatherhood of the dog hero. The passage I have chosen covers the period from when Scott, about to sail for California, decides to leave White Fang with Matt, to the moment he relents on the ship:

It was in the air. White Fang sensed the coming calamity, even before there was tangible evidence of it. In vague ways it was borne in upon him that a change was impending. He knew not how or why, yet he got the feel of the oncoming event from the gods themselves. In ways subtler than they knew, they betrayed their intentions to the wolf-dog that haunted the cabin-stoop, and that, though he never came inside the cabin, knew what went on inside their brains.

'Listen to that, will you!' the dog-musher exclaimed at supper one night.

Weedon Scott listened. Through the door came a low, anxious whine, like a sobbing under the breath that has just grown audible. Then came the long sniff, as White Fang reassured himself that his god was still inside and had not yet taken himself off in mysterious and solitary flight.

'I do believe that wolf's on to you,' the dog-musher said.

Weedon Scott looked across at his companion with eyes that almost pleaded, though this was given the lie by his words.

'What the devil can I do with a wolf in California?' he demanded.

'That's what I say,' Matt answered. 'What the devil can you do with a wolf in California?'

But this did not satisfy Weedon Scott. The other seemed to be judging him in a noncommittal sort of way.

'White-man's dogs would have no show against him,' Scott went on. 'He'd kill them on sight. If he didn't bankrupt me with damage suits, the authorities would take him away from me and electrocute him.'

'He's a downright murderer, I know,' was the dog-musher's comment.

Weedon Scott looked at him suspiciously.

'It would never do,' he said decisively.

'It would never do,' Matt concurred. 'Why, you'd have to hire a man 'specially to take care of 'im.'

The other's suspicion was allayed. He nodded cheerfully. In the silence that followed, the low, half-sobbing whine was heard at the door and then the long, questing sniff.

'There's no denyin' he thinks a hell of a lot of you,' Matt said.

The other glared at him in sudden wrath. 'Damn it all! I know my own mind and what's best.'

'I'm agreein' with you, only . . .'

'Only what?' Scott snapped out.

'Only . . .' the dog-musher began softly, then changed his mind and betrayed a rising anger of his own. 'Well, you needn't get so all-fired het up about it. Judgin' by your actions one'd think you didn't know your own mind.'

Weedon Scott debated with himself for a while, and then said more gently: 'You are right, Matt. I don't know my own mind, and that's what's the trouble.'

'Why, it would be rank ridiculousness for me to take that dog along,' he broke out after another pause.

'I'm agreein' with you,' was Matt's answer, and again his employer was not quite satisfied with him. 'But how in the name of the great Sardanapolis he knows you're going is what gets me,' the dog-musher continued innocently.

'It's beyond me, Matt,' Scott answered, with a mournful shake of his head.

Then came the day when, through the open cabin door, White Fang saw the fatal grip on the floor and the love-master packing things into it. Also there were comings and goings, and the erstwhile placid atmosphere of the cabin was vexed with strange perturbations and unrest. Here was indubitable evidence. White Fang had already sensed it. He now reasoned it. His god was preparing for another flight. And since he had not taken him before, so, now, he could look to be left behind.

That night he lifted the long wolf-howl. As he had howled, in his puppy days, when he fled back from the Wild to the village to find it vanished and naught but a rubbish-heap to mark the site of Grey Beaver's tepee, so now he pointed his muzzle to the cold stars and told to them his woe.

Inside the cabin the two men had just gone to bed.

'He's gone off his food again,' Matt remarked from his bunk.

There was a grunt from Weedon Scott's bunk, and a stir of blankets.

'From the way he cut up the other time you went away, I wouldn't wonder this time but what he died.'

The blankets in the other bunk stirred irritably.

'Oh, shut up!' Scott cried out through the darkness. 'You nag worse than a woman.'

'I'm agreein' with you,' the dog-musher answered, and Weedon Scott was not quite sure whether or not the other had snickered.

The next day White Fang's anxiety and restlessness were even more pronounced. He dogged his master's heels whenever he left the cabin, and haunted the front stoop when he remained inside. Through the open door he could catch glimpses of the luggage on the floor. The grip had been joined by two large canvas bags and a box. Matt was rolling the master's blankets and fur robe inside a small tarpaulin. White Fang whined as he watched the operation.

Later on two Indians arrived. He watched them closely as they shouldered the luggage and were led off down the hill by Matt, who carried the bedding and the grip. But White Fang did not follow them. The master was still in the cabin. After a time, Matt returned. The master came to the door and called White Fang inside.

'You poor devil,' he said gently, rubbing White Fang's ears and tapping his spine. 'I'm hitting the long trail, old man, where you cannot follow. Now give me a growl – the last, good, good-bye growl.'

But White Fang refused to growl. Instead, and after a wistful, searching look, he snuggled in, burrowing his head out of sight between the master's arm and body.

'There she blows!' Matt cried. From the Yukon arose the hoarse bellowing of a river steamboat. 'You've got to cut it short. Be sure and lock the front door. I'll go out the back. Get a move on!'

The two doors slammed at the same moment, and Weedon Scott waited for Matt to come around to the front. From inside the door came a low whining and sobbing. Then there were long, deep-drawn sniffs.

'You must take good care of him, Matt,' Scott said, as they started down the hill. 'Write and let me know how he gets along.'

'Sure,' the dog-musher answered. 'But listen to that, will you?'

Both men stopped. White Fang was howling as dogs howl when their masters lie dead. He was voicing an utter woe, his cry bursting upward in great heartbreaking rushes, dying down into quavering misery, and bursting upward again with rush upon rush of grief.

The *Aurora* was the first steamboat of the year for the Outside, and her decks were jammed with prosperous adventurers and broken gold seekers, all equally as mad to get to the Outside as they had been originally to get to the inside.

Near the gang-plank, Scott was shaking hands with Matt, who was preparing to go ashore. But Matt's hand went limp in the other's grasp as his gaze shot past and remained fixed on something behind him. Scott turned to see. Sitting on the deck several feet away and watching wistfully was White Fang.

The dog-musher swore softly, in awe-stricken accents. Scott could only look in wonder.

'Did you lock the front door?' Matt demanded.

The other nodded and asked, 'How about the back?'

'You just bet I did,' was the fervent reply.

White Fang flattened his ears ingratiatingly, but remained where he was, making no attempt to approach.

'I'll have to take 'm ashore with me.'

Matt made a couple of steps toward White Fang, but the latter slid away from him. The dog-musher made a rush of it, and White Fang dodged between the legs of a group of men. Ducking, turning, doubling, he slid about the deck, eluding the other's efforts to capture him.

But when the love-master spoke, White Fang came to him with prompt obedience.

'Won't come to the hand that's fed 'm all these months,' the dog-musher muttered resentfully. 'And you – you ain't never fed 'm after them first days of gettin' acquainted. I'm blamed if I can see how he works it out that you're the boss.'

Scott, who had been patting White Fang, suddenly bent closer and pointed to fresh-made cuts on his muzzle, and a gash between the eyes.

Matt bent over and passed his hand along White Fang's belly.

'We plump forgot the window. He's all cut an' gouged underneath. Must 'a butted clean through it, b'gosh!'

But Weedon Scott was not listening. He was thinking rapidly. The *Aurora*'s whistle hooted a final announcement of departure. Men were scurrying down the gang-plank to the shore. Matt loosened the bandana from his own neck and started to put it around White Fang's. Scott grasped the dog-musher's hand.

'Good-bye, Matt, old man. About the wolf – you needn't write. You see, I've . . .!'

'What!' the dog-musher exploded. 'You don't mean to say . . .?'

'The very thing I mean. Here's your bandana. *I'll* write to *you* about him.'

Matt paused halfway down the gang-plank.

'He'll never stand the climate!' he shouted back. 'Unless you clip 'm in warm weather!'

The gang-plank was hauled in, and the *Aurora* swung out from the bank. Weedon Scott waved a last good-bye. Then he turned and bent over White Fang, standing by his side.

'Now growl, damn you, growl,' he said, as he patted the responsive head and rubbed the flattening ears.

A Last-Minute Reprieve ─────────

Sir Edwin Arnold

This legend comes from *Pearls of the Faith* by Sir Edwin Arnold (1832–1904), a scholar of Buddhism and of Sanskrit, who was famous for *The Light of Asia*, a life in verse of Gautama, the founder of the Buddhist faith. The following verses tell of a convicted woman being led to her place of execution, which was to be by stoning. When she is seen along the way, by the king, to have compassion for a dog, he

judges this act to show a side of her character unrevealed to the court,
and orders her to be pardoned and freed:

High noon it was, and the hot Khamseen's breath
Blew from the desert sands and parched the town.
The crows gasped; and the kine went up and down
With lolling tongues; the camels moaned; a crowd
Pressed with their pitchers, wrangling high and loud
About the tank; and one dog by a well
Nigh dead with thirst, lay where he yelped and fell
Glaring upon the water out of reach,
And praying succour in a silent speech,
So piteous were its eyes. Which, when she saw,
This woman from her foot her shoe did draw
Albeit death-sorrowful; and looping up
The long silk of her girdle, made a cap
Of the heel's hollow, and thus let it sink
Until it touched the cool black water's brink;
So filled th'embroidered shoe, and gave a draught
To the spent beast, which whined and fawned and quaffed
Her kind gift to the dregs; next licked her hand
With such glad looks that all might understand

He held his life from her; then at her feet
He followed close all down the cruel street,
Her one friend in that city.
                              But the King,
Riding within his litter, marked the thing,
And how the woman on her way to die,
Had such compassion for the misery
Of that parched hound: 'Take off her chain and place
The veil once more above the sinner's face,
And lead her to her house in peace!' he said.
'The law is that the people stone thee dead,
For that which thou hast wrought; but there is come,
Fawning around thy feet, a witness dumb,
Not heard upon thy trial; this brute beast
Testifies for thee, sister! whose weak breast
Death could not make ungentle. I hold rule
In Allah's stead, who is the Merciful,
And hope for Mercy; therefore go thou free –
I dare not show less pity unto thee.'

Vendetta _____

Guy de Maupassant

In the following tale, that French master of the short story, Guy de
Maupassant (1850–93), placing a dog at the centre of his plot, shows
the passionate hatred of an old Italian woman scheming for bizarre
revenge against the murderer of her beloved son:

Palo Saverini's widow dwelt alone with her son in a small, mean house
on the ramparts of Bonifacio. Built on a spur of the mountain and in
places actually overhanging the sea, the town looks across the
rock-strewn straits to the low-lying coast of Sardinia. On the other
side, girdling it almost completely, there is a fissure in the cliff, like an
immense corridor, which serves as a port, and down this long
channel, as far as the first houses, sail the small Italian and Sardinian
fishing-boats, and once a fortnight the broken-winded old steamer
from Ajaccio. Clustered together on the white hillside, the houses

form a patch of even more dazzling whiteness. Clinging to the rock, gazing down upon those deadly straits, where scarcely a ship ventures, they look like the nests of birds of prey. The sea and the barren coast, stripped of all but a scanty covering of grass, are for ever harassed by a restless wind, which sweeps along the narrow funnel, ravaging the banks on either side. In all directions the black points of innumerable rocks jut out from the water, with trails of white foam streaming from them, like torn shreds of cloth, floating and quivering on the surface of the waves.

The widow Saverini's house was planted on the very edge of the cliff, and its three windows opened upon this wild and dreary prospect. She lived there with her son Antoine and their dog Sémillante, a great gaunt brute of the sheepdog variety, with a long, rough coat, whom the young man took with him when he went out shooting.

One evening, Antoine Saverini was treacherously stabbed in a quarrel by Nicolas Ravolati, who escaped that same night to Sardinia.

At the sight of the body, which was brought home by passers-by, the old mother shed no tears, but she gazed long and silently at her dead son. Then, laying her wrinkled hand upon the corpse, she promised him the Vendetta. She would not allow anyone to remain with her, and shut herself up with the dead body. The dog Sémillante, who remained with her, stood at the foot of the bed and howled, with her head turned towards her master and her tail between her legs. Neither of them stirred, neither the dog nor the old mother, who was now leaning over the body, gazing at it fixedly, and silently shedding great tears. Still wearing his rough jacket, which was pierced and torn at the breast, the boy lay on his back as if asleep, but there was blood all about him, on his shirt, which had been stripped off in order to expose the wound, on his waistcoat, trousers, face and hands. His beard and hair were matted with clots of blood.

The old mother began to talk to him, and at the sound of her voice the dog stopped howling.

'Never fear, never fear, you shall be avenged, my son, my little son, my poor child. You may sleep in peace. You shall be avenged, I tell you. You have your mother's word, and you know she never breaks it.'

Slowly she bent down and pressed her cold lips to the dead lips of her son.

Sémillante resumed her howling, uttering a monotonous, long-drawn wail, heart-rending and terrible. And thus the two remained, the woman and the dog, till morning.

The next day Antoine Saverini was buried, and soon his name ceased to be mentioned in Bonifacio.

He had no brother, nor any near male relation. There was no man in the family who could take up the Vendetta. Only his mother, his old mother, brooded over it.

From morning till night she could see, just across the straits, a white speck upon the coast. This was the little Sardinian village of Longosardo, where the Corsican bandits took refuge whenever the hunt for them grew too hot. They formed almost the entire population of the hamlet. In full view of their native shores they waited for a chance to return home and regain the bush. She knew that Nicolas Ravolati had sought shelter in the village. . . .

One night, when Sémillante began to whine, the old mother had an inspiration of savage, vindictive ferocity. She thought about it till morning. At daybreak she rose and betook herself to church. Prostrate on the stone floor, humbling herself before God, she besought Him to aid and support her, to lend to her poor, wornout body the strength she needed to avenge her son.

Then she returned home. In the yard stood an old barrel with one end knocked in, in which was caught the rain-water from the eaves. She turned it over, emptied it, and fixed it to the ground with stakes and stones. Then she chained Sémillante to this kennel and went into the house.

With her eyes fixed on the Sardinian coast, she walked restlessly up and down her room. He was over there, the murderer.

The dog howled all day and all night. The next morning the old woman brought her a bowl of water, but no food, neither soup nor bread. Another day passed. Sémillante was worn out and slept. The next morning her eyes were gleaming, and her coat standing, and she tugged frantically at her chain. And again the old woman gave her nothing to eat. Maddened with hunger, Sémillante barked hoarsely. Another night went by.

At daybreak, the widow went to a neighbour and begged for two trusses of straw. She took some old clothes that had belonged to her husband, stuffed them with straw to represent a human figure, and made a head out of a bundle of old rags. Then, in front of Sémillante's kennel, she fixed a stake in the ground and fastened the dummy to it in an upright position.

The dog looked at the straw figure in surprise and, although she was famished, stopped howling.

The old woman went to the pork butcher and bought a long piece of black pudding. When she came home she lighted a wood fire in the yard, close to the kennel, and fried the black pudding. Sémillante bounded up and down in a frenzy, foaming at the mouth, her eyes fixed on the gridiron with its maddening smell of meat.

Her mistress took the steaming pudding and wound it like a tie round the dummy's neck. She fastened it on tightly with string as if to force it inwards. When she had finished she unchained the dog.

With one ferocious leap, Sémillante flew at the dummy's throat and with her paws on its shoulders began to tear it. She fell back with a portion of her prey between her jaws, sprang at it again, slashing at the string with her fangs, tore away some scraps of food, dropped for a moment, and hurled herself at it in renewed fury. She tore away the whole face with savage rendings and reduced the neck to shreds.

Motionless and silent, with burning eyes, the old woman looked on. Presently she chained the dog up again. She starved her another two days, and then put her through the same strange performance.

For three months she accustomed her to this method of attack, and to tear her meals away with her fangs. She was no longer kept on the chain. At a sign from her mistress, the dog would fly at the dummy's throat.

She learned to tear it to pieces even when no food was concealed about its throat. Afterwards as a reward she was always given the black pudding her mistress had cooked for her.

As soon as she caught sight of the dummy, Sémillante quivered with excitement and looked at her mistress, who would raise her finger and cry in a shrill voice, 'Tear him.'

One Sunday morning when she thought the time had come, the widow Saverini went to confession and communion, in an ecstasy of devotion. Then she disguised herself like a tattered old beggar man, and struck a bargain with a Sardinian fisherman, who took her and the dog across to the opposite shore.

She carried a large piece of black pudding wrapped in a cloth bag. Sémillante had been starved for two days and her mistress kept exciting her by letting her smell the savoury food.

The pair entered the village of Longosardo. The old woman hobbled along to a baker and asked for the house of Nicolas Ravolati. He had resumed his former occupation, which was that of a joiner, and he was working alone in the back of his shop.

The old woman threw open the door and called:

'Nicolas! Nicolas!'

He turned round. Slipping the dog's lead, she cried:

'Tear him! Tear him!'

The maddened dog flew at his throat. The man flung out his arms, grappled with the brute and they rolled on the ground together. For some moments he struggled, kicking the floor with his feet. Then lay still, while Sémillante tore his throat to shreds.

Two neighbours seated at their doors remembered to have seen an old beggar man emerge from the house and, at his heels, a lean black dog, which was eating as it went along, some brown substance that its master was giving it.

By the evening the old woman had reached home again.

That night she slept well.

Tam o'Shanter

Albert Payson Terhune

One of the best-liked American dog authors of the early years of this century was Albert Payson Terhune, who was born in Newark, New Jersey, in 1872, but who was chiefly resident in New York City during the years of his literary success. Although most celebrated for his dog stories – such as *Wolf*, *The Way of a Dog*, *Lochinvar Luck* and *Treve* – he also wrote a number of film scripts. The following passage comes from a tale called 'The Grudge' which was included in the volume published under the title *Buff: A Collie*. The setting is the Rampano Mountains in Terhune's native New Jersey.

The feral and marauding pack of black dogs has been almost annihilated by angry farmers, one of whom, Trask Frayne, owns two much-loved collies, Wisp and Tam o'Shanter. The largest and most ferocious of the wild black dogs has eluded the farmers' tactics and guns. This local menace kills Wisp. Tam dedicates himself to hunting the killer. A few days later he is accused by a neighbour of slaying his cattle, but Trask Frayne proves that, although Tam's footprints are there, so too are those of the fearsome black dog, who has been marauding up and down the valley. After missing Tam for several weeks Frayne goes up into the hills, where he tethers a sheep as a bait for the black dog and waits in ambush with his gun. The black dog duly attacks the sheep, but, as Frayne raises his gun, Tam o'Shanter appears from the shadows and a terrific fight ensues. This is the climax of the story:

The Black dived for the Collie's forelegs, seeking to crack their bones in his mighty jaws and thus render his foe helpless. Nimbly, Tam's tiny white forefeet whisked away from the peril of each dive. In redoubled fury he drove for the throat. And the two clashed shoulder to shoulder.

Then, amid the welter, came the final phase of the fight. The Black, as the two reared, lunged again for the Collie's hurt throat. Tam jerked his head and neck aside to avoid the grip. And, as once before, the Black changed the direction of his lunge. With the swiftness of a striking snake, he made the change. And, before the other could thwart or so much as divine his purpose, he had secured the coveted hold, far up on Tam's left foreleg.

No mere snap or slash this; but a death grip. The Black's teeth sank deep into the captured leg; grinding with a force which presently must snap the bones of the upper leg and leave the Collie crippled against a practically uninjured and terrible antagonist. The rest would be slaughter.

Tam knew his own mortal peril. He knew it even before Trask Frayne came rushing out from his watching-place, brandishing the gun, club-fashion. The Collie did not try to wrench free and thereby hurry the process of breaking his leg or of tearing out the shoulder-muscles. He thought, as quickly as the mongrel had lunged.

Rearing his head aloft, he drove down at the Black. The latter was clinging with all his might to the Collie's foreleg. And, in the rapture of having gained at last a disabling grip, he ignored the fact that he had left an opening in his own defence – an opening seldom sought in a fight, except by a Wolf or a Wolf's descendant. It was for this opening that Tam o'Shanter struck. In a trice his white teeth had buried themselves in the exposed nape of the Black's neck.

Here, at the brain's base, lies the spinal cord, dangerously within reach of long and hard-driven fangs. And here, Tam has fastened himself.

An instant later – but an instant too late – the Black knew his peril. Releasing his grip on the Collie's leg, before the bone had begun to yield, he threw his great body madly from side to side, fighting crazily to shake off the death-hold. With all his mighty strength, he thrashed about.

Twice, he lifted the seventy-pound Collie clean off the ground. Once he fell, with Tam under him. But the Collie held on. Tam did more than hold on. Exerting every remaining atom of his waning power, he let his body be flung here and there, in the Black's struggles; and he concentrated his force upon cleaving deeper and deeper into the neck-nape.

This was the grip whereby the Black, a month ago, had crushed the life out of friendly little Wisp. And, by chance or fate, Tam had been enabled to gain the same hold. Spasmodically, he set his fangs in a vicelike tightening of his grip.

At one instant, the Black was whirling and writhing in the fulness of his wiry might. At the next, with a sickening snapping sound, his giant body went limp. And his forequarters hung, a lifeless weight, from his conqueror's jaws.

Tam relaxed his hold. The big black body slumped to earth and lay there. The Collie, panting and swaying, stood over his dead enemy. The bitterly long quest was ended. Heavenward went his bleeding

muzzle. And he waked the solemn stillness of the summer night with an eerie Wolf howl, the awesome primal yell of Victory.

For a few seconds Trask Frayne, unnoticed, stared at his Dog. And, as he looked, it seemed to him he could see the Collie change gradually back from a wild thing of the forests to the staunch and adoring watchdog of other days. Then the man spoke.

'Tam!' he said quietly. '*Tam!* Old friend!'

The exhausted victor lurched dizzily about, at sound of the voice. Catching sight of Trask, he trembled all over.

He took a dazed step toward Frayne. Then, with something queerly like a human sob, the Collie sprang forward; and gambolled weakly about the man; licking Trask's feet and hands; springing up in a groggy effort to kiss his face; patting his master's chest with eager forepaws; crying aloud in an ecstasy of joy at the reunion.

Then, all at once, he seemed to remember he was a staid and dignified middle-aged Dog and not a hoodlum puppy. Ceasing his unheard-of demonstrations, he stood beside Frayne, looking up into Trask's eyes in silent worship.

'You've done a grand night's work, Tam,' said Frayne, seeking to steady his own voice. 'And your hurts need bathing. Come home.'

His plumed tail proudly wagging, his splendid head aloft, Tam o'Shanter turned and led the way to the house he loved.

Revenge of a Chieftain's Dog ⸻

Manly Wade Wellman

Manly Wade Wellman was born in the early years of this century in Portuguese West Africa, where his father was a medical missionary. He later settled in the mountains of North Carolina where 'devil hounds' are said to roam. 'One has three legs only,' said Wellman, 'and to see it in the twilight is a sure warning of bad luck, maybe death. So I don't go looking for it.' A distinguished expert on American folklore and superstitions, he was celebrated in the United States as a science fiction writer. His best-known novel, *Who Fears the Devil?* was later filmed as *The Legend of Hillbilly John*. This story, 'Dead Dog', based on a macabre legend from the West Africa he knew so well in his youth, ends in deathly triumph for the murdered chieftain and his dog Ohondongela:

Dead dogs may bite the careless feet – Umbundu proverb

They brought the rebel chief Kaflatala out of the jungle to Father Labossier's mud-brick house, brought him in a *tepoia* because he still limped from a Portuguese bullet in his thigh. Twenty black warriors, clicking their spears respectfully, followed the hammock-litter and formed a row outside the stockade as Kaflatala dismounted and hobbled up the path.

Springing from his seat on the porch, Father Labossier walked swiftly to meet his old friend. The chief was lean, taller by a head than the sturdy priest, and black as basalt save for a grey scar across his proud face from eye to nostril. The two men said the requisite Kalungu greetings and sat on a log under the broad-leafed fig-tree. Then Kaflatala spoke:

'Your advice came to me in my hiding. I cannot hope to win against the Portuguese soldiers; now I must surrender and save my people further punishment.'

'That is wise, Kaflatala,' nodded Father Labossier, smiling. Nine years in West Africa had not dulled the missionary zeal that had stirred him from a pleasant curé of souls near Antwerp, and moments like this repaid him for long toil.

'The white man's Saviour, of whom I told you,' he continued, 'will make your sentence a light one.'

The scar darkened on Kaflatala's face and his wide lips tightened.

'My people will suffer no more, that is all. Rodriguez, the Portuguese captain, will kill me.'

The priest held up a hand in protest. 'Not all Portuguese are cruel. It is true that Captain Rodriguez's heart is sick; he was sent here because he had sinned against the laws at home –'

'However he came here, he will kill me,' Kaflatala fairly jerked out the words, then apologized for interrupting. 'Good-bye, my father. We shall not meet again.'

Still Father Labossier argued. 'A power will save you, Kaflatala.'

'A power will avenge me,' was the bleak reply. 'That is all.'

Father Labossier brought notebook and pencil from his pocket and scribbled a note as he sat. 'This asks that you be treated kindly,' he explained. 'My fastest servant will bear it to the fort ahead of you.'

The chief thanked him courteously, and rose. 'One favour before I go.'

'Name it.'

Kaflatala emitted a chirping whistle. At once something black and swift sped from behind the row of warriors, dashed through the gate and up the path – a huge, shaggy hound, as black as thunder. It was as large as a calf, and its eyes shone with an uneasy greenish pallor. Yet it seemed gentle, thrusting its long, ugly head under the chief's hand.

'Will you keep my dog for me?' asked Kaflatala.

'Until you come back,' agreed Father Labossier.

'I do not come back,' insisted the other, and Father Labossier changed the subject by asking how the beast was called.

'Ohondongela,' replied the master.

That word means 'revenge' in the Umbundu, and Father Labossier, eyeing the dog, thought it as fierce as its name. Black, rough, lean, powerful of jaw and long of fang, it had something of the forbidding wild about it, almost like a forest beast; but all dogs were once forest beasts, at the beginning of time. . . .

Kaflatala again excused himself for cutting the visit short, spoke commandingly to Ohondongela, and smiled when the brute curled himself obediently at the feet of Father Labossier. Then he stumped to the gate, crept into his *tepoia* and gave the signal for the march to continue.

Three days later Father Labossier was wakened before dawn by the dismal howling of Kaflatala's hound. He grumbled sleepily, then reflected that a man of God must not think unkindly, even of a beast. . . .

At about four o'clock in the afternoon a chorus of shouts from his servants betokened a stranger coming up the trail.

It was a runner, bare-legged and wearing a faded khaki shirt, who advanced to the porch, saluted in clumsy military fashion, and offered a parcel sewn in rice-sacking.

'From the fort,' the runner told him. 'Captain Rodriguez has sent it.'

'Thank you.' Some answer, of course, to his plea for mercy to Kaflatala. But why a package and no letter? There must be a note inside.

Producing a clasp knife, the priest ripped the sacking.

A face looked up at him through the ragged hole – a black dead face. Upon it a pallid grey scar ran from eye to nostril. Kaflatala had been right; Captain Rodriguez had made short work of him, and thus was answering Father Labossier's recommendation of mercy.

Again rose the doleful wail of Ohondongela the hound. And just before sunset the great beast lay down and died, quietly, quickly and inexplicably.

Three moons had waned and waxed again, and the same runner from the fort met Father Labossier just outside his stockade. It was mid-afternoon, as on the runner's previous appearance, and again he had something from Captain Rodriguez – not a package this time, but a letter.

The priest took the envelope and gazed for a moment at the almost indecipherable characters that spelled his own name upon it. They had been set down by a shaking hand, a hand that he knew as the captain's. He had written to Rodriguez on the same day that he had received Kaflatala's head; he had stiffly indicted the officer as a cruel and cowardly murderer, and had sent a duplicate of the letter to the governor at Loanda. Nobody had replied – was this a belated acknowledgement of his message, perhaps a justification of Rodriguez's action or a further sneer at the priest?

He opened the letter and read it, his kindly face spreading over with wonder. For Rodriguez was praying for help and comfort in the name of Christian mercy and priestly compassion. The last phrase, in particular, was out of character: 'I know I have sinned, yet ask for the aid I do not deserve.'

The priest lifted his eyes to the waiting runner. 'Go back and say that I will come tomorrow.'

The native paused, embarrassed, then replied diffidently that his master was in dreadful case and that there was no white doctor to do magic for his healing. Could not Father Labossier come at once?

'It will be an all-night trek,' demurred the priest. Then he thought better of his hesitancy, and added. 'But a moon will shine. I shall go with you.'. . .

It was a wearying tramp by moonlight, and an eventful one. At sunrise he came to the fort, where, brooding in his quarters over untasted food, Captain Rodriguez waited for him.

Father Labossier was shocked at the sight of the Portuguese. When they had last met, four months previously, Rodriguez had been florid, swaggering, vigorous. Now he sagged shrunkenly inside his dirty white uniform. The face he lifted was pale, its eyes wild, and his once-jaunty moustache drooped.

'Father,' he mumbled hoarsely, 'I am ridden by devils.'

Father Labossier took the captain's hand. It trembled in his grasp. 'I do not doubt you, my son,' he replied gravely. 'Yours has been an evil life.'. . .

The captain clutched his face in wasted hands and his shoulders shook, as with sobs. Finally he forced himself to speak of what lay upon his soul.

Three nights before, he had retired, as usual, to his lonely bedchamber. He spoke of his habitual preparations; the examination of the windows to see if their gratings and mosquito nets were in place, his locking of the door against possible night prowlers, his placing of a service pistol beside the water glass on his bedside table. Nothing untoward had happened during the day. His thoughts before slumber had taken the form of an idle review of his work and a wistful consideration of his chances to be forgiven certain indiscretions and called home to Portugal. Then he had dozed off, to wake suddenly and in fear.

At this point in his narrative, he hid his face again and shuddered uncontrollably. Father Labossier laid a hand on the captain's arm, and strength flowed from him into that shaken frame.

'I looked towards the window, and there I saw it. Blood of the saints, I saw it! By the window – a great dog!'

'Dog!' repeated the other, leaning forward in his turn. 'What sort of a dog?'

'Large – black and shaggy. It was sitting up, and its head and shoulders rose above the window-sill, making a silhouette against the moonlight. Its eyes, like green lamps of hell, stared at me. The hate in them!' Captain Rodriguez's face twitched with the memory.

'I see. And then?'

'I screamed, a thing I have not done since I was a baby. A moment later, my orderly was pounding and calling at the door; and the dog – had gone.'

'Gone!' echoed the priest.

'Yes, vanished like a candle-flame snuffed.'

Father Labossier clicked his tongue. 'Was it not a dream, that?'

Captain Rodriguez laughed, but not merrily. He had thought that very thing, he admitted, though he was too nervous to sleep any more that night. In the morning he forced himself to forget the adventure and had gone about his duties with a heart that grew lighter as the day progressed. By nightfall the nervousness returned, and he lulled himself to sleep with a bromide.

'Again – mark me, Father – again I saw to windows, mosquito netting, lock. I put from me the troublesome vision of the night before. I slept.'

Father Labossier took a cigar from his pocket. 'The dream –'

'It was no dream, I say. When does a dream come twice in two nights?' The captain's lips twitched, showing teeth that were set as though to hold back a dreadful pain. 'The dog returned. I woke in sudden instinctive fear, and there it was as before. No, not as before.'

'What do you mean?' asked Father Labossier, biting the end of his cigar.

'It had been at the window the first time. Now it was at the foot of my bed, nearer to me by half the floor's width.' Rodriguez laid his fist to his lips, as though to crush their trembling. 'It was so large as to look over the footboard at me. Its green eyes burned into mine.'

Father Labossier said, very quietly, that a real dog could not have looked Rodriguez in the eye.

'No, and this was no real dog. It was my gaze that faltered, and I screamed aloud.'

'As before?'

'Yes, as before. And my orderly came, bearing a light that shed itself through the cracks of the door. At that beam, the thing was gone, completely and instantly. I rose to let the orderly in – never have I allowed a native to see me so upset.'

Father Labossier rubbed a match on the sole of his boot. 'And then, my son?'

'In the morning I sent for you. But last night, while you were on the trail – last night, the dreadful dog from hell visited me yet again!'

He flung out a hand, palm vertical. 'No farther away than that, it sat at my side. It breathed upon me, I heard the growl in its throat. And somehow I snatched up the pistol from my table and fired into its face – it vanished. But tonight – *it will not vanish!*'

His voice had risen to a wail. Again the priest's strong, steady hand clutched his companion's quivering one, calming the frantic shivers.

'You have fancied these things, my son.'

'But I swear they are true, by every saint in the calendar. Come, Father, to my room. You shall see for yourself.'

Still murmuring set phrases of comfort, Father Labossier followed Rodriguez back into the house. The captain's sleeping-compartment was comfortable and even luxurious beyond military requirements, appointed as he had described.

'See,' urged Rodriguez, laying an unsteady finger upon the door-jamb. 'This round hole – my bullet made it.'

'I see it,' Father Labossier assured him.

'And you observe the gratings and nets at the window? The lock on my door? Well, then –'

Father Labossier cleared his throat. He was well read, and something of an amateur psychologist. 'My son, you knew, perhaps, that Chief Kaflatala had a great black hound.'

'Did he? I never saw it.'

'You had heard, perhaps, of the beast. Its name was Ohondongela.'

Rodriguez bit his lips. 'Ohondongela – revenge.' He calmed himself and said that he might have heard of it.

'Ah, then,' said Father Labossier, 'it has become a symbol with you, my son, of the wrong your heart's core has admitted.'

Much more he said, drawing upon Freud and the Gospels in turn. Captain Rodriguez listened carefully, nodding from time to time as though he comprehended the argument and was disposed to agree.

'But if this is the truth,' he said when the priest had made an end, 'what am I to do?'

'You have begun by repenting and confessing,' Father Labossier told him. 'Tonight –'

'Tonight!' gasped Rodriguez, turning pale.

'Do not fear. Go to bed as usual, composing yourself. I shall sit up in the parlour. If the dream returns, call me – softly. We will deal with it together.'

Rodriguez drew a deep breath, as of relief. 'I am hungry,' he said suddenly. 'You, Father, have not breakfasted. Forgive me my neglect, and be my guest.'. . .

★

That night the captain said goodnight and went into his bedroom.

Sitting alone in the parlour, Father Labossier examined the bookshelf. After the Scriptures and the writings on the Saints, he enjoyed best Edgar Allan Poe, Maurice Leblanc and *The Adventures of Sherlock Holmes*. This story would help him while away the hours. He savoured a chapter, a second, a third. . . .

The calm night tore open before a blood-banishing scream of fear and agony.

Dropping the book, Father Labossier sprang to his feet. In three quick strides he crossed to the door of Rodriguez's bedroom. Even as he reached it, the scream rose higher, died suddenly, and a spatter of pistol shots rang out. Then a second voice, inhuman and savage, the jabbering snarl of a beast at the kill –

The door was locked. Father Labossier shook the knob futilely, then turned as a native orderly rushed in from the rear of the house. Together they flung their shoulders against the panel. A second time. The lock gave, the door drove in. The orderly paused to catch up a lamp, and the priest stepped across the threshold.

He shrank back, staring into the gloom. Something dark and hunched was squirming violently upon the bed. Then, as the orderly lifted the light above Father Labossier's shoulder, that shape was gone.

The two men stared and wondered. The gratings and nets were in

place. Nowhere along the tight walls could even a beetle find entrance or exit.

But Captain Rodriguez lay still among the tumbled sheets. His throat had been ripped out to the neckbone. One hand clutched his revolver, the other a tuft of shaggy black hair – such hair as had grown upon Ohondongela, the long-dead hound of the long-dead Kaflatala.

Jock and the Fighting Baboon _____

Sir Percy Fitzpatrick

Jock of the Bushveldt, surely one of the finest dog adventures ever recorded, was first published in 1907 and went into a great many editions. Its author, Sir Percy Fitzpatrick KCMG, who was born of Irish parentage in 1862, ventured to make his career in the Transvaal at the age of twenty-two. Politically a radical, he was imprisoned while honorary secretary of the Reform Committee. He accompanied and helped to organize Randolph Churchill's expedition through Mashonaland in 1891. He was in the South African Parliament from 1910 to 1920.

Fitzpatrick's red dog, Jock, was born to a brindle bull terrier bitch by a mongrel. The book, whose setting is the Kruger National Park, reflects Fitzpatrick's intimate knowledge of the veldt and of African game hunting. It is an impressive and moving tribute to an immensely brave, resilient and faithful companion. The original edition is liberally illustrated throughout with pen drawings by E. Caldwell.

I was approaching the end of the book for the first time when languishing with measles in a sickroom bed in my first year at my Surrey preparatory school. I remember the occasion well because it coincided with that dramatic night, in 1936, when the Crystal Palace burned down and there was a red glow in the northern sky. For fear of matron, I scanned the pages beneath the sheets by pen-torch. Imagining myself to be sharing all Jock's tribulations, as well as his high moments, I wept copiously that night. The opening words of the last chapter remain deeply etched on my memory: 'And Jock? But I never saw my dog again.' Fitzpatrick, having to make a journey on which Jock could not accompany him, left him with a friend. Almost every night kaffir dogs prowled round the friend's home in search of livestock. It was Jock's job to guard the livestock. One night Fitzpatrick's friend, mistaking him for a kaffir dog, shot Jock dead, but not before that great canine hero had accounted for a marauder.

Here Fitzpatrick recounts a fight to the death between his dog and a killer baboon, which is kept – mostly for the purpose of fighting and slaughtering dogs – by a villainous and callous local field cornet (a minor official) called Seedling:

It is not very clear how the trouble began. We had been sitting on the little store-counter and talking for over an hour, a group of half a dozen swapping off the news of the goldfields and the big world against that from Delagoa and the Bushveldt. Seedling had joined us early and, as usual, began the morning with drinks. We were not used to that on the road, or out hunting; indeed, we rarely took any drinks, and most of us never touched a drop except in the towns. The transport rider had opportunities which might easily become temptations – the load often consisting of liquor, easy to broach and only to be paid for at the end of the trip; but we had always before us the lesson of the failures. Apart from this, however, we did not take liquor because we could not work as well or last as long, run as fast or shoot as straight, if we did. And that was reason enough!

We had one round of drinks which was 'called' by one of the horsemen, and then, to return the compliment, another round called by one of us. A few minutes later Seedling announced effusively that it was his 'shout'. But it was only ten in the morning, and those who had taken spirits had had enough; indeed, several had only taken a sip of the second round in order to comply with a stupid and vicious custom; I would not and could not attack another bottle of sour gingerbeer; and thus Seedling's round was reduced to himself and the proprietor. No man however thirsty would drink alone in those days – it was taken as a mark of meanness or evidence of 'soaking' – and the proprietor had to be ready at any time to 'take one for the good of the house'.

A quarter of an hour passed, and Seedling, who had said nothing since his 'shout' was declined, turned away and strolled out, with hands thrust deep in the pockets of his riding breeches and a long heavy sjambok dangling from one wrist. There was silence as he moved through the doorway, and when the square patch of sunlight on the earth floor was again unbroken the man behind the counter remarked:

'Too long between drinks for him! Gone for a pull at the private bottle.'

'Is that how it's going?'

'Yah! all day long. Drinks here as long as anyone'll call, but don't do much shoutin' on his own, I tell you! That's the first time I seen him call for a week. He wanted to get you chaps on the go, I reckon. He'll be wrong all day today. I know him!'

'Cost him two bob for nothing, eh!'

'Well, it ain't so much that; ye see, he reckoned you'd all shout your turns, and drinks'd come regular; but he sees you're not on. Twig? I'm not complainin', mind you – Lord no! He don't pay anyway! It's all "chalked up" for him, an' I got to wipe it off the slate when the next load comes and he collects my customs duties. His liquor's took him wrong today – you'll see!'

We did see; and that before very long. We had forgotten Seedling, and were hearing all about the new finds reported from Barberton district, when one of the waggon boys came running into the store calling to me by my kaffir name and shouting excitedly, 'Baas, Baas! come quickly. The baboon got Jock: it will kill him!'

I had known all about the vicious brute, and had often heard of Seedling's fiendish delight in arranging fights or enticing dogs to attack it for the pleasure of seeing the beast kill the overmatched dogs. The dog had no chance at all, for the baboon remained out of reach in his house on the pole as long as it chose, if the dog was too big or the opening not a good one, and made its rush when it would tell best. But apart from this the baboon was an exceptionally big and powerful one, and it is very doubtful if any dog could have tackled it successfully in an open fight. The creature was as clever as even they can be; its enormous jaws and teeth were quite equal to the biggest dog's and it had the advantage of four 'hands'. Its tactics in a fight were quite simple and most effective: with its front feet it caught the dog by the ears or neck, holding the head so that there was no risk of being bitten, and then gripping the body lower down with the hind feet, it tore lumps out of the throat, breast and stomach – pushing with all four feet and tearing with the terrible teeth. The poor dogs were hopelessly outmatched.

I did not see the beginning of Jock's encounter, but the boys' stories pieced together told everything. It appears that when Seedling had left the store he went into his own hut and remained there some little time; on coming out again he strolled over to the baboon's pole about halfway between the two houses and began teasing it, throwing pebbles at it to see it dodge and duck behind the pole, and then flicking at it with the sjambok, amused by its frightened and angry protests. While he was doing this, Jock, who had followed me to the store, strolled out again making his way towards the waggons. He was not interested in our talk; he had twice been accidentally trodden on by men stepping back as he lay stretched out on the floor behind them; and doubtless he felt that it was no place for him: his deafness prevented him from hearing movements except such as caused vibration in the ground, and, poor old fellow, he was always at a disadvantage in houses and towns.

The baboon had then taken refuge in its box on top of the pole to escape the sjambok, and when Seedling saw Jock come out he commenced whistling and calling softly to him. Jock, of course, heard nothing: he may have responded mildly to the friendly overtures conveyed by the extended hand and patting of legs, or more probably simply took the nearest way to the waggons where he might sleep in peace, since there was nothing else to do. What the boys agree on is that as Jock passed the pole Seedling patted and held him, at the same time calling the baboon, and then gave the dog a push which did not quite roll him over but upset his balance; and Jock, recovering himself, naturally jumped round and faced Seedling, standing almost directly between him and the baboon. He could not hear the rattle of the chain on the box and pole, and saw nothing of the charging brute, and it was the purest accident that the dog stood a few inches out of reach. The baboon – chained by the neck instead of the waist, because it used to bite through all loin straps – made its rush, but the chain brought it up before its hands could reach Jock and threw the hindquarters round with such force against him that he was sent rolling yards away.

I can well believe that this second attack from a different and wholly unexpected quarter thoroughly roused him, and can picture how he turned to face it.

It was at this moment that Jim first noticed what was going on. The other boys had not expected anything when Seedling called the dog, and they were taken completely by surprise by what followed. Jim would have known what to expect: his kraal was in the neighbour-hood; he knew Seedling well, and had already suffered in fines and confiscations at his hands; he also knew about the baboon; but he was ignorant, just as I was, of the fact that Seedling had left his old place across the river and come to live in the new hut, bringing his pet with him.

It was the hoarse threatening shout of the baboon as it jumped at

Jock, as much as the exclamations of the boys, that roused Jim. He knew instantly what was on and, grabbing a stick, made a dash to save the dog, with the other boys following him.

When Jock was sent spinning in the dust the baboon recovered itself first and, standing up on its hind legs, reached out its long ungainly arms towards him, and let out a shout of defiance. Jock, regaining his feet, dashed in, jumped aside, feinted again and again, as he had learnt to do when big horns swished at him; and he kept out of reach just as he had done ever since the duiker taught him the use of its hoofs. He knew what to do, just as he had known how to swing the porcupine: the dog – for all the fighting fury that possessed him – took the measure of the chain and kept outside it. Round and round he flew, darting in, jumping back, snapping and dodging, but never getting right home. The baboon was as clever as he was; at times it jumped several feet in the air, straight up, in the hope that Jock would run underneath; at others, it would make a sudden lunge with the long arms, or a more surprising reach out with the hind legs to grab him. Then the baboon began gradually to reduce its circle, leaving behind it slack chain enough for a spring; but Jock was not to be drawn. In cleverness they were well matched – neither scored in attack; neither made or lost a point.

When Jim rushed up to save Jock, it was with eager anxious shouts of the dog's name that warned Seedling and made him turn; and as the boy ran forward the white man stepped out to stop him.

'Leave the dog alone!' he shouted, pale with anger.

'Baas, Baas, the dog will be killed,' called Jim excitedly, as he tried to get round; but the white man made a jump towards him, and with a backhand slash of the sjambok struck him across the face, shouting at him again.

'Leave him, I tell you.'

Jim jumped back, thrusting out his stick to guard against another vicious cut, and so it went on with alternate slash and guard, and the big Zulu danced round with nimble bounds, guarding, dodging, or bearing the sjambok cuts, to save the dog. Seedling was mad with rage; for who had ever heard of a nigger standing up to a Field Cornet? Still Jim would not give way; he kept trying to get in front of Jock, to head him off the fight, and all the while shouting to the other boys to call me. But Seedling was the Field Cornet, and not one of them dared move against him.

At last the baboon, finding that Jock would not come on, tried other tactics; it made a sudden retreat and, rushing for the pole, hid behind it

as for protection. Jock made a jump and the baboon leaped out to meet him, but the dog stopped at the chain's limit, and the baboon – just as in the first dash of all – overshot the mark; it was brought up by the jerk of the collar, and for one second sprawled on its back. That was the first chance for Jock and he took it. With one spring he was in; his head shot between the baboon's hind legs, and with his teeth buried in the soft stomach he lay back and pulled – pulled for dear life, as he had pulled and dragged on the legs of wounded game; tugged as he tugged at the porcupine; held on as he had held on when the koodoo bull wrenched and strained every bone and muscle in his body.

Then came the sudden turn! As Jock fastened on to the baboon, dragging taut the chain while the screaming brute struggled on its back, Seedling stood for a second irresolute, and then with a stride forward raised his sjambok to strike the dog. That was too much for Jim; he made a spring in and grasping the raised sjambok with his left hand held Seedling powerless, while in the right the boy raised his stick on guard.

'Let him fight, Baas! You said it! Let the dog fight!' he panted, hoarse with excitement.

The white man, livid with fury, struggled and kicked, but the wrist loop of his sjambok held him prisoner and he could do nothing.

That was the moment when a panic-stricken boy plucked up enough courage to call me; and that was the scene we saw as we ran out of the little shop. Jim would not strike the white man: but his face was a muddy grey, and it was written there that he would rather die than give up the dog.

Before I reached them it was clear to us all what had happened; Jim was protesting to Seedling and at the same time calling to me; it was a jumble, but a jumble eloquent enough for us, and all intelligible. Jim's excited gabble was addressed with reckless incoherence to Seedling, to me, and to Jock!

'You threw him in; you tried to kill him. He did it. It was not the dog. Kill him, Jock, kill him. Leave him, let him fight. You said it – let him fight! Kill him, Jock! Kill! Kill! Kill!'

Then Seedling did the worst thing possible; he turned on me with,

'Call off your dog, I tell you, or I'll shoot him and your—nigger too!'

'We'll see about that! They can fight it out now,' and I took the sjambok from Jim's hand, and cut it from the white man's wrist.

'Now! Stand back!'

And he stood back.

The baboon was quite helpless. Powerful as the brute was, and formidable as were the arms and gripping feet, it had no chance while Jock could keep his feet and had the strength to drag and hold the chain tight. The collar was choking it, and the grip on the stomach – the baboon's own favourite and most successful device – was fatal.

I set my teeth and thought of the poor helpless dogs that had been decoyed in and treated the same way. Jim danced about, the white seam of froth on his lips, hoarse gusts of encouragement bursting from him as he leant over Jock, and his whole body vibrating like an overheated boiler. And Jock hung on in grim earnest, the silence on his side broken only by grunting efforts as the deadly *tug – tug – tug* went on. Each pull caused his feet to slip a little on the smooth worn ground; but each time he set them back again, and the grunting tug went on.

It was not justice to call Jock off; but I did it. The cruel brute deserved killing, but the human look and cries and behaviour of the baboon were too sickening; and Seedling went into his hut without even a look at his stricken champion.

Jock stood off, with his mouth open from ear to ear and his red tongue dangling, blood-stained and panting, but with eager feet ever on the move shifting from spot to spot, ears going back and forward, and eyes – now on the baboon and now on me – pleading for the sign to go in again.

Before evening the baboon was dead.

Lassie Come-Home _____

Eric Knight

Eric Knight, a Yorkshireman by birth, emigrated to Philadelphia in 1912 and worked there as a newspaper journalist for many years. In 1939 he moved to a farm in Pennsylvania, where he wrote *This Above All, Now Pray We for Our Country* and *Lassie Come-Home*, which was first published in 1940. Commissioned into the United States Army, Knight was killed in a plane crash in 1943.

Lassie sold more than a million copies in the English language and was translated into twenty-four foreign languages. From it emerged an equally successful film.

Its story, which displays a profound understanding of canine courage, love and faithfulness, and of the relationship between a child and his dog, tells of a collie belonging to a Yorkshire miner called Sam Carraclough and, more especially, to his son, Joe.

Lassie always arrives at the school gate at four o'clock to accompany Joe home. One day, however, she fails to keep her rendezvous and Joe dashes home with 'Mother? Mother, something's happened to Lassie! She didn't meet me!' It transpires that Carraclough, who is now out of work and desperate for money, has sold Lassie for a handsome sum to the local grandee, the tetchy Duke of Rudling, who has had his eye on her for a long time and has already made several offers.

After a day or two Lassie, for whom the hour of four o'clock remains imperative, escapes from the Duke's kennels and meets an incredulous Joe at the school gate. A terrible family row ensues when Joe brings her home, and he is heartbroken when Hynes, the Duke's unsympathetic Cockney kennelman, comes to collect her.

The Duke moves Lassie to the kennels of his Highland estate. 'Father, is it very far to Scotland?' asks a tear-stained Joe. To which his

father replies, 'A long, long road, Joe. Much farther than tha'll ever travel, I'd say. A long, long road.' But Joe never gives up hope.

Owing to a combination of Lassie's dislike of Hynes, the man's carelessness, Lassie's ingenuity and a little collusion from the Duke's granddaughter Priscilla, Lassie slips her leash and is out of the park gates in a trice.

With unfailing determination she treks south. She learns to live off the wild, circumvents the huge expanses of Highland lochs, crosses raging torrents and suffers from a poisoned foot. She is wounded by a shepherd's rifle bullet and is picked up by collectors of stray dogs and kennelled, but eventually eludes them. She is succoured by an old couple who love her and won't let her go, until they understand the urgency of her desire to travel.

She is set upon by farm dogs, stoned by boys and harried through unfriendly villages. She joins Rowlie, the travelling potter, his horse and cart and Toots, his terrier. She sees off two thieves who kill Toots and threaten Rowlie. On the north English moors she nearly dies in a snowstorm. But at last, after many months and over 1000 miles journeying, she arrives once more at the school gate. Joe is overwhelmed with joy – until the Duke arrives at the Carraclough's front door looking very stern. But he has not come for Lassie – he does not even recognize her in her reduced state. He has sacked Hynes from his post of kennelman and is offering it to Carraclough. The family move into one of the Duke's cottages and are financially secure again. Meanwhile, Lassie gives birth to a fine litter of puppies. Joe rechristens his beloved dog 'Lassie Come-Home'. This is how the author portrays Lassie's homecoming:

Sam Carraclough had spoken the truth early that year when he told his son Joe that it was a long way from Greenall Bridge in Yorkshire to the Duke of Rudling's place in Scotland. And it is just as many miles coming the other way, a matter of four hundred miles.

But that would be for a man travelling straight by road or by train. For an animal how far would it be – an animal that must circle and quest at obstacles, wander and err, back-track and side-track till it found a way?

A thousand miles it would be – a thousand miles through strange terrain it had never crossed before, with nothing but instinct to tell direction.

Yes, a thousand miles of mountain and dale, of highland and moor, ploughland and path, ravine and river, beck and burn; a thousand miles of tor and brae, of snow and rain and fog and sun; of wire and thistle and thorn and flint and rock to tear the feet – who could expect a dog to win through that?

Yet, if it were almost a miracle, in his heart Joe Carraclough tried to believe in that miracle – that somehow, wonderfully, inexplicably, his dog would be there some day; there, waiting by the school gate. Each day as he came out of school, his eyes would turn to the spot where Lassie had always waited. And each day there was nothing there, and Joe Carraclough would walk home slowly, silently, stolidly as did the people of his country.

Always, when school ended, Joe tried to prepare himself – told himself not to be disappointed, because there could be no dog there. Thus, through the long weeks, Joe began to teach himself not to believe in the impossible. He had hoped against hope so long that hope began to die.

But if hope can die in a human, it does not in an animal. As long as it lives, the hope is there and the faith is there. And so, coming across the schoolyard that day, Joe Carraclough would not believe his eyes. He shook his head and blinked, and rubbed his fists in his eyes, for he thought what he was seeing was a dream. There, walking the last few yards to the school gate was – his dog!

He stood, for the coming of the dog was terrible – her walk was a thing that tore at her breath. Her head and tail were down almost to the pavement. Each footstep forward seemed a separate effort. It was a crawl rather than a walk. But the steps were made, one by one, and at last the animal dropped in her place by the gate and lay still.

Then Joe roused himself. Even if it were a dream he must do something. In dreams one must try.

He raced across the yard and fell to his knees, and then, when his hands were touching and feeling fur, he knew it was reality. His dog had come to meet him!

But what a dog this was – no prize collie with fine tricolor coat gleaming, with ears lifted gladly over the proud, slim head with its perfect black mask. It was not a dog whose bright eyes were alert, and who jumped up to bark a glad welcome. This was a dog that lay, weakly trying to lift a head that would no longer lift; trying to move a tail that was torn and matted with thorns and burrs, and managing to do nothing very much except to whine in a weak, happy, crying way. For she knew that at last the terrible driving instinct was at peace. She was at the place. She had kept her lifelong rendezvous, and hands were touching her that had not touched her for so long a time.

Indian Hospitality ——————————

Sheila Burnford

Sheila Burnford's book, *The Incredible Journey*, tells of the 300-mile walk made by Luath, a golden Labrador, Bodger, a half-blind white bull terrier and Tao, a Siamese cat, across the wilds of Canada. The marathon, which is filled with hair's–breadth escapes and terrifying encounters, in days that alternate regularly between joy and despair, and is threaded by the love bond of the three animals, ends happily with their being reunited with their owners. But the story may need no introduction. The Walt Disney company made a film of it and by 1983 the book had sold well over a million copies and had gone into twenty-nine impressions.

The passage I have chosen describes how hungry Bodger is welcomed to an Indian camp fire:

The scent on the evening breeze was a fragrant compound of roasting rice, wild-duck stew and wood smoke. When the animals looked down from a hill, tantalized and hungry, they saw six or seven fires in the clearing below, their flames lighting up a semicircle of tents and conical birch-bark shelters against a dark background of trees; flickering over the canoes drawn up on the edge of a wild rice marsh and dying redly in the black waters beyond; and throwing into ruddy relief the high, flat planes of brown Ojibway faces gathered around the centres of warmth and brightness.

The men were a colourful lot in jeans and bright plaid shirts, but the women were dressed in sombre colours. Two young boys, the only children there, were going from fire to fire shaking grain in shallow pans and stirring it with paddles as it parched. One man in long soft moccasins stood in a shallow pit trampling husks, half his weight supported on a log frame. Some of the band lay back from the fires, smoking and watching idly, talking softly among themselves; while others still ate, ladling the fragrant contents of a black iron pot on to tin plates. Every now and then one of them would throw a bone back over a shoulder into the bush, and the watching animals gazed hungrily after. A woman stood at the edge of the clearing pouring grain from one bark platter to another, and the loose chaff drifted on the slight wind like smoke.

The old dog saw nothing of this, but his ears and nose supplied all that he needed to know: he could contain himself no longer and picked his way carefully down the hillside, for his shoulder still pained him. Halfway down he sneezed violently in an eddy of chaff. One of the boys by the fire looked up at the sound, his hand closing on a stone, but the woman nearby spoke sharply, and he waited, watching intently.

The old dog limped out of the shadows and into the ring of firelight, confident, friendly, and sure of his welcome; his tail wagging his whole stern ingratiatingly, ears and lips laid back in his nightmarish grimace. There was a stunned silence – broken by a wail of terror from the smaller boy, who flung himself at his mother – and then a quick excited chatter from the Indians. The old dog was rather offended and uncertain for a moment, but he made hopefully for the nearest boy, who retreated nervously, clutching his stone. But again the woman rebuked her son, and at the sharpness of her tone the old dog stopped, crestfallen. She laid down her basket then, and walked quickly across the ring of firelight, stooping down to look more closely. She spoke some soft words of reassurance, then patted his head gently and smiled at him. The old dog leaned against her and whipped his tail against her black stockings, happy to be in contact with a human being again. She crouched down beside him to run her fingers lightly over his ears and back, and when he licked her face appreciatively, she laughed. At this, the two little boys drew nearer to the dog, and the rest of the band gathered around. Soon the old dog was where he most loved to be – the centre of attention among some human beings. He made the most of it and played to an appreciative audience; when one of the men tossed him a chunk of meat he sat up painfully on his hindquarters and begged for more, waving one paw in the air. This sent the Indians into paroxysms of laughter, and he had to repeat his performance time and time again, until he was tired and lay down, panting but happy.

The Indian woman stroked him gently in reward, then ladled some

of the meat from the pot on to the grass. The old dog limped towards it; but before he ate he looked up in the direction of the hillside where he had left his two companions.

A small stone rebounded from rock to rock, then rolled into the sudden silence that followed.

When a long-legged, blue-eyed cat appeared out of the darkness, paused, then filled the clearing with a strident plaintive voice before walking up to the dog and calmly taking a piece of meat from him, the Indians laughed until they were speechless and hiccupping. The two little boys rolled on the ground, kicking their heels in an abandonment of mirth, while the cat chewed his meat unmoved, but this was the kind of behaviour the bull terrier understood, and he joined in the fun. But he rolled so enthusiastically that the wounds reopened: when he got to his feet again his white coat was stained with blood.

All this time the young dog crouched on the hillside, motionless and watchful, although every driving, urgent nerve in his body fretted and strained at the delay. He watched the cat, well fed and content, curl himself on the lap of one of the sleepy children by the fire; he heard the faint note of derision in some of the Indians' voices as a little, bent, ancient crone addressed them in earnest and impassioned tones before hobbling over to the dog to examine his shoulder as he lay peacefully before the fire. She threw some cattail roots into a boiling pot of water, soaked some moss in the liquid, and pressed it against the dark gashes. The old dog did not move; only his tail beat slowly. When she had finished, she scooped some more meat on to a piece of birchbark and set it on the grass before the dog; and the silent watcher above licked his lips and sat up. But still he did not move from his place.

But when the fires began to burn low and the Indians made preparations for the night, and still his companions showed no sign of moving, the young dog grew restless. He skirted the camp, moving like a shadow through the trees on the hill behind, until he came out upon the lake's shore a quarter of a mile upwind of the camp. Then he barked sharply and imperatively several times.

The effect was like an alarm bell on the other two. The cat sprang from the arms of the sleepy little Indian boy and ran towards the old dog, who was already on his feet, blinking and peering around rather confusedly. The cat gave a guttural yowl, then deliberately ran ahead, looking back as he paused beyond the range of firelight. The old dog shook himself resignedly and walked slowly after – reluctant to leave the warmth of the fire. The Indians watched impassively and silently and made no move to stop him. Only the woman who had first befriended him called out softly, in the tongue of her people, a farewell to the traveller.

The dog halted at the treeline beside the cat and looked back, but the commanding, summoning bark was heard again, and together the two passed out of sight and into the blackness of the night.

That night they became immortal, had they known or cared, for the ancient woman had recognized the old dog at once by his colour and companion; he was the White Dog of the Ojibways, the virtuous White Dog of Omen, whose appearance heralds either disaster or good fortune. The Spirits had sent him, hungry and wounded, to test tribal hospitality; and for benevolent proof to the sceptical they had chosen a cat as his companion – for what *mortal* dog would suffer a cat to rob him of his meat? He had been made welcome, fed and succoured: the omen would prove fortunate.

Rats, Soldier Dog of Ulster _____

Max Halstock

At the time of writing, Rats the soldier dog is still alive. During his active service days, spent mostly at Crossmaglen, in Northern Ireland, he was handed over from battalion to battalion as each was posted away; so he kept coming into new ownership, a terrible wrench for any dog. Day after day, night after night, he was with the troops in the 'front line', lying with ambush parties, flying with helicopter-borne sections, going out on patrol, crouching at the feet of sentries or just keeping off-duty soldiers company.

He was blown up by a booby trap, shot at 'more times than anybody could count' and was twice run over. Four pieces of metal were embedded in his spine, there was gunshot in his chest and he had a broken leg. He made many enemies among the IRA, who well knew him to be the troops' mascot and morale raiser *par excellence*. He had seen off dogs five times his size that were set on him by Republican sympathizers. He was awarded two medals for gallantry; and, when he retired, the Welsh Guards staged a full-dress parade in his honour. This passage from Max Halstock's biography, *Rats*, gives some idea of how the little terrier endeared himself so easily to the troops:

A B B C T V crew arrived to make a brief film about the lives of the troops 'in the front line' and, in the course of their visit, they discovered Rats. As a result, Rats became something of a T V star. The little dog's warmth and personality, his ability to merit newspaper headlines or appearances on T V, made the Company more aware than ever of the valuable boost he was giving to the troops' morale.

In his honour, therefore, a special medal was struck and he was formally given an army number. The medal, made from a dog disc, had the Queen's head on one side, and the legend 'Rats. Delta 777' – Delta for Delta Company, 777 because three sevens were considered lucky – on the other side. Along with the medal went a red and white ribbon with his 'army number' on it.

Rats received his medal at a special ceremony. The entire Company paraded outside the walls of their 'Submarine', while a piper played 'Scotland the Brave' and other Highland airs, and the company sergeant major pinned the medal on the dog-collar of the army's most unusual recruit. The medal was later removed and hung on the board at the entrance to the base for all to see, before being later taken to H Q at Bessbrook to be placed among other mementoes of the Army's stay in Crossmaglen.

For Corporal O'Neil, Rats's newfound fame proved a mixed blessing. His two sons, young Joseph (aged five) and Kevin (aged three), had seen what they called 'Daddy's dog' on T V and 'nothing would do but that I would promise to bring him back to Glasgow. I had a terrible time explaining to them that I couldn't do that – so I had to promise them their own pup instead.' Rats took up much of the time that O'Neil spent chatting on the telephone with his family. 'And, of course, I had to send several photographs home.'

A sad moment came for him when the time arrived for the Queen's Own Highlanders to leave Crossmaglen, handing over to the Prince of Wales Company, 1st Battalion, Welsh Guards.

'I asked Corporal Arwel Lewis, of the Welsh Guards, if he would be prepared to look after Rats, and he agreed that he would. So he did patrols with me for a few days, getting to know the dog in the way I had. I felt pretty angry that I wasn't allowed to take Rats with me – and a lot of the other chaps felt the same way. Some of them urged me, "Go on, take him in your kitbag and to hell with it!" but I had been warned that I was to do no such thing.'

Rats, of course, sensed that the Q O H were about to leave and that he was not going with them.

'When he saw all the cases and kit being loaded aboard the helicopter he realized it was happening to him again,' recalls Corporal O'Neil. 'You know, I don't think anybody has realized how much and how often Rats must have been hurt in his lifetime. I'm not talking now about his physical injuries, but the way he struck up so many close friendships and then saw his friends leave him, without knowing why or where they were going.

'If a dog has any mind at all, he must have been badly hurt, for he had to keep finding a new friend all the time. He was prepared to stick to a man. But no man ever stuck to him – not permanently, that is. So he gave out all the love and affection he had – and then his master would disappear, and he would be left to find somebody else to whom he could give his affection.'

On this occasion, Rats travelled up to Bessbrook, thus avoiding the poignancy of another Crossmaglen farewell.

'He just jumped into the helicopter and sat, as usual, beneath my seat. But at Bessbrook, it was very, very sad. Rats had cried when the corporal I had taken him from went away, and now he cried again. It's a strange and disturbing thing to see a dog cry – whining miserably. I was crying myself, of course, and doing my best not to let anybody see. Then we jumped into the back of the army lorry and off we drove. Corporal Lewis, who had come up to Bessbrook specially, had to lift Rats in his arms and hold him there as he struggled to follow us. And that's the last I ever saw of Rats – that little face peeping up above the arms of the corporal. I just kept waving until we were out of sight.'

To Corporal O'Neil his friendship with Rats 'still seems like a fairy-tale'.

Rats, he thought, had given every soldier in Crossmaglen something that they would always value; they could never forget him.

'I think everybody else thought I was a bit batty the way I used to talk to Rats – but, you know, he was almost like a human being to me.'

Why Rats, though? Why not Fleabus or Nutter or some other dog? Surely he was just a cross-breed, a mongrel? What made Rats so especially attractive?

'I think it was because he *was* so scruffy that he became the soldiers' dog he did. A pedigree dog would have been no good in these circumstances. Rats was a dog who could be a normal soldier's dog. When a chap returns from a patrol, he isn't neat and tidy – so he doesn't want a posh dog.

'Rats was often filthy and dirty, of course – he couldn't be anything else in all that mud. I washed or showered him about once a week, although he hated it. As soon as he knew was going into the water, he

was off – whoosh.

'Sometimes I'd have to do it two or three times a week. When he was washed, though, he looked completely different, really lovely. He was pure white on the toes and under the stomach and the rest was a brownish, rusty colour. To me anyway,' said Joseph O'Neil, 'he'll always be a small legend.'

ADVERSITY

Beth Gêlert

William Robert Spencer

Based on true history, the tragic narrative verse 'Beth Gêlert', otherwise known as 'The Grave of the Greyhound', was the inspiration of William Robert Spencer, son of the first Earl Spencer.

> The spearmen heard the bugle sound,
>   And cheerily smiled the morn;
> And many a brach, and many a hound
>   Obeyed Llewellyn's horn.
>
> And still he blew a louder blast,
>   And gave a lustier cheer,
> 'Come, Gêlert, come, wert never last
>   Llewellyn's horn to hear.
>
> 'O where does faithful Gêlert roam
>   The flower of all his race;
> So true, so brave – a lamb at home,
>   A lion in the chase?'
>
> In sooth, he was a peerless hound,
>   The gift of royal John;
> But now no Gêlert could be found,
>   And all the chase rode on.
>
> That day Llewellyn little loved
>   The chase of hart and hare;
> And scant and small the booty proved,
>   For Gêlert was not there.
>
> Unpleased, Llewellyn homeward hied,
>   When, near the portal seat,
> His truant Gêlert he espied
>   Bounding his lord to greet.
>
> But when he gained the castle door,
>   Aghast the chieftain stood;
> The hound all o'er was smeared with gore;
>   His lips, his fangs, ran blood.

Llewellyn gazed with fierce surprise;
  Unused such looks to meet,
His favourite checked his joyful guise
  And crouched, and licked his feet.

Onward, in haste, Llewellyn passed,
  And on went Gêlert too;
And still, where'er his eyes he cast,
  Fresh blood-gouts shocked his view.

O'erturned his infant's bed he found,
  With blood-stained covert rent;
And all around the walls and ground
  With recent blood besprent.

He called his child – no voice replied –
  He searched with terror wild;
Blood, blood he found on every side,
  But nowhere found his child.

'Hell-hound! my child's by thee devoured,'
   The frantic father cried;
And to the hilt his vengeful sword
   He plunged in Gêlert's side.

Aroused by Gêlert's dying yell,
   Some slumberer wakened nigh;
What words the parent's joy could tell
   To hear his infant's cry!

Concealed beneath a tumbled heap
   His hurried search had missed,
All glowing from his rosy sleep
   The cherub boy he kissed.

Nor scathe had he, nor harm, nor dread,
   But, the same couch beneath,
Lay a gaunt wolf, all torn and dead,
   Tremendous still in death.

Ah, what was then Llewellyn's pain!
   For now the truth was clear;
His gallant hound the wolf had slain
   To save Llewellyn's heir.

Flush Secluded

Virginia Woolf

All dog-lovers should read *Flush*, in which Virginia Woolf (1882–1941) explains most poignantly, but with a good deal of novelist's licence, first why Mary Russell Mitford (1787–1855) – the author of *Our Village* and much else – was obliged, in her reduced circumstances, to dispense with her spaniel, who, until then, had enjoyed an ecstatic life in the country. Then how poor Flush was given to the invalid Elizabeth Barrett (1806–61), the future wife of the poet Robert Browning. How he then languishes for years as a sedentary London dog, spending most of his time on a Wimpole Street settee, at Miss Barrett's feet.

How he is stolen by a ruffian Whitechapel dog dealer; how he is retrieved from that misery; how he accompanies the Brownings to Italy, to a better existence, albeit to an environment that is too hot for him, and one hazardous with fleas and disease. And how, in 1854, he dies:

Mrs Browning was growing old now and so was Flush. She bent down over him for a moment. Her face, with its wide mouth and its great eyes and heavy curls, was still oddly like his. Broken asunder, yet made in the same mould, each perhaps completed what was dormant in the other. But she was a woman; he was a dog. Mrs Browning went on reading. Then she looked at Flush again. But he did not look at her. An extraordinary change had come over him. 'Flush!' she cried. But he was silent. He had been alive; he was now dead. That was all.

Here, Virginia Woolf's version of Flush's arrival at Wimpole Street is followed by Elizabeth Barrett Browning's own tribute to the spaniel, which is written not in a tragic mood, but with love and joy:

Miss Barrett's bedroom – for such it was – must by all accounts have been dark. The light, normally obscured by a curtain of green damask, was in summer further dimmed by the ivy, the scarlet runners, the convolvuluses and the nasturtiums which grew in the window-box. At first Flush could distinguish nothing in the pale greenish gloom but five white globes glimmering mysteriously in midair. But again it was the smell of the room that overpowered him. Only a scholar who has descended step by step into a mausoleum and there finds himself in a crypt, crusted with fungus, slimy with mould, exuding sour smells of decay and antiquity, while half-obliterated marble busts gleam in midair and all is dimly seen by the light of the small swinging lamp which he holds, and dips and turns, glancing now here, now there – only the sensations of such an explorer into the buried vaults of a ruined city can compare with the riot of emotions that flooded Flush's nerves as he stood for the first time in an invalid's bedroom, in Wimpole Street, and smelt eau-de-Cologne.

Very slowly, very dimly, with much sniffing and pawing, Flush by degrees distinguished the outlines of several articles of furniture. That huge object by the window was perhaps a wardrobe. Next to it stood, conceivably, a chest of drawers. In the middle of the room swam up to the surface what seemed to be a table with a ring round it; and then the vague amorphous shapes of armchair and table emerged. But everything was disguised. On top of the wardrobe stood three white busts; the chest of drawers was surmounted by a bookcase; the bookcase was pasted over with crimson merino; the washing-table had a coronal of shelves upon it; on top of the shelves that were on top of the washing-table stood two more busts. Nothing in the room was itself; everything was something else. Even the window-blind was not a simple muslin blind; it was painted fabric with a design of castles and gateways and groves of trees, and there were several peasants taking a walk. Looking-glasses further distorted these already distorted objects so that there seemed to be ten busts of ten poets instead of five; four tables instead of two. And suddenly there was a more terrifying confusion still. Suddenly Flush saw staring back at him from a hole in the wall another dog with bright eyes flashing, and tongue lolling! He paused amazed. He advanced in awe.

Thus advancing, thus withdrawing, Flush scarcely heard, save as the distant drone of wind among the tree-tops, the murmur and patter of voices talking. He pursued his investigations, cautiously, nervously, as an explorer in a forest softly advances his foot, uncertain whether that shadow is a lion, or that root a cobra. At last, however, he was aware of huge objects in commotion over him; and, unstrung as he was by the experiences of the past hour, he hid himself, trembling, behind a screen. The voices ceased. A door shut. For one instant he paused, bewildered, unstrung. Then with a pounce as of clawed fingers memory fell upon him. He felt himself alone – deserted. He rushed to the door. It was shut. He pawed, he listened. He heard footsteps descending. He knew them for the familiar footsteps of his mistress. They stopped. But no – on they went, down they went. Miss Mitford was slowly, was heavily, was reluctantly descending the stairs. And as she went, as he heard her footsteps fade, panic seized upon him. Door after door shut in his face as Miss Mitford went downstairs; they shut on freedom; on fields; on hares; on grass; on his adored, his venerated mistress – on the dear old woman who had washed him and beaten him and fed him from her own plate when she had none too much to eat herself – on all he had known of happiness and love and human goodness! There! The front door slammed. He was alone. She had deserted him.

Then such a wave of despair and anguish overwhelmed him, the irrevocableness and implacability of fate so smote him, that he lifted up his head and howled aloud. A voice said 'Flush'. He did not hear it. 'Flush', it repeated a second time. He started. He had thought himself alone. He turned. Was there something alive in the room with him? Was there something on the sofa? In the wild hope that this being, whatever it was, might open the door, that he might still rush after Miss Mitford and find her – that this was some game of hide-and-seek such as they used to play in the greenhouse at home – Flush darted to the sofa.

'Oh, Flush!' said Miss Barrett. For the first time she looked him in the face. For the first time Flush looked at the lady lying on the sofa.

Each was surprised. Heavy curls hung down on either side of Miss Barrett's face; large bright eyes shone out; a large mouth smiled. Heavy ears hung down on either side of Flush's face; his eyes, too, were large and bright; his mouth was wide. There was a likeness between them. As they gazed at each other each felt: Here am I – and then each felt: But how different! Hers was the pale worn face of an invalid, cut off from air, light, freedom. His was the warm ruddy face of a young animal; instinct with health and energy. Broken asunder, yet made in the same mould, could it be that each completed what was dormant in the other? She might have been – all that; and he – But no.

Between them lay the widest gulf that can separate one being from another. She spoke. He was dumb. She was woman; he was dog. Thus closely united, thus immensely divided, they gazed at each other. Then with one bound Flush sprang on to the sofa and laid himself where he was to live for ever after – on the rug at Miss Barrett's feet.

To Flush, My Dog

Elizabeth Barrett Browning

Loving friend, the gift of one
Who her own true faith hath run
  Through thy lower nature;
Be my benediction said
With my hand upon thy head,
  Gentle fellow creature!

Like a lady's ringlets brown
Flow thy silken ears adown
  Either side demurely
Of thy silver-suited breast,
Shining out from all the rest
  Of thy body purely.

Darkly brown thy body is
Till the sunshine, striking this,
  Alchemise its dullness, –
When the sleek curls manifold
Flash all over into gold,
  With a burnished fulness.

Underneath my stroking hand,
Startled eyes of hazel bland,
  Kindling, growing larger,
Up thou leapest with a spring.
Full of prank and curveting,
  Leaping like a charger.

Leap! thy broad tail waves alight.
Leap! they slender feet are bright,
   Canopied in fringes;
Leap! those tasselled ears of thine
Flicker strangely, fair and fine,
   Down their golden inches. . . .

This dog, if a friendly voice
Call him now to blyther choice
   Than such chamber-keeping,
'Come out!' praying from the door. –
Presseth backward as before,
   Up against me leaping.

Therefore to this dog will I,
Tenderly, nor scornfully,
   Render praise and valour!
With my hand upon his head,
Is my benediction said
   Therefore, and for ever.

Owd Bob and Red Wullie _____

Alfred Ollivant

Alfred Ollivant (1874–1927) was a regular officer in the Royal Artillery, but resigned his commission, following a back injury when he fell from his charger. He began writing his best-known work, *Owd Bob*, when he was only twenty years old. This was published, in 1898, under the title *Bob, Son of Battle*, in the United States, where it was an immediate and prominent success. But ten years elapsed before the English edition, *Owd Bob*, enjoyed similar acclaim. The critics were fulsome in their praise: 'The best dog story ever written' (William Lyon Phelps); 'Not only one of the best realistic stories of animal life, but the only one' (Frederick Taber Cooper). The book was filmed much later under the title *To the Victor*, starring Will Fyffe.

Written in the spirit of the Victorian melodrama, the story is as much about the clash of human good and evil as it is about the canine race. It is set in the Scottish dales. James Moore, of Kenmuir, the owner of Owd Bob, is a fine upright dalesman, whose lineage is 'traced level with the noble Grey Dogs of Kenmuir'. He has a beautiful daughter, Maggie. His neighbour, another widower and fellow sheep farmer, Adam M'Adam, the owner of Red Wullie, 'the Tailless Tyke', is a mean, jealous, vindictive mischiefmaker. He is endowed with a good strong-minded son, David, whom he bullies unmercifully. David is in love with Maggie.

The coveted Shepherd's Trophy, for the victor of the annual sheep trials, glitters at the centre of the plot. When both dogs are entered for the first time they are unanimously considered by the local dalesmen to be the chief rivals. Then Moore, respecting the memory of his recently deceased wife, withdraws Owd Bob, and Red Wullie wins. But, on the following two occasions, to M'Adam's consuming resentment, the prize goes to the superior Owd Bob. M'Adam sets his heart on regaining the trophy, stopping at nothing, including attempts on both Moore's and Owd Bob's life, and trying to steal it from Moore's house. Meanwhile the plot expands with a seemingly irreparable lover's tiff between David and Maggie and the introduction of a mystery sheep killer. Everything points to Red Wullie being the criminal. But one moonlight night, when both men reach the scene, it appears for a moment that Owd Bob is the culprit. But, on closer inspection, it is patently clear that Owd Bob, catching Red Wullie in the act, has defeated him in battle. In the end all the dogs in the vicinity, hating Red Wullie, hound him to death. M'Adam dies soon after. This is the climax:

'Wullie! ma Wullie!' screamed M'Adam, bounding down the slope a crook's length in front of the rest. 'Wullie! Wullie! to me!'

At the cry the huddle below was convulsed. It heaved and swayed and dragged to and fro, like the sea lashed into life by some dying leviathan.

A gigantic figure, tawny and red, fought its way to the surface. A great tossing head, gory past recognition, flung out from the ruck. One quick glance he shot from ragged eyes at the little flying figure in front; then with a roar like a waterfall plunged towards it, shaking off the bloody leeches as he went.

'Wullie! Wullie! I'm wi' ye!' cried that little voice, now so near.

Through – through – through! an incomparable effort and his last.

They hung to his throat, they clung to his muzzle, they were round and about him.

Down he went again with a sob and a little suffocating cry, shooting up at his master one quick beseeching glance as the sea of blood closed over him – worrying, smothering, tearing, like foxhounds at the kill.

They left the dead, and pulled away the living. And it was no light task; for the pack were mad for blood. At the bottom of the wet mass of hair and red flesh was old Shep, stone-dead. And as Saunderson pulled the body out, his face was working; for no man can lose in a crack the friend of a dozen years and remain unmoved.

The Venus lay there, her teeth clenched still in death; smiling that her vengeance was achieved. Big Rasper, blue no longer, was gasping out his life. Two more came crawling out to find a quiet spot where they might lay them down to die. Before the night had fallen another had gone to his account; while not a dog who fought upon that day but carried the scars of it to his grave. The Terror o' th' Border, terrible in his life, like Samson, was yet more terrible in his dying.

Down at the bottom lay that which once had been Adam M'Adam's Red Wull.

At the sight the little man neither raved nor swore. It was past that for him. He sat down, heedless of the soaking ground, and took the mangled head in his lap, very tenderly.

'They've done ye at last, Wullie – they've done ye at last,' he muttered, convinced that the attack had been organised while he was detained in the tap-room.

On hearing that little voice, the dog gave one weary wag of his stump-tail. And with that, the Tailless Tyke, Adam M'Adam's Red Wull, the Black Killer, went to his long home.

One after one the Dalesmen bore away their dead, and the little man was left alone with the body of his last friend.

Dry-eyed he sat there, nursing the dead dog's head; hour on hour; alone; crooning to himself –

'"Monie a sair daurk we twa hae wrought,
An' wi' the weary warl' fought!
An' monie an anxious day I thought
We wad be beat" –

An' noo we are, Wullie – noo we are!'

So he went on, repeating the lines over and over again, always with the same sad termination.

'A man's mither – a man's wife – a man's dog they three are a' little M'Adam iver had to back him. D'ye mind the auld mither, Wullie? and her "Niver be doon hearted, Adam; ye've aye got your mither" –

and ae day I had not. And Flora, Wullie (ye remember Flora, Wullie? Na, na; ye dinna), wi' her laffin' daffin' manner, cryin' to me, "Adam, ye say ye're alone. But ye've me – is that no' enough for ony man?" And God kens it was – while it lasted.' He broke down, and sobbed awhile. 'And you, Wullie – and you! the only man friend iver I had'. He sought the dog's bloody paw with his right hand.

'"And here's a hand, my trusty fier'
And gie's a hand o' thine;
And we'll tak' a right guid willie-waught,
    For auld lang syne."'

He sat there, stroking the poor head upon his lap, bending over it like a mother over a sick child.

'They've done ye at last, lad – done ye sair. And noo I'm thinkin' they'll no' rest content till I'm gone. And oh, Wullie!' he bent down and whispered, 'I dreamed sic an awful thing: that ma Wullie – But there! 'twas but a dream.'

So he sat on, crooning to the dead dog; and no man approached him. Only Bessie of the inn watched the little lone figure from afar.

It was long past noon when at length he rose, laying the dog's head reverently down, and tottered away towards that bridge which once the dead thing on the slope had held against a thousand.

He crossed it and turned: there was a look upon his face, half hopeful, half fearful, very piteous to see.

'Wullie, Wullie, to me!' he cried; only the accents, formerly so fiery, were now weak as a dying man's.

He waited: in vain.

'Are ye no' comin', Wullie?' he asked at length, in quavering tones. 'Ye're not used to leave me.'

He walked away a pace, then turned again and whistled his shrill sharp call; only now it sounded like a broken echo of itself.

'Come to me, Wullie!' he implored very pitifully. ''Tis the first time iver I kent ye not come and me whistlin'. What ails ye, lad?'

He recrossed the bridge, walking blindly like a sobbing child; and yet dry-eyed.

Over the dead body he stooped.

'What ails ye, Wullie?' he asked again. 'Will you too leave me?'

Then Bessie, watching fearfully, saw him bend, sling the great body on to his back, and stagger away.

Limp and hideous, the carcase hung down from his shoulders. The huge head, with grim, wide eyes and lolling tongue, jolted and

swagged with the motion, seeming to grin a ghastly defiance at the world it had left. And the last Bessie saw of them was that bloody, rolling mask, with the puny legs staggering beneath their load, as the two passed out of the world's ken.

In the Devil's Bowl, next day, they found the pair; Adam M'Adam and his Red Wull, face to face; dead not divided; each save for the other alone. The dog, his saturnine expression glazed and ghastly in the fixedness of death, propped up against that hump-backed boulder beneath which, a while before, the Black Killer had dreed his weird; close by, his master, lying on his back, his dim dead eyes staring up at the heaven where now he had appeared, one hand still clasping a crumpled photograph; the weary body at rest at last, the mocking face – mocking no longer – alight with a whole-souled, transfiguring happiness.

A Tie So Strong Between Us . . . ————

Emile Zola

The novelist Emile Zola, who has been described as 'the principal figure in the French school of naturalist fiction', was born in 1840 and died in 1902. His most important work was *Les Rougon-Macquant*, a series of twenty novels, in which he departed from the limited themes of the fictional works of his day to display the whole panorama of nineteenth-century French life. As a champion of justice he played a prominent part in the Dreyfus case. His compassion for his fellow creatures could not be better exemplified than in this little memoir:

I had a little dog, a griffon of the smallest kind, whose name was Fanfan. One day, at the dog-shows at Cours-la-Reine, I saw him in a cage, with a large cat as a companion. He regarded me with eyes so full of sadness, that I asked the attendant to let him out of his cage for a little while. As soon as he was on the ground he commenced to walk like a little toy dog. Enthusiastically I bought him. It was a little mad dog. One morning, after I had him about a week, he commenced to turn in a circle without ceasing, round and round without ever stopping. When he had fallen with fatigue, in appearance drunk, he would painfully raise himself and set to turning again. When, seized by pity, I took him in my arms, his paws would keep up the movement of the continual round, and when I placed him on the ground, he commenced turning again, turning always. I called in a veterinary, who spoke of an injury to the brain. Then he offered to poison him. I refused. All the animals who live with me die a natural death, and they all sleep in a tranquil corner of my garden. Fanfan appeared recovered after this first attack. During the next two years that it entered into my life, it was so much to me that I cannot find words to describe it. It never quitted me, crouching near to me, in the bottom of my armchair, in the morning during my four hours of work; it had become, thus, part of my agony, part of my joys, raising its little nose at the moments of repose, and regarding me with its little clear eyes. And then it took part in all my walks, going before me with his gait of little toy dog, which used to make all the passers-by laugh, sleeping, when we returned, under my chair, passing the night upon a cushion at the foot of my bed. There was a tie so strong between us that, even at the shortest of separations, I missed him as much as he missed me.

And shortly Fanfan became again mad. He had two or three attacks at different intervals. Then the attacks were so frequent that our life was frightful. When the madness was upon him, he would turn and turn without ceasing. I was not able to keep him in my chair. A demon seemed to possess him. And I have seen him turn for two hours around my table. But it was in the night that I suffered the most, hearing him do this involuntary round, head-strong and savage, with the continual noise of the fall of his little paws upon the carpet. I have often risen and taken him in my arms, keeping him thus for an hour, two hours, hoping that the attack would subside, but as soon as I put him to the ground he would commence to turn.

People laughed at me, and said I was mad myself to keep the dog in my room. I could not do otherwise. My heart melted at the idea that I should not be there to take him and try to calm him, and that he would regard me no more, with his little clear eyes, his eyes distracted by misery, yet which thanked me.

It was thus, in my arms, one morning, that Fanfan died while regarding me. He had but a slight shock, and all was finished. I felt simply his little convulsed body become of the suppleness of chiffon. The tears came to my eyes, and I felt it was a loss to me. An animal, nothing but a little animal, and to suffer thus at its loss! To be haunted by its recollection to such an extent, that I wished to write of my sorrow, certain of leaving the impression of my heart on the page! Today, all that is distant, and other sorrows have come, and I feel that the things I have said are cold. But then it seemed to me that I had so much to say, that I should have said the things profound, definite, upon this love of animals – so obscure and so powerful, at which I see people around me smile, and which pains me to the extent of troubling my life.

And why was I attached so profoundly to this little mad dog? Why have I fraternised with it as one fraternises with a human being? Why have I cried as one cries for a lost friend? Is it not that the unquenchable tenderness which I feel for everything which lives and feels is a brotherhood of suffering? A charity which inclines one towards the most humble and disinherited.

Kennelled to Fight —————————————

K. F. Barker

K. F. Barker was a writer and artist with a deep feeling for animal emotion. *Just Dogs, Himself, The Wood by the Water* and many other animal stories came from his pen. *His Mother's Son* is a terrible indictment of that (still existing) host of men who keep dogs as fighting machines to satisfy their own warped minds. The awful Snapper, who, like Seedling in *Jock of the Bushveldt*, keeps all manner of animals in order to watch them inflict injury and death on other animals, bets Jack Springs, the landlord of the Fox and Hounds, that he can lure Jack's mighty dog Champion, half bull terrier, half sheepdog, out of the pub and away. If Snapper fails he must pay the landlord two pounds. If he wins he keeps Champion. Snapper covers himself in a tantalizing odour – and wins the bet, leading the dog out to a life of hell. But Champion's initial fate, which I have quoted, does not last.

His father was a sheepdog. When two marauding dogs attack a flock of sheep within sight of Champion's kennel, the instinct he has inherited from him surfaces. He tugs at his chain, breaks his collar and kills the attackers. In starting his escape home, however, he is intercepted on the moor by Snapper, who has been poaching. Snapper, believing Champion to be the sheep worrier, strikes him with a stone, then knocks him unconscious with a club. But, as he is about to drown him, he hears voices down the lane. He drops Champion in a ford and runs. The dog, revived by the water, regains consciousness and limps home to Jack Springs and happiness. Here is the beginning:

Champion hadn't been at the Fox and Hounds very long, but already was becoming quite a favourite now that the novelty of his breed had worn off a little.

To all appearances a typical bull-terrier, ostensibly bred back for generations to the old fighting strain, Champion in reality was not, as the fanciers have it, 'true blue'. His mother, a pure-bred bull-terrier, had had the bad taste to fall in love with a little sneaking yellow cur collie. Why she had chosen such a humble member of the canine race, as Tom Pilcher, her owner, and breeder of high-class bull-terriers, pathetically put it, only Gawd knew – but perhaps Ch. Laughing White Girl had her reasons; who shall say?

However, as her son had wisely elected to resemble her in every particular instead of his lowly papa, Mr Pilcher had kept the pup until he was just over a year old; furthermore he had, in the privacy of his little office, concocted a wonderful pedigree in readiness for when a purchaser should turn up.

The landlord of the Fox and Hounds, Mr Jack Springs, who now owned Champion, was an ex-huntsman, a genial soul, who was delighted with his purchase. Champion's subtle, tight-lipped smile, modelled on the Mona Lisa pattern, was a source of perpetual pride to his master.

'Brings custom it does, he's like a bit o' sunshine about the place; all helps trade,' he would aver to Tom, his ex-kennelman, barman and general factotum, a weathered, wrinkled man of some fifty summers.

But that worthy, ever since Champion's destruction of a long-cherished dishcloth, had viewed the bull-terrier with a certain reserve.

'I ain't saying,' he would stubbornly retort, in reply to Mr Springs's periodical enquiries as to what exactly he thought of Champion.

But whatever doubts Tom harboured with regard to the bull-terrier there was no question about Mr Springs's feelings on the point; he was never tired of showing off the son of Ch. Laughing White Girl in the tap-room of an evening to admiring 'patrons'.

'I'd lay yond beggar could do summat in t'fightin' line,' offered one worthy as he slowly absorbed his customary pint of nourishment.

A little yellow-faced man who had been closely observing Champion for some evenings looked up now and smiled over the rim of his glass.

''E might,' he observed, meditatively sucking a hollow tooth. 'An' then again he might be just muck at t'job; t'aint allus them as looks most like doin' things as is best at 'em, particularly when it comes to the scrappin' stuff.' He paused, and his small bright eyes swivelling round discovered the landlord of the Fox and Hounds stop in the act of drawing a half-pint to listen to the doubts cast on the fighting powers of his favourite.

'Ye see,' resumed Snapper o' Scartop, which was the only name by which the patrons of the Fox and Hounds had ever known the little yellow-faced man, 'ye see, a lot o' the present-day bull-terriers is all wrong; instead of red blood i' their veins they're stuffed wi' nowt but sawdust.'

'Well, I don't know,' exclaimed Snapper's neighbour; 'that sounds a rum go ter me,' and his heavy face, with its round, prominent eyes, gazed in blank amazement into the lined countenance of Snapper who clicked his teeth irritably.

'O' course, that's speaking figgerative,' he resumed with what patience he could muster. 'Wat I meant is this 'ere: ter get looks, long 'eads an' 'ard feet, an' a lot o' other things not worth rotten apples, breeders 'as chucked away brains an' guts, them's wot yer want in a bull-terrier, mate; if a bull-terrier ain't cramfull ter bustin' with guts, he ain't worth salt.' Snapper emphasised the last words by bringing his glass down with a bang on the little table.

'What's yours, sir?' enquired the landlord politely.

'Another o' the same,' briefly replied Snapper, whose eyes were appraising Champion with the critical, knowledgeable gaze of one who knew to a nicety just what a bull-terrier should look like.

As Mr Springs returned with his order, Snapper once more addressed his stolid companion.

'There's only one line o' bull-terriers as yer can put yer b— shirt on, Mister, take my word for it, an' that's the Battlin' Hector lot, stiff wi' Staffordshire pit blood they be, an' them sort knew all ther was ter know about the fightin' game; the've forgot more'n than the other sort of bull-terriers 'ull ever know.'

He paused, and burying his thin, hooked nose deeply in his glass, waited patiently for that which he guessed would follow.

'How should you think that dog yonder was bred?' enquired the landlord of the Fox and Hounds, jerking a thumb in the direction of Champion, who was stretched out in one corner of the tap-room.

Snapper turned with a well-feigned start of surprise.

'Eh?' he said. 'That dog o' yourn? Well, you're askin' me summat now, Mr Springs; bull-terriers is bred all ways now, as I were just sayin' to my friend 'ere,' went on Snapper smugly. 'The old fightin' pit strains is like good old vintage port, very rare and 'ard to come by.'

'Wot'd you say if I was to tell you that dog is out of a Battlin' Hector bitch by a Wild Fire dog?'

'Say?' retorted Snapper scornfully. 'Why, I'd say when them as bred 'im told yer that, they'd seen yer comin'. Battlin' Hector terriers is about as rare as blackberries growin' on gooseberry bushes,' concluded Snapper, winking at his audience in a cocksure manner.

'Well,' persisted Mr Springs, 'I'll lay you drinks all round, Snapper, that dog is one of the Battlin' Hector and Wild Fire strain.'

'Done with yer,' instantly replied Snapper o' Scartop, 'but,' he added slyly, 'seein' as 'ow we've a bit o' a bet on ye'll 'ave ter prove it, Mister.'

'That,' replied the owner of Champion, 'is just what I'm going to do, not but what takin' your bet's the same as robbin' a baby of its bottle.'

But Snapper only smiled, he knew that he was about to see that for which he had been working all the evening – Champion's pedigree.

If it was 'right', then he, Snapper, was going to get possession of the bull-terrier; but just how this was to be accomplished he was not as yet quite sure.

'There you are, Mister, all down in black and white *and* signed by the breeder,' said Mr Springs, slapping a paper down in front of an apparently discomfited Snapper o' Scartop, who, however, read it very closely, his curiously lined face betraying nothing of what was in his mind.

There was a respectful, interested silence in the tap-room, everyone was secretly rather pleased, firstly, because the cocksure Snapper had for once been caught napping, and secondly, at the certain prospect of a free glass in the immediate future.

At last Snapper looked up. 'You've won, Mister,' he announced with a crestfallen air, 'but it's that rare nowadays ter come across that perticler strain, gentlemen,' he spoke in a slightly apologetic tone, as he looked round at the grinning faces gazing expectantly in his direction, and then shaking off his chagrin, resumed gaily, 'Well, gents, all name yer poison; no one can say as Snapper o' Scartop don't stand by 'is bets.'

II

Snapper o' Scartop's scheme for gaining possession of the bull-terrier was fast nearing completion – tonight he was adding the finishing touches. . . .

In one of his curiously twisted but efficient hands he held an odd-looking object roughly of the same size and shape as a Brazil nut; in the other hand was a file, and spread over his knees a newspaper. As he used his file, a soft greyish powder fell on to the newspaper.

When the little heap of powder looked big enough for his purpose, Snapper's actions appeared stranger than ever; scooping up a generous pinch of the powder, he scattered it inside the turn-ups of his trousers, working it thoroughly into the greasy cloth with hard, bony fingers. He treated the cuffs of his shirt and coat in the same way, finally replacing the file and the queer nut-like object in an inside pocket.

Timing his arrival at the Fox and Hounds rather late, he slipped in with a few others, and took his usual place in the corner. Under cover of lighting his pipe he took a reassuring sniff at his hands, which still reeked of that strange penetrating scent.

Talk presently turned on the non-appearance of one of the 'regulars', George, a young shepherd who had recently taken himself a wife.

'Happen she's found young George a job up at whoam,' volunteered a friend of George's, who since the wedding had seen but little of his former boon companion.

'Ay, trust a woman for that; they can't thole ter see a chap 'appy an' carefree, some of 'em, they like ter mak other folk's lives as sour as wot their own are; but tak my word for't, George 'ull be back afore so long, lookin' for a bit o' peace and quiet,' volunteered another of the company, a confirmed 'woman-hater'.

'Nay, I doan't know abart that. I reckon 'e'll traipse round arter that wench 'e's gotten wed to, same as 'is owd dog goes arter 'im,' volunteered George's friend loyally, if a little mournfully.

'Ay, wunnerful faithful critters dogs be, they'll stick ter one boss better nor a wench will,' replied the cynic. 'I reckon no one cud mak that owd dog o' George's foller 'im same as 'e does George.'

'I could.' The voice belonged to Snapper o' Scartop.

For the space of a minute or so there was a heavy disapproving silence, as Snapper's boastful challenge revolved its slow way round the crowded tap-room.

Then from George's friend: 'Easy ter talk, Mister, seein' as 'ow neither George nor 'is dog's 'ere,' voicing to a nicety the feeling of every man present.

'Wot I said,' replied Snapper, 'goes with any dog, not only George's' – with a grin towards George's friend. 'Bring any dog you fancy,' went on Snapper, 'an' I bet I'll make 'im foller me outer this 'ere room inside five minutes, now then.'

Mr Springs laughed. 'That's talking big, ain't it, Snapper?' he remarked. 'You're a bit of a card at handlin' dogs, but there's dogs *and* dogs, you know.'

Snapper o' Scartop grinned. 'There ain't a power o' dogs 'ere tonight, but there's Mr Springs's bull-terrier. Now bull-terriers ain't everybody's friend, but I bet as I can mak that feller foller me outer this room inside five minutes, now then.'

'And I'll lay you can't, Mister,' instantly replied Champion's owner.

'Ay, but wot's bet goin' to be, drinks all round?' queried Tom hopefully.

There was a chorus of approval, but Snapper raised his voice.

'Nay,' he said scornfully. 'Yon's no sort o' bet; we'll mak a sportin' do of it while we're on t'job. Now listen 'ere, Mr Springs: if I can mak that dog o' yourn foller me outer this room wi'out touchin' 'im, inside five minutes, dog's mine, but if 'e wean't foller me, I pay you a couple o' quid, ow's that?'

A fleeting doubt crossed the ex-hunstman's mind, and he hesitated.

''E don't trust 'is dog seemin'ly,' laughed Snapper to the man next to him, thus neatly turning the feeling of the crowd in his own favour.

From all round the bar came cries of 'Nay, Mr Springs, be a sport, go on lad.'

Mr Springs made up his mind.

'All right, done with you; get on, an' let's see you make t'dog follow you same as you said,' he added to get the stupid business over.

'Ay,' put in a shepherd, 'let's see thee do summat, lad.'

'So,' remarked Snapper o' Scartop, and got on to his feet. Walking across towards Champion, he halted about a yard from the bull-terrier and, advancing one of those curiously gnarled hands of his, he said coaxingly, 'Come on, Champion, lad.'

The bull-terrier raised his head, and lifted a lid preparatory to a growl – Snapper was no favourite of his – when all in a moment his attitude changed.

The strong muzzle tilted, the nostrils twitched, and the small dark eyes became intent. Getting abruptly to his feet, he pushed his muzzle into Snapper's outstretched hand.

'Poor old feller,' murmured Snapper's low, soothing voice as he started to move step by step towards the door.

As one man the tap-room leaned forward.

'Gawd,' muttered Mr Springs, his eyes fixed entreatingly on the muscular white form as though by the concentration of his gaze he could stop that fateful walk to the door. But the soul of the bull-terrier was far away, beyond the reach of any man.

'I allus knowed 'e were a sorter fool dog,' murmured Tom, and clicked his false teeth disparagingly.

'Blast your guts, shut your jaw,' snarled his agitated employer, his eyes fixed pathetically on the slowly receding white shape.

The tap-room was silent, all watched the little drama being played out to its inevitable end.

They had reached the door now, and with his left hand Snapper unlatched it, still keeping his other hand outstretched towards Champion; they passed through, the door closed again softly, and a cracked voice came through the panels. ''E's mine now, I reckon.'

'By Gow! 'e's won! Yond chap's a fair knockout wi' dogs.'

Loudly the comments crashed on the ears of Champion's owner – he straightened up, and walking across, picked up the two dirty notes deposited by Snapper, and handed them to the shepherd. 'Take him his b— brass, Sam,' he said, briefly.

''Tain't natteral,' observed the shepherd, moving heavily towards the door.

In a little while he was back. ''E's gorn,' he said, 'an' dog as well,' he added with the merciless exactitude of his kind.

'I reckon you've lost yer dog, Mister,' put in an old man sitting near the door.

'Ay, it seems like it,' replied Champion's master, and he went outside, and watched Snapper and the bull-terrier go down the hill. 'Gawd blast him, and his devil's tricks; it wasn't a fair deal, and if I was a dyin' man I'd say the same,' he muttered, and turned heavily back into the tap-room, noisy now with every man voicing his opinion of the evening's episode.

And away on the fell, a white bull-terrier padded silently up the road made long and long ago by Roman hands. His nose and brain were full of a wonderful scent, a scent that he would follow to pain and death, and world's end. Whimpering, Champion pressed his quivering, longing nose into the hand that had betrayed him, and Snapper o' Scartop laughed until the lonely moor, echoing as to a kindred spirit, seemed to be laughing with him.

III

That Snapper was no fool where dogs were concerned was proved by his first action after conducting Champion into a dark shed at the back of his cottage.

Instead of trusting to a rope the little man picked up a rusty chain, the end of which was already secured to an iron staple in the wall; the swivel he now attached to the bull-terrier's collar.

He then departed, slamming the door, and – worst of all – taking with him the soul-enslaving smell.

And on that instant Champion came to himself. Immediately the scent left his nostrils the cloud lifted from his brain.

Crouching there in the darkness, that most lonely of all animals – a dog without a familiar scent about him – Champion suddenly raised his head and sniffed anxiously. A warm, rank smell drifted past his nostrils. Standing rigid, he peered into the gloom, and as he stood staring, he caught the gleam of shining eyes, and heard the grating slither of long claws on wood.

Again a wave of fetid scent filled his wide nostrils, a scent that roused long dormant desires, chief among which was the lust to kill. Lunging forward, he was brought up short by the chain, and stood for a moment trembling with excitement.

And as he stood, two shining green eyes suddenly materialised out of the surrounding blackness; they glared malevolently; the age-old hatred of the cat tribe for that of the dog was reflected in the unwinking emerald orbs. Champion jumped sideways all abristle to this new menace, and as the chain clanked the eyes disappeared.

Morning brought Snapper, who entered the shed and approached the bull-terrier. 'I reckon ye'd better be interjuiced to yer room-mates, Champion; good beginnings makes good endin's – that is, some-times,' and chuckling as though at some secret thought, Snapper released the chain and, leading the bull-terrier across to a dark corner, halted him in front of a roughly made wooden cage.

A creature utterly unlike anything Champion had ever seen crouched the other side of the bars. It had a reddish grey body and a white head fantastically barred with black. But although the bull-terrier showed a certain amount of curiosity, there was none of that savage lust to kill for which Snapper had hoped.

Gritting his teeth with disappointment, the little man stood for a moment, and, as always when things were not turning out to plan, all the bad blood in Snapper bubbled to the surface.

'We'll see wot Rasper 'as ter say to yer,' he muttered at last, and conducted the bull-terrier to another cage which housed a great grey ragged-coated tom cat. Bred half-wild, always kept hungry, and systematically teased by Snapper, it now possessed a truly diabolical temper. The moment he saw Snapper and Champion approaching he arched his mangy, scarred back, opened his wide-hinged jaws, and screeched his rage, spitting like a snake.

Seeing that the bull-terrier evinced no apparent eagerness to make the closer acquaintance of Rasper, Snapper, clutching him by the collar, forcibly dragged him up to the iron bars – whereupon the infuriated cat made a lightning thrust at the dog's eyes, but, missing this objective by a fraction, the raking claws scored instead a deep cut over Champion's left cheekbone.

The son of Ch. Laughing White Girl gave a yelp of pain and surprise, and Snapper chuckled, well pleased.

'P'raps that'll wakken yer up a bit,' he grunted, regarding with deep satisfaction the trickle of scarlet staining the white of the bull-terrier's cheek. Before chaining Champion up again he administered a freshened prod of his stick to Rasper, who responded in a manner that caused even Snapper o' Scartop, tough little sinner that he was, to step back rather appalled at the result of his handiwork.

Screeching and yowling its bubbling, seething hatred, the ragged-coated monster hurled itself against the bars, biting and tearing at the unyielding iron with savage but impotent teeth and claws, that very soon showed red and foam-flecked, as drops of bloody froth fell from the gaping, panting jaws and dripped onto the spread claws that ripped now at the iron, now at the empty air.

'Red in tooth and claw, grand words them,' muttered Snapper, gazing fascinated on the spectacle of demoniacal rage presented by Rasper.

It is perhaps not very difficult now to guess Snapper's secret hobby; it was seeing animals fight, kill and maim each other; nothing else in the world afforded his warped soul quite the same exquisite pleasure as seeing an animal in its death throes still fighting desperately, hopelessly; to this end Snapper had formed his menagerie, composed of all the gamest fighters amongst the smaller animals: weasels, rats, a badger, a fox, Rasper the half-wild cat, and now the bull-terrier.

Mongrel's Memoir _____

Mark Twain

Samuel Langhorn Clemens, alias Mark Twain (1835–1910), the author of *The Innocents Abroad*, *Tom Sawyer* and *Huckleberry Finn*, was perhaps the most famous of all the American humourists. Here he is contrasting man's cruelty with dog's devotion – imagining a mongrel's reminiscing:

My father was a St Bernard, my mother was a collie, but I am a

Presbyterian. This is what my mother told me; I do not know these nice distinctions myself. To me they are only fine large words meaning nothing. My mother had a fondness for such; she liked to say them, and see other Dogs look surprised and envious, as wondering how she got so much education.

You can see by these things that she was of a rather vain and frivolous character; still, she had virtues enough to make up, I think. She had a kind heart and gentle ways, and never habored resentments for injuries done her, but put them easily out of her mind and forgot them; and she taught her children her kindly way, and from her we learned also to be brave and prompt in time of danger, and not to run away, but face peril that threatened friend or stranger, and help them the best we could without stopping to think what the cost might be to us. And she taught us, not by words only, but by example, and that is the best way and the surest and the most lasting.

When I was well grown at last, I was sold and taken away, and I never saw her again. She was broken-hearted, and so was I, and we cried; but she comforted me as well as she could, and said we were sent into this world for a wise and good purpose, and must do our duties without repining, take our life as we might find it, live it for the best good of others and never mind about the results; they were not our affair.

So we said our farewells, and looked our last upon each other through our tears; and the last thing she said – keeping it for the last to make me remember it the better, I think – was 'In memory of me, when there is a time of danger to another, do not think of yourself; think of your mother and do as she would do.'

Do you think I could forget that? No.

Mr Gray was thirty-eight, and tall and slender and handsome, a little bald in front, alert, quick in his movements, businesslike, prompt, decided, unsentimental, and with that kind of trim-chiselled face that just seems to glint and sparkle with frosty intellectuality! He was a renowned scientist.

The laboratory was not a book, or a picture, or a place to wash your hands, as the college president's Dog said – no, that is the lavatory; the laboratory is quite different, and is filled with jars, and bottles, and electrics, and wires, and strange machines; and every week, other scientists came there and sat in the place, and used the machines, and discussed, and made what they called experiments and discoveries; and often I came too, and stood around and listened, and tried to learn, for the sake of my mother, and in loving memory of her, and although it was a pain to me, as realizing what she was losing out of her life and I gaining nothing at all; for, try as I might, I was never able to make anything out of it at all.

Other times, I lay on the floor in the mistress's bedroom and slept, she gently using me for a footstool, knowing it pleased me, for it was a caress; other times I spent an hour in the nursery, and got well tousled and made happy; other times I watched by the crib there, when the baby was asleep, and the nurse out for a few minutes on the baby's affairs; other times I romped and raced through the grounds and the garden with Sadie till we were tired out, then slumbered on the grass in the shade of a tree while she read her book; other times I went visiting the neighbour Dogs – for there were some most pleasant ones not far away, and one very handsome and courteous and graceful one, a curly-haired Irish setter by name of Robin Adair, who was a Presbyterian like me, and belonged to the Scotch minister.

The servants in our house were all kind to me and were fond of me, and so, as you see, mine was a pleasant life. There could not be a happier Dog than I was, nor a gratefuller one. I will say this for myself, for it is only the truth: I tried in all ways to do well and right, and honour my mother's memory and her teachings, and earn the happiness that had come to me, as best I could.

By and by, came my little Puppy, and then my cup was full, my happiness was perfect. It was the dearest little waddling thing, and so smooth and soft and velvety, and had such cunning little awkward paws, and such affectionate eyes, and such a sweet innocent face; and it made me so proud to see how the children and their mother adored it, and fondled it, and exclaimed over every little wonderful thing it did. It did seem to me that life was just too lovely to –

Then came the winter. One day I was standing a watch in the nursery. That is to say, I was asleep on the bed. The baby was asleep in the crib, which was alongside the bed, on the side next the fireplace. It was the kind of crib that has a lofty tent over it made of a gauzy stuff that you can see through. The nurse was out, and we two sleepers were alone. A spark from the wood-fire was shot out, and it lit on the slope of the tent. I suppose a quiet interval followed, then a scream from the baby woke me, and there was that tent flaming up toward the ceiling! Before I could think, I sprang to the floor in my fright, and in a second was halfway to the door; but in the next half-second my mother's farewell was sounding in my ears, and I was back on the bed again. I reached my head through the flames and dragged the baby out by the waist-band, and tugged it along, and we fell to the floor together in a cloud of smoke; I snatched a new hold, and dragged the screaming little creature along and out at the door and around the bend of the hall, and was still tugging away, all excited and happy and proud, when the master's voice shouted –

'Begone, you cursed beast!' and I jumped to save myself; but he was wonderfully quick, and chased me up, striking furiously at me with his cane, I dodging this way and that, in terror, and at last a strong blow fell upon my left foreleg, which made me shriek and fall, for the moment, helpless; the cane went up for another blow, but it never descended, for the nurse's voice rang wildly out, 'The nursery's on fire!' and the master rushed away in that direction, and my other bones were saved.

The pain was cruel, but, no matter, I must not lose any time; he might come back at any moment; so I limped on three legs to the other end of the hall, where there was a dark little stairway leading up into a garret where old boxes and such things were kept, as I had heard say, and where people seldom went. I managed to climb up there, when I searched my way through the dark amongst the piles of things, and hid in the secretest place I could find. It was foolish to be afraid there, yet still I was; so afraid that I held in and hardly even whimpered, though it would have been such a comfort to whimper, because that eases the pain, you know. But I could lick my leg, and that did me some good.

For half an hour there was a commotion downstairs, and shoutings, and rushing footsteps and then there was quiet again. Quiet for some minutes and that was grateful to my spirit, for then my fears began to go down; and fears are worse than pain – oh, much worse. Then came a sound that froze me! They were calling me – calling me by name – hunting for me!

It was muffled by distance, but that could not take the terror out of it, and it was the most dreadful sound to me that I had ever heard. It went all about, everywhere, down there; along the halls, through all the rooms, in both storeys, and in the basement and the cellar; then outside, and farther and farther away – then back, and all about the house again, and I thought it would never, never stop. But at last it did, hours and hours after the vague twilight of the garret had long ago been blotted out by black darkness.

Then in that blessed stillness my terrors fell little by little away, and I was at peace and slept. It was a good rest I had, but I woke before the twilight had come again. I was feeling fairly comfortable, and I could think out a plan now. I made a very good one, which was to creep down, all the way down the back stairs, and hide behind the cellar door, and slip out and escape when the iceman came at dawn, whilst he was inside filling the refrigerator; then I would hide all day, and start on my journey when night came; my journey to – well, anywhere where they would not know me and betray me to the master. I was feeling almost cheerful now; then suddenly I thought, why, what would life be like without my Puppy!

That was despair. There was no plan for me. I saw that; I must stay where I was; stay, and wait, and take what might come – it was not my affair; that was what life is – my mother had said it. Then – well, then the calling began again! All my sorrows came back. I said to myself, the master will never forgive. I did not know what I had done to make him so bitter and so unforgiving, yet I judged it was something a dog could not understand, but which was clear to a man and dreadful.

They called and called – days and nights, it seemed to me. So long that the hunger and thirst near drove me mad, and I recognized that I was getting very weak. When you are this way you sleep a great deal, and I did. Once I woke in an awful fright – it seemed that the calling was right there in the garret! And so it was; it was Sadie's voice, and she was crying; my name was falling from her lips all broken, poor thing, and I could not believe my ears for the joy of it when I heard her say,

'Come back to us, – oh, come back to us, and forgive – it is all so sad without our . . .'

I broke in with *such* a grateful little yelp, and the next moment Sadie was plunging and stumbling through the darkness and the lumber, and shouting for the family to hear, 'She's found! she's found!'

The days that followed – well, they were wonderful. The mother and Sadie and the servants – why, they just seemed to worship me. They couldn't seem to make me a bed that was fine enough; and as for the food, they couldn't be satisfied with anything but game and delicacies that were out of season; and every day the friends and neighbours flocked in to hear about my heroism – that was the name they called it by, and it means agriculture. I remember my mother pulling it on a kennel once, and explaining it that way, but didn't say what agriculture was, except that it was synonymous with intramural incandescence; and a dozen times a day Mrs Gray and Sadie would tell the tale to newcomers, and say I risked my life to save the baby's, and both of us had burns to prove it, and then the company would pass me around and pet me and exclaim about me, and you could see the pride in the eyes of Sadie and her mother; and when the people wanted to know what made me limp, they looked ashamed and changed the subject, and sometimes when people hunted them this way and that with questions about it, it looked to me as if they were going to cry.

And this was not all the glory; no, the master's friends came, a whole twenty of the most distinguished people, and had me in the laboratory, and discussed me as if I was a kind of discovery; and some of them said it was wonderful in a dumb beast, the finest exhibition of instinct they could call to mind; but the master said, with vehemence, 'It's far above instinct; it's *reason*, and many a man, privileged to be saved and go with you and me to a better world by right of its possession, has less of it than this poor silly quadruped that's fore-ordained to perish,' and then he laughed, and said, 'Why, look at me – I'm a sarcasm! Bless you, with all my grand intelligence, the only thing I inferred was that the Dog had gone mad and was destroying the child, whereas but for the beast's intelligence – it's *reason*, I tell you – the child would have perished!'

They disputed and disputed, and *I* was the very centre and subject of it all, and I wished my mother could know that this grand honor had come to me; it would have made her proud.

Then they discussed optics, as they called it, and whether a certain injury to the brain would produce blindness or not, but they could not agree about it, and said they must test it by experiment by and by; and next they discussed plants, and that interested me, because in the summer Sadie and I had planted seeds – I helped her dig the holes, you know – and after days and days a little shrub or a flower came up there, and it was a wonder how that could happen; but it did, and I wished I could talk – I would have told those people about it and shown them how much I knew, and been all alive with the subject; but I didn't care for the optics; it was dull, and when they came back to it again it bored me, and I went to sleep.

Pretty soon it was spring, and sunny and pleasant and lovely, and the sweet mother and the children patted me and the Puppy good-bye, and went away on a journey and a visit to their kin, and the master wasn't any company for us, but we played together and had good times, and the servants were kind and friendly, and we got along quite happily and counted the days and waited for the family.

And one day those men came again, and said now for the test, and they took the Puppy to the laboratory, and I walked three-leggedly along, too, feeling proud, for any attention shown the Puppy was a pleasure to me, of course. They discussed and experimented, and then suddenly the Puppy shrieked, and they set him on the floor, and he went staggering around with his head all bloody, and the master clapped his hands and shouted:

'There, I've won – confess it! He's as blind as a Bat!'

And they all said,

'It's so – you've proved your theory, and suffering humanity owes you a great debt from henceforth,' and they crowded around him, and wrung his hand cordially and thankfully, and praised him.

But I hardly saw or heard these things, for I ran at once to my little darling, and snuggled close to it where it lay, and licked the blood, and it put its head against mine, whimpering softly, and I knew in my heart it was a comfort to it in its pain and trouble to feel its mother's touch, though it could not see me. Then it drooped down, presently, and its little velvet nose rested upon the floor, and it was still, and did not move any more.

Soon the master stopped discussing a moment, and rang in the footman, and said, 'Bury it in the far corner of the garden,' and then went on with the discussion; and I trotted after the footman, very happy and grateful, for I knew the Puppy was out of its pain now, because it was asleep. We went far down the garden to the farthest end, where the children and nurse and the Puppy and I used to play in the summer in the shade of a great elm, and there the footman dug a hole, and I was sure he was going to plant the Puppy, and I was glad, because it would grow and come up a fine handsome Dog, like Robin Adair, and be a beautiful surprise for the family when they came home, so I tried to help him dig, but my lame leg was no good, being stiff, you know, and you have to have two, or it is no use. When the footman had finished and covered little Robin up, he patted my head, and there were tears in his eyes, and he said, 'Poor little Doggie, you SAVED *his* child.'

I have watched two whole weeks, and he doesn't come up! This last week, a fright has been stealing upon me. I think there is something terrible about this. I do not know what it is, but the fear makes me sick, and I cannot eat, though the servants bring me the best of food; and they pet me so, and even come in the night, and cry, and say, 'Poor Doggie – do give it up and come home; *don't* break our hearts!' and all this terrifies me the more, and makes me sure something has happened. And I am so weak; since yesterday I cannot stand on my feet any more. And within this hour, the servants looking towards the sun where it was sinking out of sight and the night chill coming on, said things I could not understand, but they carried something cold to my heart.

'Those poor creatures! They do not suspect. They will come home in the morning, and eagerly ask for the little Doggie that did the brave deed, and who of us will be strong enough to say the truth to them: "The humble little friend is gone where go the beasts that perish." '

The Captain ————————————————

Walter Emanuel

Walter Emanuel was writing stories about dogs, some tragic, some very amusing (he was a regular contributor to *Punch*) at the turn of the century. The anthropomorphic one I have chosen, *The Dogs of War*, is a wistfully sad example of much of his work. The narrator, the self-effacing Ears, is elected to the exclusive mongrels' club, known as 'The Dogs of War', by his hero, the club's Captain. 'As a matter of fact,' says Ears, 'he [the Captain] was a dog who, though of small stature, would attract attention in any assemblage. His face was the face of a setter, with something of the added dignity of a bloodhound, and all the intelligence of a St Bernard. His body was a fox-terrier's, and his tail, like his brain, his own.' Ears worships the Captain and is never the same again after his hero dies:

The Captain was the beginning of a new era in my life – or rather, I should say, the beginning of my life. Almost from the first, when I was in the Captain's company, the streets ceased to have any terrors for me, and the day came ultimately when not only did I not fear any man, dog, or thing in the world, but when most men and all dogs feared me. Of course this came gradually. At first, not even cats ran away from me. Then to my delight – which seems childish to me now – one windy day a number of leaves in the road took flight when they saw me. Then birds, then cats. And at length – a dog!

I have even barked defiantly at a whole troop of mounted soldiery, any one of whom could have run me through or shot me, had he possessed the necessary pluck. . . .

I was now constantly in the Captain's company, and, when I think of it, how good and noble of him it was for a dog in his position to consort with one who, after all, at that time was a mere ignorant yokel – a bumpkin! Never, I realized, could I repay what I owed him, though I should try to do so by a life-long devotion. He put me on my legs. He showed me about town. But for him, I, a simple countryman, would have been victimised one hundred times, for the Cockneys are a sharp race.

When I thanked him, he merely said, 'I have taken a fancy to you, Ears' – for that was the nickname he gave me.

I soon discovered that the Captain was a dog of immense influence, and the effect of his friendship was instantaneous. When I first came to town, the natives cold-shouldered me. As soon as it was noticed how much I was with the Captain, a marked change took place. Innumerable little dogs now paid me court – kowtowed to me – as being a favourite of the Captain. It was most pleasant.

The Captain was the most entertaining of companions, for he was so wonderfully well informed. He knew all about everything. His astonishing accumulation of knowledge was mainly due, he told me, to a habit his mistress had of reading out the most interesting items from the newspaper at breakfast to the rest of the family. The Captain would always listen attentively – in which respect, by the way, he was more polite than the others. Thus it came about that there was nothing you could ask the Captain which he could not answer. He knew all the big words, and I still remember my delight when he told me I was a 'quadruped', for I had no idea that I was anything so important. Half an hour's conversation with the Captain was a liberal education in itself, and whatever I have of polish and choice of diction, I owe to the Captain. . . .

He was not slow to mark the change in me, and, eight weeks after my first meeting him, he made me a member of his Club. This was the greatest distinction that could be conferred upon a dog. My gratitude knew no bounds; but all that the Captain said in reply to my protestations was, 'I like you, Ears.'

It was the most famous Dogs' Club in the world. I need scarcely say that I refer to 'The Dogs of War' – known to our rivals as 'The Mongrelians', 'The Hooligans', 'The Gargoyles', and other soubriquets as insulting as they are stupid. This Club, as is well known, was founded by the Captain as a monument to his mother. The Captain's mother had made a love-match. She was considered, however, to have married out of the pale, was cut by all thorough-breds, and fretted herself to death.

To avenge this heartless piece of snobbery, 'The Dogs of War' was formed. Its motto was 'Defiance not Defence', and all thorough-breeds giving themselves airs were to be attacked on sight.

The rules and regulations of the Club were many, and I do not propose to set them out at length. In all of them the master-mind of the Captain was apparent.

Females and children were ineligible for membership. A proposal to form a junior branch was rightly rejected by the Captain. As he pointed out, the youngsters, with their constant infantile complaints, would be more bother than they were worth. And, unless a special dispensation – the word is the Captain's – were obtained, the members must remain bachelors. And no black dogs were admitted; the line was drawn at coloured gentlemen.

The Captain alone chose the members. If a likely young fellow applied to him, or was introduced by a member, the Captain would place the candidate on probation for a month. During those four weeks the Captain would receive reports on its habits and customs, and would personally test it in many ways. For instance, he would meet one of the little novices out with its mistress. The Captain would beckon to it. The novice would advance towards the Captain. The mistress would call it back. The Captain would beckon again. The novice would once more run to the Captain. The Captain would detain it for five minutes, and say, 'Now you may go back.' It would get a beating from its mistress. The Captain would meet the same dog in similar circumstances the next day, and if then it did not come at the first summons, the Captain would let it know that he had no use for it.

Nor did we have the rule of 'Once a member, always a member'. The Captain reserved to himself the right of expulsion. It was the only way, he explained, to keep us up to the mark. One member was expelled, soon after I joined, for cowardice. It was a painful affair. He was a personal friend of the Captain, but the Captain felt he must make an example of him. He was a small dog, known as 'The Barrel' from his shape. One day a Newfoundlander, who came up suddenly behind him, cried out: 'Hullo, here's one of the dirty Mongrelians.' The Barrel turned round and looked at the Newfoundlander, and found him so big that he decided that the insult was not intentional. The incident, however, was reported, and The Barrel had to leave. The Captain took an especially serious view of the matter, as the insult was to the Club and not to the member personally. I used to see the outcast occasionally afterwards, but if he caught sight of one of us he would always slink away; and I used to pity him, he looked so miserable.

Expulsion, too, used to take place occasionally for slackness and disobedience. Without obedience, the Captain held, nothing was possible. We were never to question his commands. He was a stern disciplinarian, and the message 'The Captain wants to speak to you' has made many a dog tremble in his day. And with it all the Captain was scrupulously just; and this, I think, was appreciated by the members, and was perhaps the secret of his marvellous influence over us. We have seen how he would not spare even his personal friend. His impartiality was wonderful. I have even known him decide against me in a dispute with another member. And once he threatened to expel me because I growled when he asked me to give him my bone, greedy brute that I was!

He was a splendid Dictator. No wonder he so often led us to victory. . . .

The thought of the Captain's end still cuts me like a knife. Yes, he died, did this great dog whose portrait I have attempted to draw. Would that I had been taken in his place, for the world could have better spared me! One cannot understand these things.

How vividly I remember it all! How strange that he who had never had a serious day's illness in his life should go out suddenly as he did!

On the evening before the end he came round to me. I offered him food. He refused it. 'Captain,' I said, 'you're ill.' He then told me that all the afternoon he had been suffering from dreadful pains in the underneath. He had come round to me in the hope that a little walk might do him good. Even as he told me this he was shaken by a dreadful spasm, and I advised him to get home as quickly as he could and go to bed. It was evident that he had eaten something which had disagreed with him. I then saw him home, though it was only with the greatest difficulty that he could walk, so frequent now were the spasms. I did not offer to go in, as I could see he would rather be left alone. So, with a 'Good-bye, old man, keep yourself warm, and I'll be round in the morning,' I left him, little thinking that that would be the last time I should see the dear fellow. I remember that as I spoke to him he looked gratefully at me.

Stupidly, I did not realise how serious the matter was. The Captain had had similar attacks in a small way before, and they had always passed off overnight. I had often told him that he was not sufficiently particular as to what he ate. Sometimes when very hungry he would pick up things in the road.

Yet in a vague sort of way I seemed to have a kind of premonition of what was going to happen. I could not sleep, and as soon as the gate was unlocked in the morning I rushed to the Captain's house. When I came to the corner where the Captain, with his bright little face, usually ran down to meet me, there was no Captain there, and all the wag went from my tail. I walked up to his door, but there was still no Captain. With sinking heart I sat down and whined until a servant opened the door. Her eyes were red with weeping. She patted my head, and all she said was, 'Poor, poor doggie!'

Then I knew.

I do not know how I dragged myself home. I was as one stunned. The sense of overwhelming misfortune seemed to numb me, and my legs almost gave way under me. I could not eat anything, and I remember my master, who did not know what had happened, tried to joke with me. In the afternoon my people must have heard the news, for they were both extra nice to me, and my mistress petted me and

tried in vain to tempt me with all sorts of niceties from her special sugar-biscuit box.

Later in the afternoon I made another journey to the house, for on thinking it over I could not believe it. Somehow I thought the Captain had so much influence that he would never die. And on reaching his street my heart gave a great leap, for I noticed that in none of the houses were the blinds drawn. In my excitement I scratched the door impatiently, and when it was opened I rushed into every room, crying 'Captain! Captain!' But the only answer I received were the servant's sobs, and then indeed I knew that my dear friend was no more.

Subsequently I learned that he had passed away early in the morning; and the doctor who was called in said it was gastritis. So I was wrong in thinking it was stomach trouble. The Captain, I fancy, would have liked the big word.

He was buried in the dead of night at some unknown spot. By reason of his being hurried into a secret grave, I was prevented, to my eternal regret, from carrying out his last wishes. The Captain had always feared lest he should be buried alive, and he had made me promise that, if he predeceased me, the most approved scientific method of ascertaining whether there was still life in him should be employed. So I was to have offered him a biscuit.

Dear old fellow, I hope he knows it was not my fault!

The suddenness of it all was appalling.

On the day following his death I was summoned to a mass meeting of the Club which had been hastily called together by interested parties. It was the fullest meeting ever held. It had been rumoured that the Captain had been poisoned by one of the rival Clubs and there were angry threats of reprisals. But there was very little geniune affection for the Captain shown. It seemed to me that I was the only one who was really heart-sore. The question of a new Captain was raised with indecent haste, and I think I was the only one not mentioned for the post, as I did not mention myself. As a matter of fact the Captain had once said, while dining at my house, that, if anything were to happen to him, he wished me to be his successor. But I did not speak. I came away before the meeting was over, for it sickened me to hear them wrangling over the leadership, and the Captain scarcely gone. Mongrels!

I had done with them. This was the respect they paid to the memory of the Captain who had made them what they were – who had slaved for them and watched over them like a father. Never again would I have anything to do with the petty crew. Blood will tell, after all. Bids were subsequently made for me by the thorough-breeds, but their advances too were rejected by me. I owed that to the Captain. I was willing to become a social outcast. Thanks to the Captain, I was now strong enough to stand alone.

The Club survived the Captain for about a week. Then it split up into a dozen different societies and associations, some of which comprised only two members, each with the rank of Captain.

So the Captain's life's-work perished with him.

I too nearly died. For days I could not touch food, and it was only thanks to the loving care of my mistress and the gentle concern of Smith that I was brought round. At times I even thought of doing away with myself, and that the first motorcar I met might have me. But my mistress and Smith made me feel that they would miss me. They, and even my master, were very good to me, so that I began to see that the Captain was right in his opinion of humans – as, of course he was right in everything.

What a rare fellow he was! The dear Captain! Have I pictured him, I wonder? It is impossible, I fear, with my poor vocabulary; and my memory is not what it was.

Were I a sculptor, what a statue I would raise to him! Seated on his own doorstep, surrounded by devoted friends, all looking up to him, the wise head on the young shoulders. How fine he looked then!

By the by, it is good to know that his name will not die out. In a grocer's shop the other day I saw a tin of his favourite biscuits. They are now called 'Captain biscuits'.

Sometimes I try to persuade myself that the Captain's death was all for the best. Latterly the poor old fellow had been haunted by the fear that he was getting stout. He often asked me whether it was so, and I always said, 'No.' But it was so.

Still, that does not make me miss him the less. I am always thinking of him. I have never recovered from the blow of his loss. I am fond of my mistress and I am fond of Smith, but I have only been in love once, and that was with the Captain.

No one, I suspect, would recognize in me now the former dog of spirit. My master calls me jestingly 'The Fire Dog', for in the long winter evenings I sit staring into the fire and thinking of the Captain, and wondering whether I bored him with my love, and reproaching myself for ever having been cross with him even for a minute. Sometimes I dream of him. Only last night I had been sleeping, and I woke up barking with joy, and I pranced about the room and made my master open the street door, for I had dreamt that the Captain was without. But I only found Darkness there. My people seemed to understand, and when I cried they patted me and tried to soothe me.

Well, well, I expect I am getting a foolish old fellow now, and soon, I suppose, I shall solve that question of whether there is a Paradise for dogs. Of one thing, at any rate, I am certain, that if Paradise there be, then the Captain is there – and he is looking out for me.

Flax Overboard —————————————

Svend Fleuron

The Danish author, Svend Fleuron, had a wonderful compassion for animals and a considerable knowledge of dog handling. In his novel *Flax, Police Dog* the hero is the son of an Alsatian bitch, belonging to a tough blacksmith, who presents him to his oldest apprentice. Finding the puppy unmanageable the apprentice gives him to a farmer, Old Tollerod, with the parting words, 'he's a bit quick in the teeth'. Tollerod keeps him chained up and subjects him to a variety of ill-treatment, rendering him wilder and more vicious than ever.

Tollerod hands Flax on to Klyn 'the higgler', an egg and cheese dealer, a far worse scoundrel, whose aim is to mould Flax into a ferocious guard dog and fighter. The methods of this 'slow, thick-set Jutlander' are brutal. When Klyn is warned by the police to keep Flax under closer control, he decides he cannot do so, and will therefore shoot him. But he dies of a heart attack on the way to the wood where the deed was to have been done. The 'Public trustee' then sells Flax to a pleasant young policeman, and the dog undergoes a long and rigorous training which he enjoys. He serves his master beautifully. But the police chief considers him to be overconscientious and eventually tells the constable to sell him.

Flax spends the next year or so guarding against poachers on a large estate where he is mostly lonely and unhappy. He escapes from there and, after some wandering, is adopted by a tenant of Old Jolly, a cattle farmer called Henrik, with whom he enjoys a very full life. In particular he gains supremacy over a turbulent bull, Ut, which no one has been able to handle. After Flax has been at the farm for two years Ut is sent aboard a ship, to be delivered to a foreign buyer. Flax is told to lie by the bull's stall and keep him in order until Henrik, who has some business in the port, returns to collect him. But Henrik misses the boat and Flax finds himself sailing away with the bull.

Aboard the ship is a gang of men with criminal records who recognize Flax as a former police adversary of theirs; so they throw him overboard. But the dog is rescued, clinging to a raft, by some artillerymen from a coastal fort. Flax spends a contented old age as a beloved member of the garrison.

The moral of this fine story is that there are no good dogs or bad dogs, but only good men and bad men. A good dog is made, not born. A dog is ever ready to love and, given the right treatment, will respond with infinite devotion and faith. *Flax* illustrates, as well as any story I know, how a dog is absolutely at the mercy of a negligent, heartless or cruel owner.

The book was first published in Denmark in 1931, the English edition appearing in 1940. The passage I have selected tells how Flax is thrown overboard:

Flax lived on intimate terms with his master, and Old Jolly's big herds. Sometimes he had unpleasant encounters with young bulls, but he had two gifts that helped him against all four-footed trouble-makers, just as they had helped him against two-footed rascals; he was light on his feet, noiseless as a wolf, and his coat had a wonderful protective colouring – no one heard him or saw him before he was on the spot.

In addition to that, he had all the courage of the old German dogs when they sprang up at the muzzles of enemy horses. Pluck shone out of his eyes, and no threats or blows could make him lower them.

He loved his life among all those animals, both in the warm stalls and out in the open. He felt at home among those placid cud-chewers, whose long-horned heads, with their surprised faces, seemed filled with a strange mysticism. He enjoyed drinking in their warm, close atmosphere; a cow, ah! He pricked up his ears! But he always maintained his superiority as a dog. Cows were all very well in their place.

Ut was going to leave the farm; he had been sold to a foreign owner, and, with a big draft of other animals, was to be put on board a cattle-boat at the nearest port.

Flax helped the stockman to get the dangerous bull down to the boat, and on board. Then Henrik ordered him to lie down outside Ut's pen, to keep him in order – then, too, Henrik knew where Flax was. He had to go to the bank, and to several other places for Old Jolly.

Whether Henrik made a mistake in the time of sailing, or whether he met some friends in a public house, Flax, to whom it mattered the most, never knew.

Dark fell, and he still lay outside Ut's pen, watching and waiting. Then the boat got under way. No one had noticed the dog.

When they were some way out, several half-naked, coaly men, with dirty rags round their necks, came up from the engine-room; they spat far over the side, and stared up at the stars shining out of an August sky.

As one of them, a Finn, passed Flax, the dog growled at him. Then they saw him, several more were called up, and matches were struck in front of him, and behind him. They examined him, and talked together – he was just like the 'Terror of the Docks'!

Under this examination, Flax grew uneasy, and, when the last match flare had gone out, he left his place and went off in search of his master. He thought Henrik was still on board, and snuffed all the places the man had been in; as the door was open he even went into the second mate's cabin, where they'd handed over the bull's papers.

Suddenly the door clanged to behind him.

'Damned police dog!' muttered the Finn outside.

The mate who had had a lot to do, had gone straight from his cabin to the bridge, the animals were bellowing, the engines throbbing, and so no one heard the dog's barks and howls.

Not till the boat was in the open sea did they discover Flax. They took him for a stowaway – well, such things did happen; he could come back with the boat!

But he wasn't wanted amidships; go forward!

Bewildered and discouraged, he went back to his place by Ut, and as the bull felt as lonely as he did, they somehow comforted one another.

A couple of hours after midnight he suddenly heard hoarse voices. They were whispering, but he couldn't mistake the tone of their voices. A strange, tarry, sooty smell, mingled with the sharp smell of spirits that conjured up his fights on the docks, puffed in his face. An iron port-hole in the side of the vessel opened close behind him; he felt the cold spray from the sea.

Puzzled, Flax got up, intending to step to one side, when suddenly a Negro, with huge arms almost like a pair of horns, gripped him round the body. His teeth closed on an arm, but his jaws had no grip. A kick, and he hurtled overboard!

He heard coarse laughter, and the port-hole slammed shut. When he got his head above water, the black ship, its lights glowing like bulls' eyes, was gliding away in the darkness.

Gun-Shy Jimmy ⸻

Sir Arthur Bryant

Early in the Second World War, Sir Arthur Bryant, the historian and *Illustrated London News* columnist, and his wife, were walking along the North Cornish cliffs when they were 'adopted' by 'a white shaggy terrier with brown cap and ears and a stump of a tail'. In his charming little book, *Jimmy, the Dog in My Life*, Sir Arthur relates how the terrier's gun-shyness – probably incurred during the Blitz and from which he was never to recover – was manifested in his later years:

One episode in Jimmy's London life sticks particularly in my memory. It occurred four years before his death, just before old age began to take the fire out of him. It was the morning of Queen Elizabeth's proclamation, and he and I were walking in Hyde Park. Suddenly there was a detonation, causing Jimmy to swerve from his path among the trees of Rotten Row. Having recovered himself, he looked up at me as though to enquire whether some active expression of fidelity and devotion was demanded. Then the detonation was repeated and he jumped again. This time, however, he did not allow it to pass unanswered, and, after a moment's pause, barked back, though still a little uncertainly. Then the gun fired again, and this time he jumped forward defiantly, as a terrier does when challenged, raised his small, resolute head and barked loudly. A duel then began between the invisible gunners and the dog, each mechanical explosion being followed by a canine one of growing ferocity. This continued all down the Row, and no threats or entreaties on my part would make him desist.

By this time we had left the Row and were crossing the Park in the direction of the firing. As we came up through the still, wintry mist towards the high ground beyond the Serpentine, we saw first the

flashes of guns and then the gun detachments of the King's Troop standing around their guns. And at that moment a most beautiful thing happened. Without word spoken, and with the most exquisite skill and alacrity, the gun teams galloped forward out of the mist and halted by the guns. Then, before I could recover from my surprise, the guns were limbered up, and the six teams started once more to gallop, now with the guns and the gunners behind them.

In a great sweep, and still without any sound but the thud of flying hooves on the grass, they made off westwards across the empty centre of the Park, towards Lancaster Gate, and then swung northwards and eastwards until they vanished from sight behind the trees of Marble Arch. It might have been Mercer's Battery – 'Left limber up and as fast as you can!' – galloping into the inferno of smoke and heat on the ridge at Waterloo. Though, unlike his master, Jimmy was no reading dog, but a simple, fighting one, some such thought may have passed through his mind, for in a flash he was after the guns. But, being an old dog, he presently realized that he could not catch them up, and returned, wagging his tail, his duty done. A few years earlier, he would have followed them into the Edgware Road and probably laid hold of a gun!

In a sense that protest against England's artillery was prophetic, for a few months later a tragedy happened in Jimmy's life. Hitherto his happiest moments, and mine, had been when we set off for the country together: to that other home, furnished with rabbits, rats, well-populated ricks and haystacks, compost-heaps, and everything a sporting dog could require to fulfil his destiny. When such moments came and the long railway or motor journey was over, and the car climbed the steep slope of the rabbit-haunted Purbeck hills, a chant of exultation would break from the quivering throat. It was a kind of royal proclamation to all the vermin for miles round to take precipitately to their burrows or suffer the worst! But a shadow now fell on all this happiness and bravado – a shadow of inexplicable terror and anxiety. For this uncontrollable little dog, once a silent and haunted-looking stray, was not the only maker of noise in the green and tawny vales between the limestone hills and the dark cliffs of shale where his hunting paradise lay.

Beyond the chalk ridge on the horizon, mysterious monsters lurched and slithered about a sandy wilderness of little heathy hills, discharging their detonating missiles from long, thin shafts as they practised incessantly for the next – or perhaps, in keeping with age-long military tradition, the last – war to end war. And, having for years treated heavy artillery with the fearlessness with which he normally treated every manifestation of man or nature, Jimmy one August day reacted to the morning's first shots from the Bovington Gunnery Range with a display of fear that no one had ever witnessed in him. Instead of ignoring them as he had always done, or boldly barking back at them as he had done to the guns in the Park, he gave one terrified look and fled to the coal cellar. A few minutes later, covered with coal dust, he emerged and, panting with anxiety, started to circle round my legs.

All day, while the bombardment lasted, he continued to alternate between furious digging and scrabbling in cupboards and dark corners, and trotting, like a crazy automaton, round me. Work became virtually impossible, for, apart from the agony of seeing a beloved friend in such a plight, whenever I started to settle myself to my task, he would fling himself into my lap and lie there panting and trembling, until out of sympathy I found myself trembling too. If I moved to fetch a book or folder of notes, he would run in circles between my legs, bringing me more than once to the ground. Nor would the poor animal, usually so full of intelligence and sensitivity and eager for every pleasurable experience, pay the slightest attention to the familiar heralds of his wonted treats. The sight of his lead and the magic word 'walk'; the opening of the sacred tin in which his chocolates lived and before which he would often lie, like a Trafalgar

Square lion, for hours at a stretch, growling at every unlicensed person who approached; the rattle of keys that announced the opening of the car in which he so loved to ride. Nothing could comfort him or restore him to consciousness of anything but the ungovernable terror riding through his poor, crazed mind.

Occasionally, when the guns became temporarily silent, he would recover sufficient composure to creep up from the cellar, bedraggled and ashamed of himself, and lie miseraby in a corner, listening for the dreaded sound. And next morning he was listening apprehensively even before they began. The moment they did so, the same manifestations of terror occurred. After a day or two we took him away.

Thereafter Jimmy's pleasure in the country never returned. Nothing seemed to avail against the terror which the guns, reverberating among the Purbeck hills, aroused in him. The secret of his fear – so pathetic to behold – seemed to lie in some cause beyond our curing; perhaps in some episode in his now remote and, to us, unknown youth. And watching him listening intently for the cruel thunder to begin beyond the encircling hills, and trying to comfort and reassure him, it was not hard to guess what that memory might have been. It was something that must have happened to many a bewildered dog in England's blitzed cities: the roaring from the skies, the shaking streets and houses, the sudden and disintegrating thunder and fire that, in a flash and cascade of falling masonry and rubble, robbed a little creature – with as great a capacity for love and fidelity as any human – of all it had known and loved.

I suspect that it may have been that memory that caused Jimmy, as he lay cowering in the cellar to emerge every few minutes from his shelter and hurry, shuddering and trembling, into the room where his foolish master, disregarding all warnings, sat at his work to assure himself that he was still alive and to implore him to take shelter before the tragedy of his youth was re-enacted.

Fugitives from Vivisection _____

Richard Adams

The name Richard Adams first sprang to fame with *Watership Down*, which was awarded the Carnegie medal and the *Guardian* award for children's literature in 1972. His book *The Plague Dogs*, although not so well received by the critics, was soon on the bestseller lists, into paperback and on celluloid as a cartoon film. The author's feel for the Lakeland fells, which provide almost the entire setting of the book, as well as his profound compassion for animals and his outrage at man's inhumanity, shine vividly through on every page.

The book's heroes, Rowf and Snitter, are escapees from a scientific laboratory specializing in experiments on animals. When the scientists admit that the dogs pose a serious threat from the virulent disease they may be carrying, the hunt for them is stepped up and so is Mr Adams's fine gift for suspense. One of the dogs is mutilated by a test gadget let into its skull, the other is haunted by terrible memories of a drowning experiment. Both are semi-demented as well as being close to death from starvation by the time the army joins the police in the search:

The wind, veering round into the east, carried to the sleeping Rowf's

unsleeping nostrils the smells of rifle oil, leather and web equipment. A moment more and his waking ears caught the sound of human voices. He stared in terror at the extended khaki line crossing the sands.

'Snitter! The red-hat men are here – they're coming!'

'Oh, Rowf, let me go to sleep.'

'If you do, you'll wake up on the whitecoats' glass table! Come on, run!'

'I know they're all after us – I know they're going to kill us, but I can't remember why.'

'You remember what the sheepdog said. He said his man believed we had a plague, a sickness or something. I only wish I had – I'd try biting a few of them.'

In and out of the undulant dunes, the marram, gorse and sea holly, dead trails of bindweed and dry patches of club-rush. Down winding, sandy valleys doubling back on themselves, catching sight once more of the soldiers now horribly nearer; dashing through deep, yielding sand, over the top and down; and so once more to the sea – wet shore, long weeds, gleaming stones, flashes and pools; and beyond, the breaking waves.

'Snitter, I won't go back in the tank! I won't go back in the tank!'

Rowf ran a few yards into the waves and returned, a great, shaggy dog whining and trembling in the wind.

'What's out there, Snitter, in the water?'

'There's an island,' said Snitter desperately. 'Didn't you know? A wonderful island. The Star Dog runs it. They're all dogs there. They have great, warm houses with piles of meat and bones, and they have – they have splendid cat-chasing competitions. Men aren't allowed there unless the dogs like them and let them in.'

'I never knew. Just out there, is it really? What's it called?'

'Dog,' said Snitter, after a moment's thought. 'The Isle of Dog.'

'I can't see it. More likely the Isle of Man, I should think, full of men –'

'No, it's not, Rowf. It's the Isle of Dog out there, honestly, only just out of sight. I tell you, we can swim there, come on –'

The soldiers appeared, topping the dunes, first one or two, here and there, then the whole line, red berets, brown clothes, pointing and calling to each other. A bullet struck the rock beside Rowf and ricocheted into the water with a whine.

Rowf turned a moment and flung up his head.

'It's not us!' barked Rowf. 'It's not us that's got the plague!'

He turned and dashed into the waves. Before the next shot hit the sand he was already beside Snitter and swimming resolutely out to sea.

Panicked and Lost _____

Al Dempsey

Touring the USA and Canada on a Winston Churchill Travelling Fellowship in the context of Animal Welfare, in 1982, I enjoyed an interesting dialogue with the American Humane Association who are based in Denver, Colorado. One of the salient problems confronting the AHA is the plight of stray dogs and the nuisance they cause, especially when they form into packs. The worst effect of that is when they turn feral, roam the farms and forests, take livestock, pull down deer and interfere with the wildlife in general.

Dr Martin Passaglia, the AHA's director, kindly gave me a copy of Al Dempsey's novel, *Dog Kill*, a frightening indictment against that host of owners who carelessly lose or deliberately abandon their dogs when they are bored with them or find they can no longer cope with them.

Mr Dempsey shows, one by one, how a number of dogs come to join a pack. Apart from the categories I have mentioned, one dog is released from an experimental laboratory by Animal Rights campaigners, another is allowed by his owners to roam, to 'sow his wild oats'. In the case I have quoted, a Labrador, accompanying his family on holiday, simply loses his head in an encounter with another dog, then panics in the traffic and is lost:

The Noel Roberts family from Chicago had no idea they were about to become part of an enormous national statistic; they were merely trying to begin a vacation that they hoped they could enjoy. But, with about thirty-five million dogs in the United States, it is predictable that some of them are going to do something to mess up the best planned holiday.

For the Roberts's three little girls, the trip was a chance to play hookey from school with their parents' permission. For Noel and Sue Roberts, the parents, the trip was a romantic quest for memories; they had gone to Mammoth Cave National Park in Kentucky on their honeymoon exactly twelve years before.

Of course, back when they had first been married, the elegant, easy-to-travel Interstate Highway 65 had not been constructed, so driving from Chicago to Kentucky had been more difficult. This time Noel's pleasure was enhanced by the fall scenery that lined the broad highway ahead.

Earlier in the day, a few hours after they had left Chicago, there had been a tumultuous uproar when daughter Paddy was accused by daughters Lucy and Claire of drinking an extra Coke. Neither Noel nor Sue had been maintaining any type of inventory control or supervised disbursement program, so there was no way to establish the truth, though there was circumstantial evidence in the form of an odd number of remaining cans. There was also the possibility of self-incrimination in Paddy's urgent plea, 'I've *got* to go to the *toilet!*' But Noel, a lawyer by profession, acted with Solomonic wisdom and replaced the missing soft drink with one purchased when they stopped to replenish the gas tank.

They were riding in their huge Chevvy station wagon with the back seat folded down to give the girls plenty of room to loll around, play games, and annoy their dog, Beau. There had been discussions about putting the dog into a kennel for the week they would be away, but Beau was so much a part of the family that the idea had been summarily dismissed. He was a mixed Labrador retriever who had received every Lab characteristic his pure-bred father possessed except size. His mother had been a small mongrel, so Beau was only about twenty inches tall rather than the ideal twenty-four inches, and he weighed only about forty-five pounds instead of the ideal seventy. But the Roberts family did not really care about his physical dimensions or his lack of pedigree; he was an excellent watchdog, he loved the children, and he was insane over automobile trips.

Beau was incredibly patient with the little girls. While he refused to sleep in the car – or even to lie down while it was moving – he constantly moved out of the girls' way when they tossed their feet, squirmed around, or demanded to sit right where he was standing. It was as if he was so absolutely grateful for being allowed to come on the trip that he would allow himself to be subjected to virtually any discomfort.

'Beau will go crazy christening all those trees,' Sue said to Noel. Beau had a mania for defining his boundaries with his urine, and he seemed to have resource capabilities that measured in gallons, because he was constantly busy whenever they stopped near a wooded area.

Sue caught a glimpse of bright orange far ahead and said, 'I think there's an "H-J" ahead.'

Her attempted code for the restaurant went for naught; the three girls exploded with excitement, and it was ordained that they would have to stop for lunch there.

'Okay, okay,' Noel chided cheerfully, 'we'll stop.'

Squeals of glee greeted the surrender; the girls cheered and Beau wagged a furious tail.

The rear-compartment passengers all crowded against the back of the front seat, the girls chattering loudly and Beau rubbing his cold, wet nose against the back of Noel's neck.

Sternly, Noel ordered, 'Now, stop the noise. And, Beau, stop soaking my neck.' Unaffected, the girls continued what they were doing, as did Beau, who had heard the words but was confident that his master surely did not mean what he was saying.

Noel began to slow the car as he approached the exit that would take them to the Howard Johnson's. He drove down around the ramp, waited at the stop sign for traffic to clear, then turned left to approach the restaurant's parking lot.

As he made his final turn onto the asphalt driveway, a dog came running at the car. Noel had not seen where the dog had come from; it could have been in the deep grass of a drainage ditch or it could have come from behind one of the cars parked in the gas station. There was no danger because the dog was well clear of the front of the car; however, it ran alongside and then cut in back very near the rear fender.

Beau went crazy.

It was not the first time he had barked at another dog, and it was routine for Beau to bark when any animal or person came towards the car when the children were inside. But, this time, Beau's bark carried a different timbre, something more violent.

'Beau! Stop it!' Noel shouted just as the other dog slammed into the rear window of the station wagon.

Noel assumed that Beau could not hear the order over his own noise, so he repeated it. Beau stopped barking, but, through the rear-view mirror, Noel could see the hair on the back of the dog's neck standing up, hackles raised more markedly than ever before.

'Easy, boy,' Noel said softly, and he saw Beau's tail give a few wags. But the hackles remained raised.

Noel pulled the car into the parking area beside the restaurant. He opened the door, and was suddenly deluged with petitions from his daughters. Through the confused trio of voices, he gathered that each wanted the right to take Beau on his lead so he could relieve himself.

He leaned back into the car and patiently explained that it was a totally strange place, and that maybe this time Daddy should walk the dog.

He was facing the girls and smiling at their arguments, so he really should have seen what was happening. But he didn't.

The other dog had done something – no one ever knew what – but something snapped in Beau's self-control and he made a leap for the front seat. He literally flew between Paddy and Claire before he landed beside Sue, and in almost the same motion he leaped over Noel and through the open door. Noel grabbed for Beau's collar, but the dog had moved with such speed that his hand missed by a foot. Beau was out of the car and running.

Noel yelled, 'Beau! Come!' The command had always been effective, but it did not work this time. Beau sped across the parking lot after the other dog.

The next thing that happened was one of those quirks of timing that can never be anticipated.

The other dog had made a rapid escape and, almost as if he realized the chase was futile, Beau slackened his pace. Just then, from off the

main road, a huge maroon truck with black trim and bundles of laundry piled on the top turned in to make a delivery to the Howard Johnson's. The driver saw Beau in plenty of time to stop easily, but he was tired and annoyed with his job and slammed on the truck's brakes with slightly more pressure than was really necessary. Beau froze at the squeal of tires and his head whipped in the direction of the truck. At that same instant, the driver smacked his hand down on the horn and, from the force of the fast stop, a bundle of dirty sheets rolled forward, dropped onto the truck's hood, and popped open like a parachute.

The combination of the tires screeching, the horn blaring, and the exploding cloud of dirty sheets fused together in Beau's hearing and vision. He panicked.

One time, as he saw the sheets fluttering toward him, he did hear his name being called. He tried very hard to gather that friendly voice of his master into his mind, but the other sounds were overpowering. Beau ran.

He headed away from Noel and out onto the street. There were no cars coming, so he had a clear field. Noel cursed his cigarette-smoking as his breath faltered, but still he kept after his dog. He thought of running back to get the car, but he felt certain Beau would stop at any moment and he would catch up.

Beau, driven by some mysterious force, was not about to stop. He cut off to the other side of the road and headed up the embankment leading to the Interstate Highway. In a couple of seconds he was out of sight over the lip of the embankment. Noel stopped running and stood, panting hard, trying to decide what to do. From up on the highway, a high-pitched, piercing noise of tires made his decision for him: a car had slammed on its brakes; Beau might have been hit.

Noel ran back to his own car as fast as he could, told Sue to take the children into the restaurant, and sped out of the parking lot toward the entrance ramp to the Interstate Highway. In less than two minutes he had reached the area where the brakes had squealed. There was no sign of Beau, but a woman was standing beside her car, which had slid sideways across the highway and come to rest on the rock-covered verge.

Noel pulled up near the woman and stopped. 'Are you okay?'

The woman nodded visibly shaken, but she managed to answer. 'Yes . . . yes . . . thank you,' she said. Then she added, 'Some damned dog just –'

Noel interrupted her. 'Where'd he go?' he demanded.

The woman whirled toward him, her face angry. 'Was that your dog? You ought to be arrested.'

'I'm sorry,' Noel said. 'But where did the dog go?'

The woman glared, but finally pointed a finger across the highway.

Noel dropped the car into 'Drive' and swerved across the grass median. He sped back along the side of the road, looking for his pet.

After searching nervously for several minutes, Noel went back to the restaurant. He told Sue to feed the girls while he looked again for the dog.

He was to spend the next two hours searching for Beau. Finally he had to admit the obvious: the dog was gone. He gave up reluctantly.

He spent another hour with the local police, reporting the loss and reaching out for some encouragement. The Robertses were told to check back by telephone, but little hope was offered: 'There's a lot of dogs out there,' the desk officer had observed. 'No telling if we'll find yours.'

The Roberts family sadly continued their vacation, which no longer seemed to be what they had planned. Beau's departure had left a great void.

The sense of loss was reciprocal. Beau found no pleasure in being on his own.

He had heard his master's frantic voice back in the restaurant parking lot, but there were some commands that Beau simply had to ignore. Anything that interfered with protecting the children could not be obeyed.

The screeching and flying white forms had thrown him into a blind panic, and he had simply run – into a strange countryside with no landmarks. He had stopped at last, and had wandered in confusion until weariness overcame him and he slept. When he awoke the next morning after his exhausting, panic-driven escape, his first sensation of loneliness was instantly replaced with pangs of hunger. He was used to pieces of toast, chunks of bacon, and remains of breakfast eggs as the Roberts children competed to give Beau his morning treats.

After less than five minutes of orientation, Beau headed across a nearby field on a compass bearing of three hundred forty degrees – a straight-line course for the Roberts's home in Chicago. The line of travel was such that it kept him well clear of automobile hazards, yet it passed enough farmhouses and small towns to provide enough garbage for his food needs. It never occurred to him to forage among the available wildlife; predation had not yet surfaced in his personality.

Just south of Seymour, Indiana, he happened across another dog, a young beagle bitch, and they roamed together through the winter. Eventually they found their way to Brown County State Park.

The Fate of Redeye ——————————

Henry Williamson

After serving in the Army through the First World War Henry Williamson, then aged twenty-three, settled in a Devon cottage and began writing his childhood autobiography. The three volumes that resulted, *The Beautiful Years*, *Dandelion Days* and *The Dream of Fair Women*, formed a trilogy under the title *The Flax of Dream*. From time to time he put that work aside to continue on his nature stories, the first collections of which were *The Peregrine's Saga* (1923), *The Old Stag* (1929) and *Tales of Marsh and Estuary* (1932). His two most celebrated novels were *Tarka the Otter* (1927), which won him the Hawthornden Prize, and *Salar the Salmon* (1935).

Perhaps no writer in the world has described the lives and adventures of animals so freshly and with such insight as Henry Williamson. The shorter of the stream of tales which he wrote in his twenties were republished under the title *Collected Nature Stories*, in 1970, when the author was seventy-five. (He died in 1977.) Concluding my review of that book for *Country Life*, I wrote: 'Middleton Murry advised the youthful Williamson not to waste his talent "writing of nature red in tooth and claw". But thankfully for the rest of us, that is how he has spent his time these last fifty years. And as prodigiously as nature.'

Among those tales is a tragic gem called 'Redeye', the lurcher of the title being unfortunate to be chosen in puppyhood by a rough, callous beer-swilling youth by the name of Tom Fitchey, who beats and kicks Redeye on whim and changes him 'from a playful creature into a snarling cur'. In the course of his sad career Redeye makes a bitter enemy of a foxhound called Lightfoot. One day Redeye bitterly disappoints his master by failing to catch a certain hare in country in which there is a scarcity of hares. So Fitchey gives Redeye a vicious kick. That is enough for the lurcher. He deserts Fitchey and mankind in general.

Redeye earns a sinister and widespread reputation as a sheep-stealer. By chance he is hunted by the local foxhounds, is put to ground, kills the terrier sent to bolt him, and flies for his life. His old adversary, Lightfoot, then leads the pack on a very long hunt. This is the denouement:

Sirius, the great star-hound of the winter heavens, woke and yawned silver in his kennel of evening-blue space. Dusk came, and the mighty Dogstar broke the chain of day, and gave tongue in green music, and glared fire i' th' eye, and bounded after Orion, and together they began the hunt of strange spirits over the horizon of time, where no mortal may follow.

But earthly chase lasts not for ever. Under the glimmering stars Tom Fitchey's runaway lurcher slunk into a farmyard not very far from his native village, and avoiding a particular spot between a wall and a haystack, collapsed.

A minute's run away the hound Lightfoot padded mute, nose to ground, on a weak scent. Scent was weak because Redeye was weak – it failed as his strength failed. On the high ground behind him a fog had come with the changing wind, creeping over Exmoor. In twos and threes the pack was wandering home to the kennels at Brendon, led by Moonstone and the lazy ones – Mayfly, Sorrel, Queenie, Trumpeter, Cornflower. Only Lightfoot kept on, with two and a half couple of hounds three minutes behind him – Magpie, Charmian, Pensioner, Emerald and Sundew.

Redeye lay still. A bat passed by the stack. A rat rustled in the straw. The puffy legs twitched. He shivered. It was thus that his old enemy found him, giving a great snarl and rushing at him, stern straight, hackles raised, teeth bared.

Redeye leapt up silently. He sprang a yard over the spot he had avoided, and turned to meet the hound. Lightfoot dashed at him, seized his ear, but was abruptly checked by a metallic snapping noise that seemed to pitch him forward. He gave a scream of pain. A shudder passed over him; then he was snapping wildly the air, Redeye, the straw, his paw, the iron thing that held him. In the dark distance hounds gave tongue, but Redeye had him by the cheek and was tearing the skin. His hackles too were raised. His tail too was straight. The two dogs worried and snarled at each other's throats. Redeye fought with the fury and rage of a mad dog. He was chopped and bitten, but all he cared was to tear out the throat of the hound that had hunted him. He drew back; but Lightfoot did not leap at him. The hound in a whimpering fury of pain and fear snapped at the iron thing that clung to his broken leg, at the chain that held the fox-gin to the peg driven into the ground. He broke his teeth on the steel spring; and now Redeye's teeth sank into his throat, and he had him, worrying, shaking, twisting – *clump, clump, clump* went the fox-gin whose iron teeth had broken the leg bone. The struggles of the trapped hound weakened, but Redeye still shook and worried, his teeth set like those of the gin. His ear was bitten off, but he did not know it, or feel anything. He had the hound by the throat, and only when hair, skin and flesh, grasped in the bite, came away was Lightfoot released. Redeye gulped down the mouthful and slunk away from the dying hound lying twisted across the gin set by the farmer to catch the animal (presumably a fox) that had been taking his fowls.

He slunk away, but half a minute later was loping over field and hedge, with five hounds following, running mute – Magpie, Charmian, Pensioner, Emerald and Sundew.

Muggy saw the beer spilling from the gennulmun's pot, and looked again at the open door, where stood an animal with the light of a smoky oil lamp glazing its eyes.

Hearing the baying of hounds again, and nearer, Tom Fitchey leapt and closed the outer door, just in time. Hounds flung themselves against it, scratching, snarling, and whimpering.

Redeye stood motionless. One forefoot was advanced. His fangs were bared. Only his tail moved downwards, almost imperceptibly, as though with relief. Hounds bayed at the outer door. He stood still on the threshold, facing the lamp. They watched for ten seconds, twenty seconds, half a minute. He never moved. His snarl was fixed. He stared straight. Slowly, very slowly, his tail went down till the tip touched the floor.

Hounds went on baying. Still Redeye stood in the doorway. Tom Fitchey touched him. He fell over dead – run stiff – heart burst and broken – muscles set. He lay as though frozen on the stone floor of the Nightcrow Inn.

Niki

Tibor Dery

The setting for *Niki, the Story of a Dog* – written by the Hungarian author, Tibor Dery, and beautifully translated into English by Edward Hyams in 1958 – is communist Budapest in the late 1940s and early 1950s. Neglected by her owner, a retired colonel of the *ancien regime*, Niki ('a fox terrier, possibly a cross between a wire-haired and a short-haired terrier') is adopted by (or rather adopts) Mr and Mrs Ancsa in the spring of 1948. Janos Ancsa, a highly qualified engineer and a faithful member of the Communist Party, is living with his wife – at the start of the story – in the outer suburbs of Budapest, close to open country. But a new posting obliges them to move into the capital.

Dery graphically describes Niki's passionate attachment to the Ancsas and how, after giving birth to a litter of puppies at the colonel's house, she moves in with the young engineer and his wife, and is sublimely happy – until they transfer to the city. Niki is particularly devoted to Janos Ancsa. Her catalogue of woes begins in earnest when, with no explanation and no trial, her master is sent to prison. Mrs Ancsa, like her husband, adores the bitch. But she is left with very little money and goes through all manner of trials and tribulations in her efforts to feed and exercise and generally succour the young terrier who is bursting with energy and yearning for the wide open spaces of her puppyhood. Almost every day the bitch anticipates her master's return, but in vain.

In the fifth year of Janos Ancsa's imprisonment, a kind friend of Mrs Ancsa's offers to drive her and the terrier to spend a day in the suburban countryside where she and her husband and Niki had been so happy together. Niki lives that day in a state of wild abandoned joy; all her forgotten youth comes flooding back. But, from the moment she returns to Budapest that evening she becomes ill, refusing to eat or play, only moping behind one piece of furniture or another. Mrs Ancsa rightly deduces that the bitch's symptoms are not the effects of any ordinary illness, but are rather the result of her having resigned herself to the fact that the flat in dreaded Budapest, minus the company of her beloved master, is to be her fate for ever. The realization is brought home to her by the conviction that that one ecstatic day in the country can never be repeated. 'She turned in on herself and nursed a desperate sadness that could only lead to an early death.' She dies the day that Janos Ancsa, again with no explanation, is released from prison and reunited with his wife.

It seems almost as though the storyteller is using Niki as a metaphor of her mistress's anguish, so that when Janos returns, the anguish (Niki) can die. The passages which I have repeated are from the account of the Ancsas' going to live in the city and of Niki's difficult adaptation to that existence:

They were not able to move into Budapest until the first couple of weeks in October, that is to say three whole months later than even Mrs Ancsa, in her calm pessimism, had foreseen. . . . The bitch fortunately had not taken any part in the excitement of settling in, that being an exclusively human interest. She adapted herself quite quickly to her new quarters, and, rather more slowly and with a kind of alarmed curiosity, to city life.

The world to which she was introduced was utterly strange to her. During the first few days her tail was constantly between her legs as she walked the streets. She learnt what it was to be on a lead. This, however, she bore very well; indeed, we fancy that she accepted it willingly, for the lead created a direct physical contact with her master or mistress in her state of alarm, and seemed a kind of protection. And it was clear that, in this new place, she needed protection. The protection offered by her owners was, in fact, not enough; for to it she added, in self-defence, an incessant, wild barking. By barking she gave herself courage, just as a bugle call rallies the spirits of troops setting out for war. The more fearful she was, the louder and more furiously she barked. When a tram thundered past her in a clatter of bell-ringing, she was so frightened that she flattened herself, at one bound, against the house walls, thereafter barking bravely after the retreating mastodon. Making herself tense against the resistance of her rigid forepaws, and with her tail sticking out horizontally, the whole of her little white body trembling, she barked so fiercely, seemed so ready to attack and even pursue the monster, that the taut leash almost choked her. She even barked at carts, and she had one kind of bark for the horse, another for the cart. But if a cart stopped near her, drawing up to the kerb, she was so scared that she would almost pull Mrs Ancsa off her feet, in her efforts to reach the shelter of the nearest doorway. She also barked at motorcars but, which was strange, she was less afraid of them than of horses-and-carts. Among these she had established some kind of hierarchy, for she clearly showed more respect for the powerful carthorses of the nationalised industries, than

for the broken-down, half-starved old screws of private enterprise, wretchedly dragging the miserable effects of some family engaged in moving house.

Niki also barked when bicycles passed her, especially when their bells were rung; she barked at pedestrians when there were too many of them together, or when they raised their voices; she barked at every dog, cat or sparrow she saw, using that method of auto-suggestion well known to all animals, as to Shakespeare's great captains declaiming before a battle. In the daytime she barked if light flashed from the pane of an opening window; and at night she barked at shadows. She barked against the entire capital. During her first days in the new days she must have felt much like a young peasant girl who, for the first time, quits her village for a great metropolis.

It was about a week after their establishment in Budapest that the engineer took in hand his bitch's education, or rather adaptation to city life. As it happened, he had ample time, for he was no longer going to his office. About the middle of October, without a word of warning, he had been relieved of his post as Director of the Mining Equipment Factory, and he had not yet been appointed elsewhere. This was as unexpected as it would have been if his wife, after twenty-eight years of conjugal happiness, had suddenly left him. There was no reason for his dismissal, but it had given rise to vague rumours which Ancsa refused to listen to. In August, as a disciplinary measure, he had been obliged to dismiss an office worker of the 'section of workers risen from the ranks,' who was on good terms with a high official of the Party. It was now being said that the latter had scuppered Ancsa by making an unfavourable 'section report' on him, which had caused the responsible but overhasty ministerial department to dismiss him.

Seeking the fault, rather, in himself, Ancsa found dozens, as usually happens in the case of a man afflicted with a sensitive conscience. These examinations of his conscience were usually made in the company of his dog and in the course of long walks, which they took together along the Danube embankment, where there were neither trams nor motorcars to try Niki's nerves, and her imagination, like her muscles, was free to roam at will. There, moreover, she had the chance to make the acquaintance of other dogs, of diverse kinds and conditions. The embankment, of course, was paved, which certainly made it less suitable than the hills of Csobanka for wild racing and giddy leaping. But further afield, up-stream, beyond the church in Pozsonyi Avenue, began an extent of wasteland with a sandy and friable soil in which grew tufts of rust-coloured grass and dwarfish acacia bushes.

That October was fine and sunny: the scents of autumn which rose from the warmed water of the river purified the smoky city air and from time to time the ruddy hills of the Buda bank wafted the scent of dead leaves across the river as a greeting to Pest. When the street lamps were lit the waters of the Danube cradled and rocked their moon-coloured reflections. Or a breath of wind frayed them into slender golden gleams which, riding the barely perceptible waves, were at last lost far out between the two banks.

Sometimes a new companion joined them for their evening walks, new only for the dog, however, for, as we shall see, he was one of the engineer's oldest friends.

He was a giant, well over six feet tall, with a round head covered with short fair hair which had never known a hat; a colossus with a thick, fleshy nose and sticking-out ears. These ears, furthermore, he could move both up and down and backwards and forwards; they were incredibly mobile as if moved by a special set of muscles, a fact which gave much pleasure to children and simple-hearted adults. This man joined the engineer one evening as he was leaving the house for his walk, and his enormous mass frightened the little bitch. At the sight of him she backed away so suddenly that she tumbled off the pavement. And faithful to her method of auto-suggestion, she set up a furious barking.

The man, who was called Jegyes-Molnar, turned round and spent a moment or two examining the excited little hound.

'Is it yours?' he asked the engineer.

During the walk which followed Ancsa's 'Yes', the colossus hardly uttered another word, and if we have been careful to quote the three words he *did* speak, it was to prove that we are not dealing with a deaf-mute. . . .

Jegyes-Molnar, then, uttered barely fifty words in the whole course of the evening. Moreover this was the first time he had come to call on the engineer at his flat. It looks very much as if by thus offering his company – if the mere presence of his physical mass can be so called – his intention was to console Ancsa in his misfortune. Clearly, he did not think that his superiors would take an ill view of his intimacy with the disgraced engineer; or, if he did think so, he did not care. In the course of the following weeks he went to call on his former director every two or three days.

Niki had difficulty in getting used to him. So long as they were all walking along the embankment Niki, busy with other matters, paid the man hardly any attention; but when he sat down next to her master on the steps up to the parapet, she drew near and smelt his feet.

Lowering his massive head, Jegyes-Molnar looked at the bitch in silence, while she went on with her investigation. When, after a few seconds, the bitch raised her eyes to look at Jegyes-Molnar's face, the engineer's friend moved his ears, first up and down, then backwards and forwards.

At first Niki seemed petrified. As usual, the examiner remained silent. But when he again started to waggle his ears, the hair of Niki's coat stood on end and she backed away from him, whining. Jegyes-Molnar stopped moving his ears. Niki looked at him for a while with an air of distrust and then, very cautiously, drew near again, lifting her paws very high as if she were walking among pointed stakes. She was a living picture of close attention. With her head stretched forward and tail stiffly backward, she pricked up both brown ears, which as a rule were left limp, while her black and ferret-like eyes stared at the man's face without blinking. He, then, for the third time, waggled his ears.

The effect of this was unexpected. The bitch, howling, leaping, snapping, into the air, very nearly fell into the water. Then she whipped round and, with her tail between her legs and her ears flat to her head, showing every outward sign of extreme canine terror – the kind of terror only provoked by a threat of eternal damnation – she shot off like a streak of lightning. In a moment she had vanished. The two men remained seated for a few more seconds, and then set out to look for her. The embankment was ill lit and deserted. There was nothing to be heard but the droning of a tram in the Avenue Pozsonyi and, even less often, a motor horn. Ancsa whistled, then called the dog by name in a carrying voice. For an hour they looked for her, but Niki had disappeared. As it might be supposed that once her terror had subsided she would return home, the engineer took leave of his friend, who set off in the direction of Wahrmann Street – subsequently Victor-Hugo Street. Ancsa continued along the embankment. When he got to Rudolf Square, later to bear the name of Mari Jaszai, as we already know, he heard a soft little trotting sound behind him, and the little bitch rejoined him in silence. She was in rather poor shape, her tail hanging low, and her coat wet with sweat. She had no doubt hidden herself until the stranger had left her master and then, having prudently made sure he was not coming back, showed herself when she felt that it was quite safe to do so.

Ancsa was not sorry for what had happened for it enabled him to get a better idea of his bitch's intelligence. The precise observation which had taught her that human beings have not, as a rule, the habit of waggling their ears bore witness to a very advanced knowledge of the human species.

Jegyes-Molnar came back the next day but one, meeting them this time, on the embankment. Niki did not see him at once. She was running a race with an old spaniel much less agile than herself, and amusing herself by turning suddenly in her tracks and leaping clean over her opponent, as if to make fun of him. When she had had enough of this game, the two men were already seated on one of the steps of the parapet, and she ran joyfully up to rejoin them. Being slightly short-sighted she did not at once recognize Jegyes-Molnar. She sniffed at his feet with an air of confidence, but immediately backed away with an expression of alarm.

The colossus did not move. It is perhaps not necessary to say that he did not speak either. Niki looked at him for a moment with an air of suspicion, then lay down at her master's feet while still keeping a close watch on his friend. For a while nothing happened. With his chin resting on his knees Jegyes-Molnar sat perfectly still. Then, suddenly, he moved his ears several times.

'What do you want to frighten her for?' the engineer asked, while Niki in a flash disappeared into the deepening dusk at the far end of the embankment.

After a certain time, with a better knowledge of men than her master, Niki did become accustomed to the ear-waggling and quite clearly became attached to Jegyes-Molnar who went so far, one day, as to pat her head. Niki trembled a little, but accepted his caress.

By that time she had already more or less resigned herself to living in Budapest, although she certainly remained, in her heart of hearts, strongly anti-urban. She showed a very marked antipathy to the major traffic centres, for instance the crossing of the boulevard St Steven and Rudolf (later Mari Jaszai) Square. When, for some reason, her master or mistress had to go that way, she would stop, look at them reproachfully, and refuse to obey, or rather show signs of a slight inclination to disobedience. It would then be necessary to tug at the lead in order to get her four paws, apparently glued to the pavement, into motion again. Furthermore she had difficulty in learning to distinguish the sidewalks from the road proper, no doubt that was a task as arduous for her as his first problem in algebra for a schoolboy. Only the trees planted along the sidewalks were some compensation, for at the base of each she could discern the appetising traces of several days' canine comings and goings. Any one of these tree-trunks conveyed to her, in a form as condensed as a pocket dictionary, more abundant and varied information on the private life of dogs than the whole main street of Csobanka. All the trees in Pozsonyi Avenue, taken together, were equal, for Niki, to one year's issue of a daily newspaper bound up into an album.

Extreme pleasures in large doses are not always salutary for the soul. Niki's behaviour with the trees was like the gluttony of a provincial on a visit to the metropolis. When one of her owners, usually Mrs Ancsa, took Niki walking down Pozsonyi Avenue, the terrier bitch dragged her mistress towards each tree with such eagerness as almost to break the lead. But after a while, saturated with pleasure, she relaxed, seemed almost to shrink in size, and slouched sulkily along behind Mrs Ancsa. The high atmospheric pressure which is usual in great cities has this effect on the healthy and rustic souls of country-folk.

Niki now found herself more in the hands of her mistress, for Ancsa had started work again at the beginning of November. He had been appointed to a rather unimportant machine-making factory in Ujpest. His position there was a subordinate one and his salary indifferent. Even so, the appointment was like a rejuvenating bath, for his enforced idleness amidst the general bustle of work had driven him to the verge of a nervous breakdown. . . .

His wife, by reason of her delicate health, dared not take a job, but she did canvassing for the local branch of the Communist Party, and undertook, in a purely honorary capacity, office work for the Democratic Union of Hungarian Women. The bitch was thus often alone. Abandoned to her own resources in the flat, which was locked up, she would mope on the cushion which had been placed for her in one corner of Mrs Ancsa's room; or, preferably, and although it had been strictly forbidden, in one of the armchairs covered with tobacco-brown rep in the living-room. And whenever Mrs Ancsa came in, even after a very short absence, Niki, drunk with joy, would welcome her with vertical leaps, an endless dance, her tail going like mad and her lungs panting, as if her mistress had returned after a very long journey, and many minutes would have to pass before her enthusiastic exultation subsided. It was impossible for Mrs Ancsa to punish or even to scold her for having dozed, despite the prohibition, in one of the armchairs. Incidentally, how did she guess this? For Niki, the moment she heard the key in the lock, was down on the floor in an instant. And Mrs Ancsa was hardly in the entrance hall when Niki her nerves stretched almost to breaking point, stood whining and trembling immediately behind the living-room door. Yet there were certain details, treacherous and infallible, which denounced her disobedience, notably the fact that the seat of the armchair would still be warm. Mrs Ancsa had only to pass her hand over it to establish her dog's guilt. But the animal would never have been able to grasp the connection, the reasoning from effect to cause, implicit in that movement of her mistress's hand, and a subsequent reprimand. She would have attributed to her mistress – in reality so simple, gentle and, on the whole, commonplace – mysterious and supernatural virtues, with which Mrs Ancsa had not the slightest desire to be credited. Had she, indeed, been willing to put her nose instead of her hand to the seat of the chair, the bitch would have been perfectly ready to suffer a scolding. But the hand – surely the hand could not be the seat of an olfactory organ? Mrs Ancsa did not want to upset Niki. In any case, when she stood by the chair and looked angrily at her dog, or even reproachfully, Niki at once lowered her tail as a mark of repentance, and made herself scarce; or she lay upon her back as a means of imploring forgiveness; and waving her four paws in the air as a sign of unconditional surrender, offered her soft, pink belly to the caress which would express that forgiveness.

Have dogs, or have they not, a conscience? This is a question we should certainly ask, if we knew the answer. As we do not, we confine ourselves to noting it down in the hope that one or other of our readers will know the answer and will have the kindness to convey it to us in a letter. Have dogs a conscience, then; or, more precisely, have they a good or bad conscience? Let us risk a hypothesis: dogs are endowed in this field only with remorse, and this remorse manifests itself in the fear which seizes them after transgressing one of the laws laid down for them. The same phenomenon is far from uncommon among men, as when they complain of the so-called pangs of conscience. But if dogs do not have a bad conscience, it follows that they cannot have a good one, unless by good conscience we mean a total want of any conscience at all, in other words, complete self-satisfaction. That, indeed, is a feeling very often met with among mankind. But if we consider conscience as an active process, which entails everyone keeping an unfailing watch on the world from the point of view of his personal responsibility, constantly deciding what must be done, issuing authorisations or prohibitions, condemning and absolving, guiding his life from the first conscious moment until the last – why, in that case the question whether animals – including Niki – have or have not a conscience, good or bad, should, in our opinion, receive a negative answer, although with reservations. It is in this that animals differ from man; man can, in the long run, develop a conscience. And thus by stating the terms of the problem with the utmost strictness, we are forced to the conclusion that, essentially, it was in this, and only in this, that Niki differed from her master, Janos Ancsa.

COMEDY

A Predilection for Toys ─────────────

J. M. Barrie

Sir James Matthew Barrie (1860–1937) put Nana into *Peter Pan* and his own St Bernard, Porthos, into *The Little White Bird*. 'It was in Lucerne that the Barries first saw that litter of St Bernard puppies,' says Denis Mackail in *The Story of J.M.B.* 'And it was Mrs Barrie, at first, who had simply got to have one. She loved animals, and they loved her, too. But it was Barrie who could put them under another of his own special spells. . . . A year later the Barries visited Kirriemuir, when Porthos, this St Bernard, distinguished and disgraced himself by following them into the South Free Kirk, mounted the pulpit and gazed quietly and nobly at the Congregation.' Back in London Mackail asks us to 'picture the two of them taking Porthos up to Kensington Gardens, Barrie in overcoat and bowler hat as worn by all . . . Mrs Barrie dressed attractively and still looking remarkably young and pretty. Porthos . . . vast, gentle and apparently melancholy, but not really. For he is not delicate yet, as he will become, alas, all too soon. He adores both his master and mistress, and this is one of the happiest times in the day. Watch him. He knows what is going to happen now. There is a toyshop and as he waits outside (he has stopped here as he always does now, and stands waving his tail) one or other of his owners will go in and buy him a toy. He likes dolls even more than a ball to take up to the Gardens. . . .'

Here is Porthos acting himself in *The Little White Bird*:

After waiting several months I decided to buy David a rocking-horse. My St Bernard dog accompanied me, though I have always been diffident of taking him to toy-shops, which overexcite him. Hitherto the toys I had bought had always been for him, and as we durst not admit this to the saleswoman we were both horribly self-conscious when in the shop. A score of times I have told him that he had much better not come; I have announced fiercely that he is not to come. He then lets go of his legs, which is how a St Bernard sits down, making the noise of a sack of coals suddenly deposited, and, laying his head between his front paws, stares at me through the red haws that make his eyes so mournful. He will do this for an hour without blinking, for he knows that in time it will unman me. My dog knows very little, but what little he does know he knows extraordinarily well. One can get out of my chamber by a back way, and I sometimes steal softly –

but I can't help looking back, and there he is, and there are those haws asking sorrowfully, 'Is this worthy of you?'

'Curse you,' I say, 'get your hat,' or words to that effect. . . .

He was a full-grown dog when I first, most foolishly introduced him to toys. I had bought a toy in the street for my own amusement. It represented a woman, a young mother, flinging her little son over her head with one hand and catching him in the other, and I was entertaining myself on the hearth-rug with this pretty domestic scene when I heard an unwonted sound from Porthos, and looking up, I saw on that noble and melancholic countenance a broad grin. I shuddered and was for putting the toy away at once; but he sternly struck down my arm with his, and signed that I was to continue. The unmanly chuckle always came, I found, when the poor lady dropped her babe; but the whole thing entranced him; he tried to keep his excitement down by taking huge draughts of water; he forgot all his niceties of conduct; he sat in holy rapture with the toy between his paws, he took it to bed with him, ate it in the night, and searched for it so longingly next day that I had to go out and buy him the man with the scythe. After that we had everything of note, the bootblack boy, the toper with the bottle, the woolly rabbit that squeaks when you hold it in your mouth; they all vanished as inexplicably as the lady; but I dared not tell him my suspicions, for he suspected also, and his gentle heart would have mourned had I confirmed his fears.

The dame in the temple of toys which we frequented thinks I want them for a little boy, and calls him 'the precious', and 'the lamb', the while Porthos is standing gravely by my side. She is a motherly soul, but overtalkative.

'And how is the dear lamb today?' she begins, beaming.

'Well, ma'am, well,' I say, keeping a tight grip on his collar.

'This blighty weather is not affecting his darling appetite?'

'No, ma'am, not all.' (She would be considerably surprised if informed that he dined today on a sheepshead, a loaf, and three cabbages, and is suspected of a leg of mutton.)

'I hope he loves his toys.'

'He carries them about with him everywhere, ma'am.' (Has the one we bought yesterday with him now, though you might not think it to look at him.)

'What do you say to a box of tools this time?'

'I think not, ma'am.'

'Is the deary fond of digging?'

218

'Very partial to digging.' (We shall find the leg of mutton some day?)

'Then perhaps a weeny spade and a pail?'

She got me to buy a model of Canterbury Cathedral once, she was so insistent, and Porthos gave me his mind about it when we got home. He detests the kindergarten system, and as she is absurdly prejudiced in its favour we have had to try other shops.

Black Gives Cook Away _____

Alexandre Dumas

Notwithstanding the affectionate care given him by the Chevalier who has adopted him, the subject of *Black, the Story of a Dog*, by Alexandre Dumas (1803–70), longs to return to his owner. He tries to sneak out of the garden door and so onto the road that will lead him home. But (according to John Farnbrook's translation):

Whilst the Chevalier occupied himself with a sweet-briar which with his own hands he had budded in the spring, but whose growth seemed to him dubious, Black, who notwithstanding the affectionate care they had given him, appeared glum about something, profited from a wide opening in the garden-door to seek the road that could lead him back to the one he held dear.

Unhappily for his scheme of flight, before he got to the street he had to cross the vestibule and pass the door of the kitchen.

Well, through this door was issuing a smell of roast meat that was truly delectable.

Black wandered into the kitchen, which seemed at first sight deserted.

He looked round for the cause of that odour.

Whilst looking, he suddenly stopped like a dog who has 'found'.

He began to bark at a big cupboard, as if he wanted to accuse that cupboard of hiding what he sought.

Marianne, at the sound of Black's barking, arrived upon the scene.

She already had in her hand her customary weapon; but Monsieur de la Graverie, who had noticed the disappearance of Black, was coming up behind her.

The figure of the Chevalier, with his air of authority, caused the cook to drop the broom.

However, the spaniel, not disturbed by what was going on, so intent was he, continued to bark with fury at the cupboard.

Monsieur de la Graverie flung open its double doors, and to his amazement discovered a cuirassier, who, recognizing in the Chevalier the master of the house, respectfully raised his hand to his helmet – which as everyone knows, is the military salute.

Marianne let herself fall upon a chair as if about to swoon.

The Chevalier understood the whole thing.

But instead of letting himself fly into measureless anger, he sensed at once the use he could make of the occasion.

He gave a caress of thanks to the dog, and bade Marianne follow him. He led her no farther than the vestibule.

There he stopped, and in a grave voice,

'Marianne,' said he, 'you get from me 300 francs in wages, and you steal 600 . . .'

Marianne tried to interrupt the Chevalier; but he stopped her with a gesture of conviction.

'You steal 600,' he went on, 'to which I shut my eyes; this gives you the best place in town; and what's more, I alone know how to put up with your unendurable character; you have just deserved to be dismissed without a reference; I shall not drive you away.'

Marianne tried to interrupt her master to thank him.

'Wait! My indulgence carries its conditions.'

Marianne bowed, to indicate she was ready to pass beneath the Caudine Forks which it pleased her master to set up.

'Here,' solemnly continued the Chevalier, 'here is a dog that I found; for reasons I need not tell you, I intend to keep him, and moreover, I wish him to be happy here; if, in consequence of your gossip, somebody gets this dog back; if, through the dislike you bear him he should fall ill; finally, if as the result of your calculated negligence he should escape, I give you my word of honour you shall immediately leave my house.

'And now, Marianne, you can, if you please, go and find your cuirassier again. I have been a soldier myself,' said the Chevalier, straightening up, 'and I am not prejudiced against the military.'

Marianne was ashamed of having been caught *in flagrante delicto*; there was such a tone of firmness and resolution in the Chevalier's words that she turned on her heels without a word and went back into the kitchen.

As for the Chevalier, he was enchanted with this episode, which, with his other safeguards, seemed to assure him the tranquil possession of the spaniel.

He was not deceived.

From that day onward, there began for Chevalier Dieudonné and his four-footed friend a life beatific in every respect.

Noble and the Empty Hole ⸻

Henry Ward Beecher

Henry Ward Beecher was no ordinary theologian, but was widely regarded as one of the ablest orators and preachers of his day. Passionately anti-slavery, he was a close adviser to Lincoln during the War Between the States. He possessed a strong tongue-in-the-cheek sense of humour, too, exemplified by this sketch:

The first summer which we spent in Lennox, we had along a very intelligent Dog, named Noble. He was learned in many things, and by his dog-lore excited the undying admiration of all the children. But there were some things which Noble could never learn. Having on one occasion seen a Red Squirrel run into a hole in a stone wall, he could not be persuaded that he was not there for evermore.

Several Red Squirrels lived close to the house, and had become familiar, but not tame. They kept up a regular romp with Noble. They would come down from the maple trees with provoking coolness; they would run along the fence almost within reach; they would cock their tails and sail across the road to the barn; and yet there was such a well-timed calculation under all this apparent rashness, that Noble invariably arrived at the critical spot just as the Squirrel left it.

On one occasion, Noble was so close upon his red-backed friend that, unable to get up the maple tree, the Squirrel dodged into a hole in the wall, ran through the chinks, emerged at a little distance, and sprang into the tree. The intense enthusiasm of the Dog at that hole can hardly be described. He filled it full of barking. He pawed and scratched as if undermining a bastion. Standing off at a little distance, he would pierce the hole with a gaze as intense and fixed as if he were trying magnetism on it. Then, with tail extended, and every hair

thereon electrified, he would rush at the empty hole with a prodigious onslaught.

The imaginary Squirrel haunted Noble night and day. The very Squirrel himself would run up before his face into the tree, and, crouched in a crutch, would sit silently watching the whole process of bombarding the empty hole, with great sobriety and relish. But Noble would allow of no doubts. His conviction that that hole had a Squirrel in it continued unshaken for six weeks. When all other occupations failed, this hole remained to him. When there were no more Chickens to harry, no Pigs to bite, no Cattle to chase, no children to romp with, no expeditions to make with the grown folks, and when he had slept all that his dogskin would hold, he would walk out of the yard, yawn and stretch himself, and then look wistfully at the hole, as if thinking to himself, 'Well, as there is nothing else to do, I may as well try that hole again.'

Thy Servant ———————————

Rudyard Kipling

Master, this is Thy Servant. He is rising eight weeks old.
He is mainly Head and Tummy. His legs are uncontrolled.
But Thou hast forgiven his ugliness, and settled him on
   Thy knee . . .
Art Thou content with Thy servant? He is *very* comfy with Thee.

Master, behold a Sinner! He hath done grievous wrong.
He hath defiled Thy Premises through being kept in too long.
Wherefore his nose has been rubbed in the dirt and his self-
   respect has been bruised.
Master, pardon Thy Sinner, and see he is properly loosed.

Master – again Thy Sinner! This that was once Thy Shoe,
He hath found and taken and carried aside, as fitting matter to
   chew.
Now there is neither blacking nor tongue, and the Housemaid has
   us in tow.
Master, remember Thy Servant is young, and tell her to let him
   go!

Master, pity Thy Servant! He is deaf and three parts blind,
He cannot catch Thy Commandments. He cannot read Thy Mind.
Oh, leave him not in his loneliness; nor make him that kitten's
   scorn.
He has had no other God than Thee since the year that he was
   born!

Lord, look down on Thy Servant! Bad things have come to pass,
There is no heat in the midday sun nor health in the wayside
   grass.
His bones are full of an old disease – his torments run and
   increase.
Lord, make haste with Thy Lightnings and grant him a quick
   release!

A Scottie and a Cairn

Mazo de la Roche

The Canadian novelist, Mazo de la Roche, who was born in 1885, was an ardent animal lover. A very shy, sensitive woman, she hated the years of childhood and early youth she was obliged to spend in her native Toronto. But she soon shared – with a cousin – a country cottage, where they kept horses and dogs. They lived in poverty, however, until Mazo's sequence of Jalna books reached the bestseller lists. This excerpt from her story 'April Day' is typical of her buoyant style:

It was seven in the morning and the Scottie and the Cairn knew that it would soon be time to get up. They heard stirrings in the house below. They slept on the top floor in the dressing-room between the bedrooms of their mistresses, Zia and Cara. The two round dog baskets, with the cretonne cushions exactly alike, stood side by side. Dan, the Scottie, was able to look into Robbie's face.

Out of his almond-shaped eyes that were set high in his hard brindle head, Dan gazed lovingly into Robbie's face, veiled in fine grey hair which stood in tremulous half-curls on his brow, curved into a tiny moustache on his lip, and turned velvet and close on his ears.

Robbie knew that Dan was staring at him, for, at this moment, he wanted nothing but to be let alone. He was savouring the last delicious

doze before the moment when he would spring out of his basket. He kept his eyes shut tight. His head rested against the side of the basket, helpless-looking, like a little child's.

Dan stared and stared. A quiver ran down his spine, making the tip of his tail vibrate. He was sixteen months old and Robbie had had his first birthday last week. Dan seemed much the older, for he often had a dour look. He poured out his soul in love to Robbie all day long.

Now a felt-slippered step shuffled outside the door and it opened a little way. The cook put in her head. 'Come, boys, come now, time to get up,' she said and held the door open wide enough for them to pass through.

Dan jumped from his basket and reared himself on his hind legs. He waved his forepaws at the cook, but she had barely a word for him. Robbie was her charmer.

Now, as he coyly descended the stairs behind her, she encouraged him with endearments. At each landing he lay on his back and rolled, talking to himself in a low pleasant growl.

'Come along, darling, do,' urged the cook, halfway down the stairs, but she had to plod back to the landing to persuade him.

Dan had gone down the two flights of stairs like a bullet. Now he stood waiting by the open front door, looking back over his shoulder. When Robbie reached the bottom step, Dan ran out and Robbie after him.

They went to their usual place under the weeping rose tree that was newly in leaf. The sun had just risen above the great shoulder of the nearest hill. The spring morning lay spread before them, to the distant mountains of Wales.

Shoulder to shoulder they trotted round the house and up the slope, pushing aside the faces of daffodils and narcissus, hastening a little as they neared the denseness of trees. Among the trees there was a moist mossy twilight and across it flitted the brown hump of a young rabbit. Dan saw it first. He gave a cry, as of agony, and hurled himself into the wood. With a little moan of bewilderment, Robbie flew after him, not yet knowing what he chased.

Head to tail, they dived into the green twilight. The rabbit whirled beneath the prickly fortress of a holly bush. Out of the other side it flew, skimming the wet grass, its ears flat in stark terror. Dan circled the holly bush, screaming. . . .

Now Robbie was sure that what they were pursuing had escaped, though he had never known what it was. He stood pensive for a moment, listening to Dan's screams, then drifted back toward the house. He found the front door shut, as the cook did against their return, so he went to the green knoll outside the kitchen window and sat there under the green-and-white spread of the sycamore tree. He looked imploringly, from under his fine fringe, into the window at the cook bending over the range, at the maid putting on her cap, tucking her curls beneath it.

He heard the clump of a step on the cobbled path and saw the milkman coming with his carrier of milk. It was a shock to find that he had drawn so near without molestation. Robbie hurled himself down the knoll, screaming and champing at the milkman's legs. The cook came out of the kitchen calling:

'Robbie! Robbie! He won't hurt you! he's as gentle as a lamb!'

She said that every morning to the milkman who never believed her but came on grumbling. The cook picked Robbie up and he let his head rest against her bosom. She still held him for a moment after the milkman had gone. He was patient but he wanted to go upstairs.

As soon as she put him down he glided along the hall and up the two flights of stairs. He scratched on the door of the dressing-room. Zia opened it and she told him how good and beautiful he was. He lay on his back looking up at them gently but haughtily, savouring their homage. His pointed grey paws hung quiet.

He saw the gas fire burning and stretched himself before it.

At first Dan did not miss Robbie, then suddenly realized that he had gone back to the house. What might not Robbie be doing without him? He tore across the grass, found the front door shut and barked insistently till it was opened by the maid.

On his short legs he pulled himself up the stairs and scratched peremptorily on the door of the dressing-room. Inside he reared and walked on his hind legs for a few steps with the sturdy grace of a pony stallion. He rolled his eyes towards the cupboard where the big glass marble lived. Zia went to the cupboard.

'Oh, must he have that?' said Cara. 'It makes such a noise.'

'He says he must,' said Zia. She laid the glass marble with the silver bear in its middle, on the floor.

With a growl of joy, Dan pounced on it. He struck it with his paw, then bounded after it. Up and down the room he chased it, pushing it swiftly with his nose then panting after it, banging it against the wall and, at last, between Robbie's paws.

Robbie hated the marble with a bitter hatred. The rolling and the noise of it made him feel sick. Now he lay, with half-closed eyes, guarding it between his paws. Dan looked up into Zia's face.

'Robbie's got my ball,' his look said.

'Get it, then,' said Zia.

Dan approached Robbie tremblingly, pretending he was afraid or really being afraid.

Zia gave him back the marble. He struck it with his muzzle, then flew after it growling. After a little he began to gnaw it.

'Enough!' said Zia, taking it from him. 'You'll ruin your teeth.'

The four went down to breakfast. The dogs' plates stood waiting, filled with bits of hard-toasted brown bread. They crunched in delight, Dan's tail waving, Robbie's laid close. The moment they had finished they ran to the table to beg. Dan sat staring up out of glowing eyes. Cara dropped bits of bacon to him which he caught with a snap. Robbie mounted the arm of the settee behind Zia's chair. He put his paws on her shoulder and his cheek close to hers, so that she gave him bits of roll and honey.

At the first whiff of cigarette smoke Dan clambered into his basket and Robbie established himself on the fender stool, with his back turned to the table. He wore a look of disdain. . . .

Now there was shopping and they sat alone in the car while Zia and Cara went into the shops. It was lonely in the car. Dan attended to his paws, licking them till his nails shone like ebony. Sometimes, by mistake, licking the cushion of the car. Robbie never licked his paws. He ignored sore spots which Dan would have licked incessantly. So, to pass the time, Robbie gnawed the polished wood of the window frame. They were nearly home when Cara discovered the tooth-marks. 'Which of you did this,' she demanded sternly.

Dan looked guilty, contrite, but Robbie knew nothing about it. His eyes spoke innocence from under his silken fringe. Cara smacked the top of Dan's lean flat skull. He burrowed into the corner, ashamed.

Presently Robbie's thoughts returned to the window frame and he gave it a last gnaw as they passed through the gate.

'So – it was you, Robbie!' cried Cara. 'Oh, poor Dan, why were you so silly?' She pulled Dan from his corner and patted him. Robbie leaped lightly from the car when it stopped and, pursued by Dan, sped into the wilderness. Soon they were chasing a rabbit and Dan's screams echoed among the trees.

They came back in time for tea. They stood shoulder to shoulder, yearning toward the teapot. They had their saucers of weak tea, then got into the basket together and slept.

The gardener stood, strong and bent in the corner of the room, the loam scraped from his boots, his hands washed clean.

'Thur's been fowls killed,' he said, 'seven of 'em. Some time this marnin', it were. I think one o' our little fellers done it.'

Cara turned pale. 'How awful! Are you sure it was one of ours?'

'Thur's been no other on t' place, ma'am. T'gates is all shut fast.'

He bent over the basket and with his gentle thick hand lifted Dan's lip and looked at the double row of white teeth laid evenly together, a little underhung, but not much.

'Nubbut there.'

As gently but less cautiously he looked in Robbie's mouth. Quickly he folded down the soft lip. ''Tis him for sartin,' he said quietly. 'There's a bit of feather between his teeth. I'm not surprised, ma'am. He killed one once before. I caught him at it. He thinks they didn't orter be running' in t'orchard. But 'tis only a puppy. Don't you fret. He'll not do it again.'

Robbie looked coyly up at them. He laid a pointed paw on each side of his face and looked up lovingly into Cara's eyes.

'He'll never do it again,' comforted the gardener.

As the sun slanted in the west window and the children were getting ready for bed, Dan and Robbie went to the nursery for their evening play. Dan romped with the children. He was rough with them, but they must not pull him about. 'Have a care how you handle me!' his warning growl came.

Robbie drifted about, always just outside the game. But, when the children caught him, he surrendered himself to be held uncomfortably in small arms, to be dandled on small hard knees.

Towards evening the air had become warmer. Without question the birds and flowers opened their hearts to the summer. Starlings walked about the lawn, staring into daisy faces. Dan and Robbie lay before the door serenely facing the great spread of hills unrolled before them. Their sensitive nostrils put aside the smell of the wallflower and drank in what rich animal scents came their way.

They lay as still as carven dogs except for the faint fluttering of the hair on Robbie's crown. Dan faced the breeze with head stark, neck arched and thick like a little stallion.

When two gypsy women clumped up the drive selling mimosa the dogs did not bark but watched their coming and their going tranquilly. They were steeped in the new sweet warmth of the evening.

But when they were turned out for a last run before bedtime, it was different. The air came sharply from the highest hill. The earth sent its quickness up into them. Robbie ran into the wildwood but Dan found a hedgehog and worked himself into a rage before its prickles. Cara and Zia found him in the blackness beneath a yew tree and turned the beam of an electric torch on him. On the bright green of grass the hedgehog sat like a bundle of autumn leaves, impervious.

'Open up! Open up!' shouted Dan, his teeth wet and gleaming.

Robbie came drifting out of the shrubbery and sat down watching the pair, knowing the hopelessness of the onslaught. Dan put his nose against the prickles, and started back, shouting still louder: 'Open up! Open up!'

But the hedgehog held itself close, impervious as a burr.

'Enough!' said Zia and tucked Dan under her arm.

Cara pounced on Robbie. The hedgehog was left to his dreams.

Snug in their baskets they lay in the dressing-room, the velvet darkness pressing closer and closer. Dan lay stretched as though running but Robbie's four feet lay bunched close together. His head was thrown back, his ears tilted alert for the whispering of dreams. What did he hear? The cry of a rabbit in a trap? Or some ghostly cackle from the poultry-yard?

He woke. He sat up in his basket and uttered a loud accusing bark at what had disturbed him. His own voice was comforting. He had never before barked so sonorously, so much like Dan. The comfort of the barking gave him a deep peace. He kept on and on. Cara came in at the door. She turned on the light.

Robbie looked at her wonderingly, his little head pillowed on his pointed paw. Dan gave a sheepish grin and hung his head. He had got out of his basket to meet her.

'Naughty, naughty, naughty!' said Cara. 'Back to your bed, Dan! Not another bark out of you!'

Dan slunk back to his basket, curled himself close. . . .

The shadows would not let Robbie be. Out of them came mysterious things to disturb him. He went to the open window and sat on the ledge, framed in ivy. He barked steadily on an even more sonorous note. He had lovely sensations. He felt that he could go on till dawn.

But he heard the door of Cara's room open and, in one graceful leap, he was back in his basket. Small and stern, Cara entered the room. In her room Zia was lying with the blankets over her head. In shame Dan went to meet Cara.

'It is the end, Dan,' she said mournfully. 'You must go into the box-room by yourself.'

She took his basket and he humbly followed her, stopping only to nuzzle Robbie as he passed. She put him in the furthest, darkest corner of the box-room where, if he did bark, he would scarcely be heard. She went back to bed. There was beautiful quiet. Zia uncovered her head.

Robbie was alone now and he gave full vent to the trouble that was in him. He forgot all but the mournful majesty of his barking as he sat on the window ledge.

When Cara came into the room he disregarded her till she took him into her arms. Then he laid his head confidingly on her shoulder and gave himself up to what might befall. It befell that he was laid on the foot of her bed. It seemed almost too good to be true. Everywhere there was peace and slumber.

At half past seven the cook heavily mounted the stairs. She opened the door of the dressing-room and saw the one empty basket. She knocked on Cara's door and opened it.

'Half past seven, madam,' she said, 'and I can't find the puppies at all!'

'Dan is in the box-room. Robbie is here.'

Dan and Robbie met in the passage. They kissed, then pranced about each other joyfully. They nipped the cook's ankles as they descended the stairs. Another April day had begun!

Please Pass the Biscuit ———————

Ogden Nash

Here are two samples of the wit of one of America's greatest writers of light verse:

> I have a little dog,
> Her name is Spangle.
> And when she eats
> I think she'll strangle.
>
> She's darker than Hamlet,
> Lighter than Porgy;
> Her heart is gold,
> Her odour, dorgy.

Her claws click-click
Across the floor,
Her nose is always
Against a door.

The squirrel flies
Her pursuing mouth;
Should he fly north;
She pursues him south.

Yet do not mock her
As she hunts;
Remember, she caught
A milkman once.

Like liquid gems
Her eyes burn clearly;
She's five years old,
And house-trained, nearly.

Her shame is deep
When she has erred;
She dreads the blow
Less than the word.

I marvel that such
Small ribs as these
Can cage such vast
Desire to please.

She's as much a part
Of the house as the mortgage;
Spangle, I wish you
A ripe old dortage.

For a Good Dog

Ogden Nash

My little dog ten years ago
Was arrogant and spry,
Her backbone was a bended bow
For arrows in her eye.
Her step was proud, her bark was loud,
Her nose was in the sky,
But she was ten years younger then,
And so, by God, was I.

Small birds on stilts along the beach
Rose up with piping cry,
And as they flashed beyond her reach
I thought to see her fly.
If natural law refused her wings,
That law she would defy,
For she could hear unheard-of things,
And so, at times, could I.

Ten years ago she split the air
To seize what she could spy;
Tonight she bumps against a chair,
Betrayed by milky eye.
She seems to pant, Time up, time up!
My little dog must die,
And lie in dust with Hector's pup;
So, presently, must I.

In Smiler's Youth

G. Clifford Ambler

Smiler was written and illustrated by G. Clifford Ambler and published in 1947. The hunt terrier, who is at once narrator and actor of the title-role and who 'wears the wide, engaging grin which earned him his name', is sent with two foxhound puppies – to complete his education – to a farm. He is taken to market 'to help with handling stock to and from the farm' and, there, stolen and bundled off to a remote mining village far from home. After a series of ups and downs he finishes his autobiography on a farm in the Lake District. This extract comes from his account of his puppyhood:

Merriment's children were a very nice lot except for one dog puppy, who was rather a nasty, mean piece of work. He would shriek to heaven if he got nipped in a scuffle, and always tried to get the best place at feeding-time; and then, when everyone was tired and wanted a sleep, he would creep round behind one and nip as hard as he could – and puppy milk-teeth are sharp! – and then run to mother for protection.

However, we cured him; or, at any rate, put him on the way to

improvement. There was a water-trough in the corner of the paddock, just deep enough for it to be difficult to climb out of, and one day when he had been particularly nasty we hustled him round to this trough and – pushed him in, and when he tried to climb out, pushed him back, till he just sat down in the middle and yelled so that the kennelboy heard him and came and lifted him out and welted him for making the water dirty! After that his manners improved quite a lot.

By this time both Merriment and my mother were feeling the strain of feeding their families, and we children were left more and more to ourselves.

The kennelboy used to feed us two or three times a day – porridge and gravy as a rule, and jolly good stuff it was too!

Here, too, I had my first lesson in ratting. It was a hot afternoon, and we were lying about in the shade of the kennel wall, when I saw something move in a patch of nettles near the water-trough.

As I watched a big old rat pushed its head out, and seeing only a few sleepy puppies, made his way quite brazenly across the yard in the direction of the stables. Then, as he reached about the halfway mark, I felt a rush from behind me, and in a flash my mother had him by the neck. One snap and it was done. The rat just hadn't a chance, and after a final shake to make sure, she threw it to one side and came back to finish her sleep.

Oh! very neat and very businesslike mother was, I can tell you!

The Pekinese _____

E. V. Lucas

Edward Verrall Lucas (1868–1938), essayist, biographer and some-time assistant editor of *Punch*, wrote this of those privileged canine products of Imperial China:

> The Pekinese
> Adore their ease
> And slumber like the dead;
> In comfort curled
> They view the world
> As one unending bed.

Labrador with a Tin-Can Fetish ——————

James Herriot

Perhaps the most successful British animal writer since the Second World War has been James Herriot, who began practising as a veterinary surgeon in North Yorkshire in the 1930s, returning to the same work after his wartime service with the RAF. To date, Mr Herriot has seven highly amusing bestsellers behind him. My quote is from *The Lord God Made them All*:

In the semi-darkness of the surgery passage I thought it was a hideous growth dangling from the side of the dog's face but as he came closer I saw that it was only a condensed-milk can. Not that condensed-milk cans are commonly found sprouting from dogs' cheeks, but I was relieved because I knew I was dealing with Brandy again.

I hoisted him on to the table. 'Brandy, you've been at the dustbin again.'

The big golden Labrador gave me an apologetic grin and did his best to lick my face. He couldn't manage it since his tongue was jammed inside the can, but he made up for it by a furious wagging of tail and rear end.

'Oh, Mr Herriot, I am sorry to trouble you again.' Mrs Westby, his attractive young mistress, smiled ruefully. 'He just won't keep out of that dustbin. Sometimes the children and I can get the cans off ourselves but this one is stuck fast. His tongue is trapped under the lid.'

'Yes . . . yes . . .' I eased my finger along the jagged edge of the metal. 'It's a bit tricky, isn't it? We don't want to cut his mouth.'

As I reached for a pair of forceps I thought of the many other occasions when I had done something like this for Brandy. He was one of my patients, a huge, lolloping, slightly goofy animal, but this dustbin raiding was becoming an obsession.

He liked to fish out a can and lick out the tasty remnants, but his licking was carried out with such sudden dedication that he burrowed deeper and deeper until he got stuck. Again and again he had been freed by his family or myself from fruit-salad cans, corned-beef cans, baked-bean cans, soup cans. There didn't seem to be any kind of can he didn't like.

I gripped the edge of the lid with my forceps and gently bent it back along its length till I was able to lift it away from the tongue. An instant later, that tongue was slobbering all over my cheek as Brandy expressed his delight and thanks.

'Get back, you daft dog!' I said, laughing, as I held the panting face away from me.

'Yes, come down, Brandy.' Mrs Westby hauled him from the table and spoke sharply. 'It's all very fine making a fuss now, but you're becoming a nuisance with this business. It will have to stop.'

The scolding had no effect on the lashing tail and I saw that his mistress was smiling. You just couldn't help liking Brandy, because he was a great ball of affection and tolerance without an ounce of malice in him.

I had seen the Westby children – there were three girls and a boy – carrying him around by the legs, upside down, or pushing him in a pram, sometimes dressed in baby clothes. Those youngsters played all sorts of games with him, but he suffered them all with good humour. In fact I am sure he enjoyed them.

Brandy had other idiosyncracies apart from his fondness for dustbins.

I was attending the Westby cat at their home one afternoon when I noticed the dog acting strangely. Mrs Westby was sitting knitting in an armchair while the oldest girl squatted on the hearth rug with me and held the cat's head.

It was when I was searching my pockets for my thermometer that I noticed Brandy slinking into the room. He wore a furtive air as he moved across the carpet and sat down with studied carelessness in front of his mistress. After a few moments he began to work his rear end gradually up the front of the chair towards her knees. Absently she took a hand from her knitting and pushed him down but he immediately restarted his backward ascent. It was an extraordinary mode of progression, his hips moving in a very slow rumba rhythm as he elevated them inch by inch, and all the time the golden face was blank and innocent as though nothing at all was happening.

Fascinated, I stopped hunting for my thermometer and watched. Mrs Westby was absorbed in an intricate part of her knitting and didn't seem to notice that Brandy's bottom was now firmly parked on her shapely knees which were clad in blue jeans. The dog paused as though acknowledging that phase one had been successfully completed, then ever so gently he began to consolidate his position, pushing his way up the front of the chair with his fore limbs till at one time he was almost standing on his head.

It was at that moment, just when one final backward heave would have seen the great dog ensconced on her lap that Mrs Westby finished the tricky bit of knitting and looked up.

'Oh, really, Brandy, you are silly!' She put a hand on his rump and sent him slithering disconsolately to the carpet where he lay and looked at her with liquid eyes.

'What was all that about?' I asked.

Mrs Westby laughed. 'Oh, it's these old blue jeans. When Brandy first came here as a tiny puppy I spent hours nursing him on my knees and I used to wear the jeans a lot then. Ever since, even though he's a grown dog, the very sight of the things makes him try to get on my knees.'

'But he doesn't just jump up?'

'Oh no,' she said. 'He's tried it and got ticked off. He knows perfectly well that I can't have a huge labrador on my lap.'

'So now it's the stealthy approach, eh?'

She giggled. 'That's right. When I'm preoccupied – knitting or reading – sometimes he manages to get nearly all the way up, and if he's been playing in the mud he makes an awful mess and I have to go and change. That's when he really does receive a scolding.'

A patient like Brandy added colour to my daily round. When I was walking my own dog I often saw him playing in the fields by the river. One particularly hot day many of the dogs were taking to the water either to chase sticks or just to cool off, but whereas they glided in and swam off sedately, Brandy's approach was unique.

I watched as he ran up to the river bank, expecting him to pause before entering. But instead he launched himself outwards, legs splayed in a sort of swallow dive, and hung for a moment in the air rather like a flying fox before splashing thunderously into the depths. To me it was the action of a completely happy extrovert.

On the following day in those same fields I witnessed something even more extraordinary. There is a little children's playground in one corner – a few swings, a roundabout and a slide. Brandy was disporting himself on the slide.

For this activity he had assumed an uncharacteristic gravity of expression and stood calmly in the queue of children. When his turn came he mounted the steps, slid down the metal slope, all dignity and importance, then took a staid walk round to rejoin the queue.

The little boys and girls who were his companions seemed to take him for granted, but I found it difficult to tear myself away. I could have watched him all day.

I often smiled to myself when I thought of Brandy's antics, but I didn't smile when Mrs Westby brought him into the surgery a few months later. His bounding ebullience had disappeared and he dragged himself along the passage to the consulting room.

As I lifted him on to the table I noticed that he had lost a lot of weight.

'Now, what is the trouble, Mrs Westby?'

She looked at me worriedly. 'He's been off colour for a few days now, listless and coughing and not eating very well, but this morning he seems quite ill and you can see he's starting to pant.'

'Yes . . . yes . . .' As I inserted the thermometer I watched the rapid rise and fall of his rib cage and noted the gaping mouth and anxious eyes. 'He does look very sorry for himself.'

His temperature was 104°F. I took out my stethoscope and ausculated his lungs. I have heard of an old Scottish doctor describing a seriously ill patient's chest as sounding like a 'kist o' whustles' and that just about described Brandy's. Râles, wheezes, squeaks and bubblings – they were all there against a background of laboured respiration.

I put the stethoscope back in my pocket. 'He's got pneumonia.'

'Oh dear,' Mrs Westby reached out and touched the heaving chest. 'That's bad, isn't it?'

'Yes, I'm afraid so.'

'But . . .' She gave me an appealing glance. 'I understand it isn't so fatal since the new drugs came out.'

I hesitated. 'Yes, that's quite right. In humans and most animals the sulpha drugs and now penicillin have changed the picture completely, but dogs are still very difficult to cure.'

Thirty years later it is still the same. Even with all the armoury of antibiotics which followed penicillin – streptomycin, the tetracyclines, and synthetics, and the new non-antibiotic drugs and steroids – I still hate to see pneumonia in a dog.

'But you don't think it's hopeless?' Mrs Westby asked.

'No, no, not at all. I'm just warning you that so many dogs don't respond to treatment when they should. But Brandy is young and strong. He must stand a fair chance. I wonder what started this off, anyway.'

'Oh, I think I know, Mr Herriot. He had a swim in the river about a week ago. I try to keep him out of the water in this cold weather but if he sees a stick floating he just takes a dive into the middle. You've seen him – it's one of the funny little things he does.'

'Yes, I know. And was he shivery afterwards?'

'He was. I walked him straight home, but it was such a freezing cold day, I could feel him trembling as I dried him down.'

I nodded. 'That would be the cause, all right. Anyway, let's start his treatment. I'm going to give him this injection of penicillin and I'll call at your house tomorrow to repeat it. He's not well enough to come to the surgery.'

'Very well, Mr Herriot. And is there anything else?'

'Yes, there is. I want you to make him what we call a pneumonia jacket. Cut two holes in an old blanket for his forelegs and stitch him into it along the back. You can use an old sweater if you like, but he must have his chest warmly covered. Only let him out in the garden for necessities.'

I called and repeated the injection on the following day. There wasn't much change. I injected him for four more days and the realization came to me sadly that Brandy was like so many of the others – he wasn't responding. The temperature did drop a little but he hardly ate anything and grew gradually thinner. I put him on sulphapyridine tablets, but they didn't seem to make any difference.

As the days passed and he continued to cough and pant and to sink deeper into a blank-eyed lethargy, I was forced more and more to the conclusion which, a few weeks ago, would have seemed impossible: that this happy, bounding animal was going to die.

But Brandy didn't die. He survived. You couldn't put it any higher than that. His temperature came down and his appetite improved and he climbed on to a plateau of twilight existence where he seemed content to stay.

'He isn't Brandy any more,' Mrs Westby said one morning a few weeks later when I called in. Her eyes filled with tears as she spoke.

I shook my head. 'No, I'm afraid he isn't. Are you giving him the halibut-liver oil?'

'Yes, every day. But nothing seems to do him any good. Why is he like this, Mr Herriot?'

'Well, he has recovered from a really virulent pneumonia, but it's left him with a chronic pleurisy, adhesions and probably other kinds of lung damage. It looks as though he's just stuck there.'

She dabbed at her eyes. 'It breaks my heart to see him like this. He's only five, but he's like an old, old dog. He was so full of life, too.' She sniffed and blew her nose. 'When I think how I used to scold him for getting into the dustbins and muddying up my jeans. How I wish he would do some of his funny old tricks now.'

I thrust my hands deep into my pockets. 'Never does anything like that now, eh?'

'No, no, just hangs about the house. Doesn't even want to go for a walk.'

As I watched, Brandy rose from his place in the corner and pottered slowly over to the fire. He stood there for a moment, gaunt and dead-eyed, and he seemed to notice me for the first time because the end of his tail gave a brief twitch before he coughed, groaned and flopped down on the hearth rug.

Mrs Westby was right. He was like a very old dog.

'Do you think he'll always be like this?'

I shrugged. 'We can only hope.'

But as I got into my car and drove away I really didn't have much hope. I have seen calves with lung damage after bad pneumonias. They recovered but were called 'bad doers' because they remained thin and listless for the rest of their lives. Doctors, too, had plenty of 'chesty' people on their books; they were, more or less, in the same predicament.

Weeks and then months went by and the only time I saw the Labrador was when Mrs Westby was walking him on his lead. I always had the impression that he was reluctant to move and his mistress had to stroll along very slowly so that he could keep up with her. The sight of him saddened me when I thought of the lolloping Brandy of old, but I told myself that at least I had saved his life. I could do no more for him now and I made a determined effort to push him out of my mind.

In fact I tried to forget Brandy and managed to do fairly well until one afternoon in February. On the previous night I felt I had been through the fire. I had treated a colicky horse until 4 a.m. and was crawling into bed, comforted by the knowledge that the animal was settled down and free from pain, when I was called to a calving. I had managed to produce a large live calf from a small heifer, but the effort had drained the last of my strength and when I got home it was too late to return to bed.

Ploughing through the morning round I was so tired that I felt disembodied, and at lunch Helen watched me anxiously as my head nodded over my food. There were a few dogs in the waiting-room at two o'clock and I dealt with them mechanically, peering through half-closed eyelids. By the time I reached my last patient I was almost asleep on my feet. In fact I had the feeling that I wasn't there at all.

'Next, please,' I mumbled as I pushed open the waiting-room door and stood back waiting for the usual sight of a dog being led out to the passage.

But this time there was a big difference. There was a man in the doorway all right and he had a little poodle with him, but the thing that made my eyes snap wide open was that the dog was walking upright on his hind limbs.

I knew I was half-asleep but surely I wasn't seeing things. I stared down at the dog, but the picture hadn't changed – the little creature strutted through the doorway, chest out, head up, as erect as a soldier.

'Follow me, please,' I said hoarsely and set off over the tiles to the consulting room. Halfway along I just had to turn round to check the evidence of my eyes and it was just the same – the poodle, still on his hind legs, marching along unconcernedly at his master's side.

The man must have seen the bewilderment in my face because he burst suddenly into a roar of laughter.

'Don't worry, Mr Herriot,' he said. 'This little dog was circus trained before I got him as a pet. I like to show off his little tricks. This one really startles people.'

'You can say that again,' I said breathlessly. 'It nearly gave me heart failure.'

The poodle wasn't ill, he just wanted his nails clipping. I smiled as I hoisted him on to the table and began to ply the clippers.

'I suppose he won't want his hind claws doing,' I said. 'He'll have worn them down himself.' I was glad to find I had recovered sufficiently to attempt a little joke.

However, by the time I had finished, the old lassitude had taken over again and I felt ready to fall down as I showed man and dog to the front door.

I watched the little animal trotting away down the street – in orthodox manner this time – and it came to me suddenly that it had been a long time since I had seen a dog doing something unusual and amusing. Like the things Brandy used to do.

A wave of gentle memories flowed over me as I leaned wearily against the door post and closed my eyes. When I opened them I saw Brandy coming round the corner of the street with Mrs Westby. His nose was entirely obscured by a large red tomato-soup can and he strained madly at the leash and whipped his tail when he saw me.

It was certainly an hallucination this time. I was looking into the past. I really ought to go to bed immediately. But I was still rooted to the door post when the Labrador bounded up the steps, made an attempt, aborted by the soup can, to lick my face and contented himself with cocking a convivial leg against the bottom step.

I stared into Mrs Westby's radiant face. 'What . . . what . . .?'

With her sparkling eyes and wide smile she looked more attractive than ever. 'Look, Mr Herriot, look! He's better, he's better!'

In an instant I was wide awake. 'And I . . . I suppose you'll want me to get the can off him?'

'Oh yes, yes, please.'

It took all my strength to lift him on to the table. He was heavier now than before his illness. I reached for the familiar forceps and began to turn the jagged edges of the can outwards from the nose and mouth. Tomato soup must have been one of his favourites because he was really deeply embedded and it took some time before I was able to slide the can from his face.

I fought off the slobbering attack. 'He's back in the dustbins, I see.'

'Yes, he is, quite regularly. I've pulled several cans off him myself. And he goes sliding with the children, too.' She smiled happily.

Thoughtfully I took my stethoscope from the pocket of my white coat and listened to his lungs. They were wonderfully clear. A slight roughness here and there, but the old cacophony had gone.

I leaned on the table and looked at the great dog with a mixture of thankfulness and incredulity. He was as before, boisterous and full of the joy of living. His tongue lolled in a happy grin and the sun glinted through the surgery window on his sleek golden coat.

'But, Mr Herriot,' Mrs Westby's eyes were wide, 'how on earth has this happened? How has he got better?'

'*Vis medicatrix naturae*,' I replied in tones of deep respect.

'I beg your pardon?'

'The healing power of nature. Something no veterinary surgeon can compete with when it decides to act.'

'I see. And you can never tell when this is going to happen?'

'No.'

For a few seconds we were silent as we stroked the dog's head, ears and flanks.

'Oh, by the way,' I said. 'Has he shown any renewed interest in the blue jeans?'

'Oh my word, yes! They're in the washing machine at this very moment. Absolutely covered in mud. Isn't it marvellous!'

Snapper

Henry Williamson

This amusing encounter comes from one of Williamson's earliest short stories, entitled 'Crime and Punishment':

The bull does not want to play with any silly little dog. He is a young bull, but recently separated from his mother the Aberdeen-Angus pedigree cow, all of whose milk he has sucked during the first eight months of his life. He is square, almost, when seen from behind; and the line of his back is straight. Shoulders all beef. He is what is called polled; he has no horns. Which is perhaps as well for Snapper; who, anyway, would not care. Was he not descended from a line of fierce and eager little earth-dogs, bred to tackle badger and fox underground?

The bull is standing in the shade of a beech tree as Snapper trots to within two yards of him. Snapper crouches in the grass.

The bull turns his head, with its curly black poll, and stares at the white crouching object with the bright eyes. Snapper makes his ears cock – or rather, he makes them stand up straight, for they are too ludicrously tall for the action to be called cocking – and lies still in the grass, taunting the bull to play.

'*Humph!*' says the bull, and swishes his tail.

'*Worro-worro-wough!*' replies Snapper, making a sort of amiable growling in his throat. The bull slowly turns away his head, and gives an extra flick to his tail. Snapper leaps up, and runs round to face him, collapsing in the grass again. The bull bends his neck and gently lifts his nose, with the copper ring, in the direction of the dog.

'*Worro-worro,*' growls Snapper, with delight. He runs to and fro before the bull several times, before collapsing in the grass, pointing himself at the bull with shining eyes, inviting him to lower his head so that he, Snapper, may have the pleasure of springing away from the thrilling snort of his nostril.

The bull turns away.

Snapper barks. Raucousness is now in his voice. The bull does not want to play, so Snapper runs twistedly at the bull showing his eye-teeth in a grin, and snapping a couple of inches away from the bull's muzzle. '*Wough wough.*'

The bull glares and snorts.

'*Ha ha!*' pants Snapper, prancing. '*Wough wough.*' He runs at the bull

244

again, leaping aside, falling over, wriggling quickly upright, and making a circle away from his glaring friend the enemy.

So happy is Snapper that he dashes round the bull half a dozen times, before crouching again at the challenge. The bull paws the ground, and pretends to graze.

Snapper, after several feints in the grass, then threatens the bull by pushing himself on his belly towards him. To lure the bull he gets up again, shakes himself, and pretends to stare at a pigeon flying over. He yawns, making a plaintive sound. Nothing happens.

The bull crops, or pretends to crop, at a tuft of rank marsh-grass, which cattle never eat. Snapper walks behind him, collapses to scratch himself, then suddenly runs in and nips the idly swinging tail at its tuft.

The bull swings round, snorting, and paws the ground. Snapper barks, crouches on his forepaws. The bull trots forward with lowered head. His eyes gleam as he runs at the dog.

Snapper flees swiftly. Only when he has scrambled under the gate does he face the bull. Very bravely he thrusts his head between the lower bars and snarls a challenge. The bull has scared him.

Gay Galliard and Miss Muffet ⸻

K. F. Barker

In 'Kennelled to Fight' we saw K. F. Barker with a grim pen. The following passage from *Me and My Dog*, shows him in a light mood. His boxer, Gay Galliard, a lonely dog, short of an animal playmate, makes bosom friends with a stray kitten:

When I carried Miss Muffet into the kitchen to meet her (possible) fate in the person of Gay Galliard, although every one of her nine lives seemed to hang by gossamer threads, she was perfectly calm and unperturbed; perhaps the possession of nine lives does make for an optimistic, carefree unconcern in a harsh and perilous world – in which one step onto a road can be a step into eternity. . . .

I, the possessor of only one life, was, on the other hand, ringed around by doubts and qualms. Standing there with the kitten under my arm, I felt something of an acutely painful anxiety that the manager of a champion featherweight would experience, who, caught up in some fantastic nightmare muddle, is compelled to watch his tiny, precious charge shake the mutton fist – preparatory to massacre – of a huge, burly heavyweight already licking his lips in anticipatory relish. It is true that Gay Galliard wasn't actually licking his lips, but he was exhibiting all the symptoms of a dog about to realise his heart's desire, and much more often than not Boxers' heart's desires centre on blood and mayhem – always on violent action of one sort or another.

In the cold, bright morning light, the kitten looked ridiculously tiny and frighteningly vulnerable; but as a counterbalance for its small size, it possessed a very special kind of 'armour'. This kitten was without fear and, judging by the expression on its small, serene face, even its curiosity appeared to be merely the mild, detached interest with which one species looks at another.

On the other hand, the curiosity of Gay Galliard, 'hotted up' by being 'bottled up', by now was like overfermented liquor, ready to explode at any moment. As he gazed avidly into the little, contemplative face of the kitten, his own face – eyebrows like surprised-looking spectacles halfway up his forehead – was just a large, excited question mark.

Looking at his face, and then at Miss Muffet, I was reminded of that familiar, heartfelt cry: 'It's a good thing your mother can't see you now!' I too felt it was fortunate – from every point of view – that Miss

Muffet's mama couldn't see her child at this tense and drama-packed moment of its career.

If I seem to have become overanxious, it is because this was, in fact, one of those nerveracking, 'hit or miss', 'no second chance' affairs. In the event of Galliard's intentions proving to be lethal ones, any chances of a rescue were practically nil – a Boxer on the job is as quick as a weasel and never more so than when a cat is the quarry.

But there was nothing to be gained by waiting. Taking a deep breath and trying at the same time to be calm and casual – it's not possible, by the way, because the two states are like oil and water, they won't get together – I placed the little victim on the sacrificial altar, in the shape of a moderately high dresser, and, taking another and even deeper breath, stood to one side.

Abandoned, and left now in the sole charge of its nine lives, that kitten took control of the situation with superb efficiency and, acting with lightning precision, managed to do four things simultaneously. Professional jugglers excepted, I had until then judged this to be an impossible feat.

As Galliard lunged forward, the kitten arched its back into roughly the shape of a croquet hoop, increased, by some personal magic, its tail to three times its ordinary size, pinned its ears back, opened its minute mouth, and swore in a very low voice. The result was as startling and odd as though the kitten had suddenly burst a paper bag – the paper bag in this case being Gay Galliard. He checked abruptly in midair, recovered a little, and immediately performed a series of face-saving, cavorting movements. Miss Muffet still disguised as some peculiar-shaped brush – the kind the enterprising salesmen try to tempt you with for removing dust from inaccessible places where you never dream of disturbing it – stood foursquare, tiny but implacable, and perfectly still.

Surprise is a wonderful weapon and, provided the surprise is really surprising, one that rarely fails; it didn't now. Galliard was not merely surprised, he was quite literally dumbfounded; never during his brief, colourful career had he experienced anything quite like the small, forceful, 'brushed up' object confronting him.

He simply didn't know what to make of it – and that's a state of mind which puts one immediately at a disadvantage. The kitten sensed this at once; cats are equipped from birth with an unerring instinct for doing the right thing at the right time for self-preservation.

It stepped daintily to the edge of the dresser and as Galliard approached – more cautiously this time – it leant down and, extending one little braceleted forepaw, administered a swift, shrewd smack to the pink triangle on top of his nose.

Rather curiously, this delighted the recipient. Standing on his hind legs, and leaning his forepaws on the edge of the dresser, he mutely asked for another of the same, which was immediately forthcoming. He was enchanted; this was a game after his own heart. He lifted a large paw and tentatively nudged the kitten in something the same way that a child nudges a toy to 'make it work'. Only this response was quicker; it was almost like pressing a button – he got results at once. Miss Muffet sat down and, balancing herself on her small striped haunches, started to bat in earnest. In a few minutes the sheer fascination of the game gripped the small player as it had the large one; completely absorbed, she had cast overboard any doubts she may have entertained and was concentrating all her skill and energy on tiny lightning uppercuts, darting right hooks and left hooks; and presently as the 'fighters' got more excited, and daring, the contest demanded a larger 'ring'. A moment later the featherweight had jumped from the dresser to the floor; but instead of going on with the boxing game, she sat down composedly on the rug in front of the fire and gazed calmly up at her heavyweight sparring partner.

Clearly Miss Muffet was deeply interested in Galliard, but equally clearly not in the least awed or impressed by his large size, cavernous mouth, or excited galumphing – he was cavorting gaily round and round her now, looking rather like a large, clumsy, biscuit-coloured liberty horse with white socks. When presently he came to a panting halt, he sat himself down and, advancing a forepaw, gave her an encouraging little push, she merely stared blandly up into his frowning, interested face. And at that moment I caught a glimpse of *her* face – it wore a tiny, subtle smile of contentment, that seemed to express her secret satisfaction, and happy confidence in that she now had the affair under control, and Gay Galliard exactly where she wanted him.

It was then, as if to set the seal on her position once and for all, and indicate plainly to Galliard that size didn't come into it – didn't in fact amount to a row of beans – that Miss Muffet played her next card. As Galliard, recollecting perhaps a mislaid bone – they were often on his mind – went through the kitchen door, she pranced up and, lifting a deft, black-padded forepaw, gave him a casual, patronising smack behind. Once again impertinence from the small and insignificant, directed against the large and important, paid off. Galliard was charmed all over again – fascinated by the incredible audacity of this

swift-acting, self-sufficient midget, whose whole head didn't measure up to one of his own ears.

But a further surprise was in store for him; a neat little joke that, I was to realise later, was typical of Miss Muffet. When Galliard came back a few minutes later, there was no kitten to be seen. After looking at me accusingly, he began hurriedly to search the kitchen. As he approached the coal bucket, a little, striped head popped up like a jack-in-the-box. 'I'm here,' it announced brightly. Galliard's ears went back, he stood with jutting lower lip, completely taken aback. The occupant of the bucket smirked.

But it turned out that Miss Muffet had yet another 'card' up her little black-braceleted sleeve; the highlight of the whole incredible affair took place later that evening.

In a corner of the kitchen, Galliard made a practice of keeping a collection of large bones, in reserve as it were, to be fetched out as and when the need arose. In something of the same way that a cigar completes and rounds off a good meal, so twenty minutes' leisurely relaxation over a ripe bone sets the hallmark on his evening programme.

On this particular evening, Galliard, having selected his bone from store, flopped down in front of the fire and arranged it firmly between his forepaws. But before he could begin operations, there was a small disturbance. Miss Muffet, determined apparently not to be left out of anything that she could be in, bustled up officiously and, with blood-chilling recklessness, gambled every one of her nine lives at one throw by establishing herself between Galliard's forelegs and wrapping her own forepaws lovingly round the big beef bone. It was one of those brave, spendthrift 'knife edge' gestures that nine times out of ten have one ending – sudden death and a few pathetic fragments of fur jacket.

Making no attempt even to dislodge the bone-snatcher, Galliard gazed down at her with deep interest, mingled – judging by his expression – with a kind of odd pleasure. That special kind of pleasure one sometimes gets from a completely new and rather fantastic experience.

And it must be an odd experience for a large dog, relaxing over a bone to match, to have a small, striped ball of fur suddenly materialise between his forepaws and wrap itself round the bone. But at the same time rather funny if you can see it like that: scores of dogs of course couldn't, because they haven't a sense of humour and, when they get hold of a bone, are apt to be a bit upstage and pompous. But not Galliard; to him even bones are a laugh, and, if, when tossed up in the air, they knock something off the table, a better joke still – better even than the 'burying a bone in your bed' one. It was probably only Galliard's unfailing sense of fun that saved Miss Muffet's skin at the very beginning.

The idea of snatching his property back from between the small sacrilegious black-braceleted paws never seemed to occur to him. Patiently he waited, while the bone was gnawed, sat upon, breathed on and rolled over. Only when Miss Muffet had finally exhausted all the bone's possibilities, and darted away to another more promising toy, did Galliard reclaim his treasure and get to work on it. . . .

It was made very clear to me, even on that first night of their acquaintance, that my ownership of the kitten – though 'ownership' is only a token term, because no one ever really owns a cat; all cats own themselves (some own human beings as well) – had passed to Gay Galliard.

Lying on the rug in front of the fire later that evening with Miss Muffet close beside him, basking in the sheltered warmth of the large frame, his frequent downward glances held all the affection and pride of ownership – as well as faint, lingering traces of that first profound astonishment.

The face of Miss Muffet herself, I noticed, again wore a small, bland smile – the proud smile of conscious achievement. For a scrap of a thing barely six inches tall, she had, when you looked back, achieved one way and another quite a lot during the past ten hours. When I looked again the smile had widened. Could it be that among her achievements was possession of one eighty-pound dog?

It was true, the unbelievable had happened; the gay swashbuckler, the tough plug-ugly, the possessor of a pedigree with thirty-six champions in it, had lost his heart to two pennorth of striped and spotted alley cat.

OBITUARY

Ancient Greece

Small Voice from the Grave

I discovered the following brief epitaph in J. W. Mackail's *Greek Anthology*:

Thou who passest on this path; if happily thou dost mark this monument, laugh not I pray thee, though it is only a dog's grave; tears fell for me and the dust was heaped above me by a master's hand, who likewise engraved these words on my tomb.

Byron's Favourite

Lord Byron

According to Byron's biographer, Frederick Raphael, the poet first acquired his huge black and white Newfoundland, Boatswain, as a Cambridge undergraduate, but was promptly reminded that the university statutes 'forbade canine company'. Whereupon he is said to have paraded a bear before the outraged Fellows, 'declaring that he had brought the beast up to sit for a Fellowship'.

When Boatswain died, aged five, in 1808, Byron's friends, who were invited to attend the dog's funeral, 'arrived hooded and cowled in monkish robes'. The poet had Boatswain buried under the high altar in the chapel of his home, Newstead Abbey, and composed this eulogy for a marble monument nearby. It is followed by Boatswain's epitaph:

Near this spot
are deposited the remains of one
who possessed beauty without vanity,
strength without insolence,
courage without ferocity,
and all the virtues of man without his vices.
This praise, which would be unmeaning
flattery
if inscribed over human remains,

is but a just tribute to the memory of
BOATSWAIN, a Dog,
who was born at Newfoundland, May 1803,
and died at Newstead Abbey, Nov. 18, 1808.

To Boatswain ————————————————

Lord Byron

When some proud son of man returns to earth,
Unknown to glory, but upheld by birth,
The sculptor's art exhausts the pomp and woe,
And storied urns record who rest below;
When all is done, upon the tomb is seen,
Not what he was, but what he should have been:
But the poor dog, in life the firmest friend,
The first to welcome, foremost to defend,
Whose honest heart is still his master's own,
Who labours, fights, lives, breathes for him alone,
Unhonour'd falls, unnoticed all his worth,
Denied in heaven the soul he held on earth:
While man, vain insect! hopes to be forgiven,
And claims himself a sole exclusive heaven.
Oh, man! thou feeble tenant of an hour,
Debased by slavery, or corrupt by power,
Who knows thee well must quit thee with distrust,
Degraded mass of animated dust!
Thy love is lust, thy friendship all a cheat,
Thy smiles hypocrisy, thy words deceit!
By nature vile, ennobled but by name,
Each kindred brute might bid thee blush for shame.
Ye! who perchance behold this simple urn,
Pass on – it honours none you wish to mourn;
To make a friend's remains these stones arise;
I never knew but one – and here he lies.

To the Memory of Little Music ⸺

William Wordsworth

Lie here, without a record of thy worth,
Beneath a covering of the common earth!
It is not for unwillingness to praise,
Or want of love, that here no stone we raise;
More thou deserv'st; but *this* man gives to man,
Brother to brother, *this* is all we can.
Yet they to whom thy virtues made thee dear
Shall find thee through all changes of the year;
This oak points out thy grave; the silent tree
Will gladly stand, a monument of thee.

We grieved for thee and wished thy end were past;
And willingly have laid thee here at last:
For thou hadst lived till everything that cheers
In thee had yielded to the weight of years;
Extreme old age had wasted thee away,
And left thee but a glimmering of the day;
Thy ears were deaf, and feeble were thy knees –
I saw thee stagger in the summer breeze,
Too weak to stand against its sportive breath,
And ready for the gentlest stroke of death.
It came, and we were glad; yet tears were shed;
Both man and woman wept when thou wert dead;
Not only for a thousand thoughts that were
Old household thoughts in which thou hadst thy share,
But for some precious boons vouchsafed to thee
Found scarcely anywhere in like degree!
For love that comes wherever life and sense
Are given to God, in thee was most intense;
A chain of heart, a feeling of the mind,
A tender sympathy, which did thee bind
Not only to us men, but to thy kind:
Yea, for thy fellow-brutes in thee we saw,
A soul of love, love's intellectual law: –
Hence, if we wept, it was not done in shame;
Our tears from passion and from reason came,
And therefore shalt thou be an honoured name!

To a Favourite Spaniel

Robert Southey

Ah, poor companion! when thou followedst last
   Thy master's footsteps to the gate
Which closed for ever on him, thou didst lose
Thy truest friend, and none was left to plead
For the old age of brute fidelity.
But fare thee well! Mine is no narrow creed;
And He who gave thee being did not frame
The mystery of life to be the sport
Of merciless man! There is another world
For all that live and move – a better one!
Where the proud bipeds, who would fain confine
Infinite Goodness to the little bounds
Of their own charity, may envy thee!

Blessed Being

Francis Jammes

Now you are dead, my faithful dog, my humble friend,
Dead of the death that like a wasp you fled,
Where under the table you would hide. Your head
Was turned to me in the brief and bitter end.

O mate of man! Blest being! You that shared
Your master's hunger and his meals as well! . . .
You that in days of old, in pilgrimage fared
With young Tobias and the angel Raphael. . . .

Servant that loved me with a love intense,
As saints love God, my great exemplar be! . . .
The mystery of your deep intelligence
Dwells in a guiltless, glad eternity.

Dear Lord! If you should grant me by Your grace
To see You face to face in Heaven, O then
Grant that a poor dog look into the face
Of him who was his god here among men! . . .

Good Nick

Sydney Smith

Here lies poor Nick, an honest creature,
   Of faithful, gentle, courteous nature;
A parlour pet unspoiled by favour,
A pattern of good dog behaviour.
Without a wish, without a dream,
Beyond his home and friends at Cheam,
Contentedly through life he trotted
Along the path that fate allotted;
Till Time, his aged body wearing,
Bereaved him of his sight and hearing,
Then laid them down without a pain
To sleep, and never wake again.

Crib Mourned

Patrick Chalmers

Crib, on your grave beneath the chestnut boughs,
Today no fragrance falls nor summer air,
Only a master's love who laid you there
Perchance may warm the earth 'neath which you drowse
In dreams from which no dinner gong may rouse,
Unwakeable, though close the rat may dare,
Deaf, though the rabbit thump in playful scare,
Silent, though twenty tabbies pay their vows.

And yet, mayhap, some night when shadows pass,
And from the fir the brown owl hoots on high,
That should one whistle 'neath a favouring star
Your small white shade shall patter o'er the grass,
Questing for him you loved o' days gone by,
Ere Death, the Dog-Thief, carried you afar!

Folly: At the Death of a Dog

Laurence Whistler

To care so much for one who gave but small
Answers to love, yet gave them, after his kind,
Completely – wild with pleasure in the giving.

To grieve so much, when he, whom love had whistled
Out of his cramped, regretless, primitive world,
Harked back, before his time, to brutal dying.

To want so much that somehow (life gone by)
This brief encounter, by the world forgotten,
Should somewhere be remembered – and be valued –
And hold one spark through all the blaze of being –
And, humbly, be.

The End of a Scotch Terrier

Mazo de la Roche

In *Portrait of a Dog* by Mazo de la Roche, published in 1930, it is as
though she is speaking to the spirit of her dead Scottie, telling him, in a
most touching and engaging manner, his whole life story. This is how
it ends:

You died at Christmas. . . . Some poison from that other sickness must have remained in you and returned swiftly, without warning, to set your brain afire. You might be saved, the doctor said, if kept quiet and inactive for some weeks. He took you to his hospital.

I went to see you once there. But you must not know that I was near you. An attendant led the way to the door and I peered in. There were a number of dogs in the room, all in separate cages. Most of them were clamorous, noisy, especially an Alsatian near the door that growled savagely when he saw me. What impressed me was your dignity. You sat small, erect, very still in your corner, quite aloof from the other dogs. I scarcely breathed lest you should hear me, but I think you felt my nearness, for you got to your feet and turned facing the door and raised your head, sniffing.

You were returned to us on Christmas morning, supposedly cured. Cured! Why, you were like a live wire. Your joy at being with us was past bearing. Your excitement at being in your home again was past bearing. It could not be borne. You raised your muzzle towards the lighted Christmas candles and uttered a deep cry, a bay, musical and full of despair.

I took you for a walk and you were beside yourself with excitement in the snow. I brought you home and left you with the other one while I went out again. When I came back I found that she had had a bad time with you. She had given you tablets from the doctor to quiet you, but nothing would quiet you. It could not be borne.

I telephoned for them to come for you. It was a nice young man who came. He wanted to put you in the box to save me the pain. But I must do it myself. It was small, even for you. As I closed it I found that your tail projected. I reopened it and curled your tail about you. Your mouth was open, showing your teeth, white as a puppy's. I closed the box. It was unbelievable that I should be doing this.

I know of a certain Canon X – who had to have a dog which he loved destroyed. He took him to the place himself and went to the very door of the room where the lethal closet was. He looked down into those trusting eyes raised to his, and the attendant saw him bow his head and murmur a short prayer. I wonder what his prayer was. Perhaps – 'O God, let him not be too much afraid when he finds himself alone in that darkness and I not there to protect him.'

We sent your body by train to Jacob that he might bury it in your own woods. It was spring before we saw the grave, a lovely soft April day when the brown fern fronds were uncurling and the air was full of birdsong. He led the way to it with an air of pride, for he had chosen the spot with great care. On a bitter December day he had trudged through the woods for a long while before he could make up his mind. Then he had found a young pine tree on a rise of ground, and there he had dug the grave. Luckily the ground was not frozen.

Now he stood looking down with solemnity at the little, carefully rounded mound he had made, over which green things were already beginning to unfold. He did not say that he would miss you about the place. I knew that without his telling me. Later on in the spring I asked him what had become of a root of a very lovely iris which I had placed by the edge of the border for planting. He answered: 'I put it by the place where little dog lies.'

As we stood looking down at the mound our hearts were filled with sadness. Not only because of the loss of you, but because your going had finally closed a chapter in our lives. Your life had been a part of many lovely things that were past. Hands beloved by us and had held you, caressed you. Your gaiety had made us smile in times when it was hard to smile. And now Jacob stood, leaning on his spade, proud of the pretty place he had chosen for your grave.

RIP

AUTHOR INDEX